D0354510

MARGO KAUFMAN is a columnist for the *Los Angeles Times*, a
frequent contributor to *The New York Times*, and a regular pan-
elist on the National Public Radio news/quiz program *Wait!
Wait! Don't Tell Me!* Her other books include *1-800-Am-I-Nuts?*
and *This Damn House!* Kaufman is the Hollywood correspondent for *Pug Talk* magazine, where she has interviewed
celebrity pug owners like Paula Abdul, and investigated
whether any pugs were mistreated during the filming of *The
Adventures of Milo and Otis*. (They weren't.) She lives in
California with her husband, son, and two pugs.

CLARA

The Early Years

The Story of the Pug Who Ruled My Life

MARGO KAUFMAN

A PLUME BOOK

This story is true, and Clara is a real pug, though she prefers not to apply such a limiting label to herself. However, to ensure that I can continue to support Clara in the manner to which she has become accustomed, I have changed the names, descriptions, geographic specifics, and distinguishing traits of some of the participants. If you think that you recognize anyone in this book, I would be deeply grateful if you would just forget all about it. —MK

PLUME
Published by the Penguin Group
Penguin Putnam Inc., 375 Hudson Street, New York, New York 10014, U.S.A.
Penguin Books Ltd, 27 Wrights Lane, London W8 5TZ, England
Penguin Books Australia Ltd, Ringwood, Victoria, Australia
Penguin Books Canada Ltd, 10 Alcorn Avenue, Toronto, Ontario,
Canada M4V 3B2
Penguin Books (N.Z.) Ltd, 182–190 Wairau Road, Auckland 10, New Zealand

Penguin Books Ltd, Registered Offices: Harmondsworth, Middlesex, England

Published by Plume, a member of Penguin Putnam Inc. This is an authorized reprint of a hardcover edition published by Villard Books, a division of Random House, Inc. For information address Villard Books, 201 E. 50th Street, New York, NY 10022.

First Plume Printing, September, 1999
10 9 8

CIP data is available.

ISBN 0-452-28136-9

Printed in the United States of America

For Nicholas with love
And of course, for Clara

Acknowledgments

Choosing who to thank for helping you write a book is as perilous as composing the guest list for your wedding. You're bound to forget a friend whose input was critical, or offend a relative by putting her in the same group as her worst enemy. Still, since writing acknowledgments is far more entertaining than revising a manuscript for the four thousandth time, I'm throwing caution to the wind.

Above all, I am indebted to my beloved husband, for his unflagging courage and Russian language skills; my sister, Laurie Goldberg, for being my reality check; my mother, Gloria Asnes, the best personal shopper in the world; Marian Bach, for holding my hand; Melinda Lewis, for her sage advice and business-class tickets; Nancy Hathaway, for her constant encouragement and willingness to talk about a writing problem until two o'clock in the morning; Lupe Padilla, nanny par excellence, for giving me the time to write; and Jon Winokur, who insisted that I write about Clara before she wrote about me.

Heartfelt appreciation to my editor, Bruce Tracy, whose suggestions enhanced both the book and my confidence; my agent, Loretta Fidel, even though she failed to get Clara the part in *Men In Black;* Clara's legion of fans at Villard Books, most notably, Brian McLendon; the wonderful women in the Santa Monica offices of Random House, especially Suzanne Wickham-Beaird and Jennifer Gaudry; and Anna Marie Wilson, editor in chief of *Pug Talk* magazine, for pushing me down the slippery slope of pug journalism.

Hugs and thanks to all of my dear, supportive friends, in particular Marjorie David, David Ewing, Susan Garfield, Marc Glassgold, Marilyn Hulquist, Deborah Levin, Suzy Slutzky, and the incomparable Blanche Roberts. Much love to my family, who welcomed their newest member with open arms. Extra kisses to Eric Mankin, Nicholas Mankin, Paul Asnes, Allan and Rose Pearlstein, Flora Pearlstein, Arthur and Shirley Mankin, Ken Goldberg, Bobby Pearlstein, and Robbie Pearlstein.

Finally, a life supply of pig's ears for Sophie, and to Clara, my undying devotion, not that she really cares.

CLARA

The Early Years

Prologue

The pug, Clara, sensed disaster. My husband, Duke, and I had two weeks to go until we departed on a journey to the ends of the earth. This wasn't unusual. We travel a lot. Yet somehow Clara had come to believe this trip marked the end of life as she knew it. Spectacularly correct, her hunch was worthy of the Psychic Friends Network, because the tangible evidence was slight. Our suitcases were still in the attic, the airline tickets locked in my desk; the only indication that something extraordinary was in the works was a growing mound of shopping bags in the laundry room.

But ever self-protective and watchful, the suspicious dog dragged her faux leopard-skin bed from its customary position in the corner of my study to a superior vantage point in front of our bedroom heater and henceforth refused to let me out of sight. Her dim pug sister, Sophie, who long ago learned to follow Clara's instincts, chirped like a dying smoke alarm until I carried her bed in too.

Never mind that I'd spent four years accustoming the dictators—excuse me, companion animals—to sleep in another room, where Sophie's compulsion to wake me at 5:30 A.M. with her insanely irritating yips and shrieks and Clara's nightly attempt to invade the sanctity of our marital bed wouldn't cause sleep deprivation. Overwhelmed with guilt, anxiety, and nostalgia, I relented. Even Duke, who isn't nearly as vulnerable to their manipulations as me—the Official Pug Lollipop—grew powerless at the sight of the matching faux leopard-skin cuddlers in a line.

"They're like the schoolgirls' beds in *Madeline*," he sighed with uncharacteristic sentimentality. Sensing weakness, Clara widened her eyes to chocolate-drop size, flattened her bat ears, and made herself look even smaller than her far-below-breed-standard twelve pounds. "The Dewdrop is looking unusually needy," Duke said reproachfully.

He had no right to complain. His days were spent downtown at the university, so Clara only stalked him on weekends and after business hours. She shadowed me round the clock. As the date of our departure grew near, she maintained a vigil over my car keys the way an alcoholic keeps tabs on all the liquor in the house. If I attempted to leave home alone, she skittered under my feet, dashed out the gate, and bounced defiantly into the passenger seat of my car. I felt like Morgan Freeman in *Driving Miss Daisy*.

I consulted my friend Blanche Roberts, a three-time winner of the title National Pug Breeder of the Year. Blanche is one of the few people I know capable of treating the usually coddled lapdogs as livestock. She assured me that Clara's behavior was reasonable. "You're making changes," Blanche said in her please-don't-be-stupid voice. "She knows it and wants to be near you when it happens. She wants to support you."

Supportive? Clara? Unlike Sophie, who exasperates me more than any living creature including my ex-husband but is goodhearted and actively prefers me to other human beings, Clara has the character and personality of her breed: that of the schemer Eve Harrington in *All About Eve*. (My husband claims that the hallmark of the pug's personality is its indifference to pleasing the master. "Where some dogs will really work to make their master happy, pugs are only in it for themselves," Duke says.)

"But I haven't even brought the suitcases out," I protested to Blanche. For good reason. Clara, who frequently travels with me, reacts to my luggage with an emotional meltdown.

"You smell different," Blanche said. "A little more stressed, a little more worried."

Pugs don't have a standard dog snout—just a snub leathery half mushroom—but I knew better than to argue with Blanche. In pug circles her word is gospel, but more important, she was going to board Clara and Sophie while we were away, for a fraction of what it would cost to send them to a swanky dog camp with hanging plants, homemade curtains, and piped-in classical music twenty-four hours a day. I'd go to any lengths to avoid getting on her bad side. Besides, there was no denying that Clara was getting less lap time than her preferred eighteen hours a day.

"Just let her do her thing," Blanche advised.

Since it is impossible to control Clara, this was easy advice to take.

My little dog caused a sensation at the Adventure Store, where I reluctantly went to be fitted for warm boots, perhaps the only pair of expensive shoes that I have no desire to own. Cedar incense wafted through the air, a sound system played a grating environmental soundtrack of chirping birds and mating whales, the floor was carpeted in Astroturf punctuated by papier-mâché redwood stumps and rocks. It evoked unhappy memories of damp sleeping bags and mosquito-filled Camp Kinni Kinnic camping trips, and I felt a panic attack coming on. The highly urbanized Clara, whose idea of communing with Mother Nature is to frolic around the orange and lemon trees and drought-resistant bushes in my in-laws' meticulously landscaped backyard in Santa Barbara, trotted past a display rack containing doggy backpacks with the slogan: SO YOUR DOG CAN CARRY HIS OWN LOAD. (As if!)

"Can I pet your pug?" asked a lanky youth with marmalade dreadlocks, dressed in khaki Patagonia shorts and a white camp shirt embroidered with the title BOOT COUNSELOR. (I think it's against the law in Los Angeles to be a regular salesperson.)

Before I could respond, he dropped to the ground and went eyeball to eyeball with Clara. She ran through her entire menu of attention-getting behaviors. Cock gnome head. Wag doughnut tail. Fold ears forward to sugar-won't-melt-in-my-mouth position. Flash crooked front tooth. By the time she came to the finale—Flop on back so Human can scratch gently rounded belly!—Clara was surrounded by the Sock Analyst and the Down-Vest Consultant, each ripping open a package of beef jerky. This is a substance that I would only eat after five weeks on a lifeboat just before turning cannibal, but Clara was most appreciative.

"Excuse me," I said, "I need lightweight boots that can withstand minus-twenty-degree cold."

The Boot Counselor sighed and took his eyes off Clara. "Are you going on a trek?" he asked hopefully. I was worried. Did I look like one of those adventurous idiots who scaled Everest for fun?

"God forbid." I shuddered. How to explain my mission without Clara learning the truth: We were flying across the world to adopt a six-month-old human baby. "It's sort of a business trip," I said evasively and ran through my boot requirements. Cute. Lightweight. Waterproof. Preferably black.

He measured my feet perfunctorily, all the while caressing Clara, who daintily pirouetted on her hind legs and devoured beef jerky at the same time. "My grandmother had a fawn pug named Pugsly," he said.

If I had a dollar for everyone who's told me that their grandmother had a pug named Pugsly, I could buy Clara and Sophie the black braided leather collars with the engraveable sterling silver locket that I admired in the Saks Fifth Avenue Christmas catalog (only $265 each!). I waited expectantly. I knew that soon I would learn Pugsly's fate.

Sure enough, the youth sadly shook his dreadlocks. "Pugsly choked to death on a chicken bone."

If I had a dollar for everyone who's told me a gruesome story about how a pug died, I could fly Clara and Sophie to Manhattan every weekend, so they could attend Central Park Pug Pals, a gathering of pugs and their pug-besotted humans that meets every Saturday and Sunday at twelve-thirty on the grassy knoll behind the Alice in Wonderland statue.

"Poor Pugsly," I said pro forma. "About my boots . . ."

Finally, he vanished into the stockroom and returned with a pair of definitely not adorable, industrial-strength black lace-up boots, which he explained would be warm enough if I wore two layers of special wicking socks. (No, he couldn't show me any; I had to consult the Sock Analyst.) "Does Clara want Gore-Tex booties?"

Clara was open to the suggestion, but despite all appearances to the contrary, I have standards. My pug's footwear is limited to a small can of Musher's Wax, which I bought in Manhattan one snowy December morning because the salt on the icy streets burned her delicate dime-sized paws. Anyway, this was one trip that Clara would definitely not be making.

"If she were mine, I'd take her everywhere," he said, and she sluttishly licked his face.

I was so guilt-ridden I pulled out my cell phone and made an emergency appointment with Dr. Pangloss, my therapist. He has seen Clara since she was a pup. (Not that she has difficulty coping; she just feels I need moral support.) Dr. Pangloss only sees one other dog regularly in his practice. "Would you believe it's another pug?" he asked.

You bet I would.

My longtime shrink is fond of gimmicks—so fond that when Tracey Ullman, playing an unconventional therapist on the TV show *Ally McBeal*, suggested that Ally needed her own theme song, I didn't even think it was strange. In the waiting room I was handed a form and asked to choose from a list of twenty-one words or phrases the one that best described my present mood. I pondered the choices: "Connected to others?" "Joyful?" "Active?" "Accepting?" "Indifferent?" "Helpless?" None seemed right, so I wrote in, "Terrified." To amuse myself, I filled out one for Clara, who sat regally beside me on the green tweed sofa, delicately sipping bottled water from a Styrofoam cup. I debated between "Good sense of self" and "Confident" before ticking off "Resourceful."

It figured. The dog was in better shape than me.

Dr. Pangloss smiled when Clara strutted into his office. "I see you've brought the good one," he said. My pugs are situated at opposite ends of the behavioral spectrum. Clara is a charmer, whereas Sophie feels it isn't worth her while to win friends and influence people. In his office are two Barcaloungers. Clara settled into the one earmarked for clients, moved over a smidgen so I could join her, and waited expectantly for the session to begin. "She seems more alert than usual," Pangloss said. "You don't look so great."

My voice cracked and tears streamed down my cheeks. "I'm about to ruin Clara's life. She knows it and it's breaking my heart." (Yes, I realized I sounded like a paranoid loon.) In a rare display of loyalty, Clara vouchsafed my sanity. She jumped off my lap, hopped onto Pangloss's knee, and gave me the evil eye, trying to vibe me out. Lest there be any doubt as to who was in charge here, she turned her mesmerizing gaze on my therapist. He made the sign of the cross and put her on the floor.

"She's like an alien with supernatural powers," Pangloss said dryly. "Don't stare at her too long, or you'll lose your will." He recalled a *Star Trek* episode in which Spock ran into a similar menace, but he couldn't remember how Spock had coped.

It didn't matter. It was comforting to know I wasn't hallucinating.

"You have rights," he continued. "She is, after all, your dog."

"She's brought me immeasurable happiness, and this is how I repay her?" I spluttered. "What if the baby is a terrible mistake?"

Pangloss reminded me that I had cold feet right before I got Clara. "You were afraid of upsetting Sophie," he said. "And she survived."

"It's not the same," I protested. "Clara is more evolved."

Pangloss brought out two gigantic magnets and demonstrated how, depending on how you held them, they either stuck together or stayed apart. It was supposed to be a consciousness-raising prop to melt away resistance, but all it brought to mind were those little Scottie dogs sold in vending machines in the bathrooms of Howard Johnson's when I was a child. "We better examine your relationship with Clara," he said.

"We only have an hour." I moaned. "And that could take years."

Girl Meets Pug

~ↄ෴ↄ~

*M*y enslavement began in June 1992, when Bess, my favorite pug for over fourteen years, developed kidney failure and had to be put to sleep. I was heartbroken. Her gluttonous sister, Stella (also fourteen), had died the previous April, and I was left with a void in my life. Blessedly, I was not left pugless, a state that I've seldom been in since I fell in love with the breed when I was nineteen. Who knew that small wrinkled dogs with pushed-in faces would prove to be the greatest commitment of my life?

A year before, after adding up all the veterinary expenses in my checkbook, I had had a revelation: The joy of pug ownership was gone. Bess and Stella were clearly on their way out, and my role had deteriorated from playing spirited games of Chase the Sock to running a pug hospice. In an effort to stave off the inevitable emotional crisis, I convinced my husband to lift his long-standing two-pug quota. After Duke made me swear that he would never have to walk all three at once, the good-looking but truculent Sophie joined the pack.

Well, she didn't exactly join—she took over like *Caulerpa taxifolia,* the mutant seaweed that is currently suffocating all marine life in its path in the western Mediterranean. It could be argued that Bess and Stella's last days were enlivened by their hatred of their new sibling, but I'd be willing to bet that euthanasia seemed more pleasurable than sharing the house with Sophie. Her favorite game was to grab Bess's leash in her teeth and sprint down the Venice boardwalk while the gallant Bess struggled to keep pace.

Within weeks, Sophie tired of tormenting her feeble sisters and turned her energies toward subjugating me. It was like living with a fourteen-pound reincarnation of Mussolini. Every morning at six o'clock Pugolini woke me like the devil's alarm clock. First, her owl-like head would rise like a periscope over the mattress and she'd monitor my rapid eye movements and breathing patterns. When she determined that sleep had reached its deepest and most relaxing state, she sprang into action, emitting a warning yelp. If I failed to respond instantly, she tore the covers off with her teeth, raked her needle-sharp claws on whichever limb happened to be most handy, and serenaded me with a piercing aria of barks. Sophie never woke me for a pressing call of nature; oh, no, she did it for sport.

After Bess died I decided to get the exasperating beast a baby sister. "You're increasing your problems exponentially," Duke warned. "Sophie's going to turn into a smoldering cauldron of jealousy."

I figured it would be my revenge for all the mornings that I couldn't sleep in. Besides, pugs are happier in pairs. You seldom see a solo pug, and people always ask why. Pugs are insanely demanding, and if you have two they can entertain each other. It's mesmerizing to watch them interact—kind of like an in-house *Wild Kingdom,* only they don't take down wounded gazelles. Best of all, when you go away, you can park two pugs in the kennel and leave with a clear conscience, knowing they will not be alone.

With Bess and Stella, I was less than rigorous about obtaining perfect physical specimens, but that was before I hung out with Blanche. And before I became Hollywood correspondent for *Pug Talk* magazine—my most absurd and yet most pleasurable professional accolade to date. Interviewing luminaries of the pug world made me far more particular. I blush to confess that I am a very superficial person. If you wanted to be charitable, you could describe me as oversensitive to my environment, but in fact I chose everything in my house—from my husband to the coffee grinder to my computer—because I liked the way it looked. So while Stella's apple head and Bess's long Betty Grable–like legs didn't diminish my love for them in any way, when choosing their replacements I adhered to a stricter set of visual standards.

Pugs come in two color combinations: a light tan coat, technically known as fawn, with black ears and mask; or pure black. (Pugs with apricot coats and black masks exist, but I've yet to see one.) I've had fawns and I've had blacks, and I prefer the latter, partly for aesthetic reasons, partly because black pugs are smarter and more adventurous, and partly for practicality. I wear black more than I wear beige, so when the pugs shed—which they do constantly—the fur doesn't show. Black pugs are rarer and a more recent import than the fawns, having been smuggled to England from China around 1880 aboard the yacht *Sunbeam*, which belonged to a Lady Brassey.

Blanche refuses to breed black pugs—"because it's like starting a new breed, they're so different," she says haughtily—and so when it came time to buy a puppy, she advised me to call the actor Paul Winfield. He lives atop a mountain in the Hollywood Hills, in a modern architect's version of a magic castle, which he shares with a pack of poorly housebroken inky gremlins. His kennel name is Avoncliffe, combining Shakespeare's home with his vertical lot, and all his pugs have Shakespearean names.

The charmless but ravishing Sophie, officially Avoncliffe's Sophia, was a Paul pug, and I was counting on Paul—who dabbles in animal husbandry when he's not winning Emmys for *Picket Fences* or making films or doing voice-overs—to supply me with an adoptive sister. Paul had just returned from filming *The Legend of Gator Face* and was low on pugs—his notorious ornamental koi pond had claimed a few less-than-expert swimmers—but he invited me to stop by. I accepted immediately. It's more mood-lifting than Prozac to see the stately six-foot-two actor walking in a sea of snuffling dramatis personae: Desdemona, Othello, Enobarbus, Iago, Portia, and Gertrude.

Paul had two pugs up for grabs: Bianca, a year-old bitch that he'd picked up at a show as breeding stock but was having difficulty integrating into his pack. "She's kind of aggressive," he conceded, and the warning bells chimed. I needed a Type B personality to compliment the bossy Sophie.

He suggested Malvolio, a chunky six-month-old male with a massive head, sweet disposition, and thick glossy coat—the result of Paul's secret fur-enhancing recipe, a high-fat casserole of chicken livers, ground turkey, garlic, and shortening, which he fries up for them daily. (When I first got Sophie, she was so spoiled she refused to eat kibble for a week. My husband, Mr. When She's Hungry Enough She'll Eat It, finally broke down and roasted her a turkey.) Paul stretched on the couch and was immediately covered with a living quilt of snorting, wheezing, sneezing muffinheads, including the handsome

Malvolio. "Blanche says he has the makings of a champion," Paul said.

More warning bells. Male dogs are not my favorites, and the last thing I wanted was a dog I had to handle in a show ring. I've attended dog shows and interviewed the participants, and never—even after living in Los Angeles in close proximity to the entertainment industry for twenty years—have I encountered such intense intramural bitchiness. Aficionados would have you poisoned for owning an animal whose nails, in their opinion, were a tad too white. Again I passed, luckily for Paul, who would ultimately finish Malvolio (dog-show speak for winning enough shows to make him a champion) and show him at the prestigious Westminster Kennel Club Show.

Paul recommended that I call Lorene, a well-respected puppy farmer. "Sophie's mother, Phoebe, came from Lorene," he said, and then he added, "Did I tell you Phoebe was kidnapped?"

I sensed a *Pug Talk* exclusive. "You're kidding?"

He shook his head. "I usually take all the pugs with me when I go to the store because they love riding in the car," Paul began, and his deep bass-fiddle voice rumbled like distant thunder. "Imagine driving down this mountain with six pugs in your lap. So anyway, I leave the windows down because I don't stay in the store very long, but someone reached in and stole Phoebe out of my car."

"How did you find her?"

"We put posters on every corner and put up a reward in the newspaper," Paul recounted. "Three weeks and no luck, driving up and down the neighborhood just looking. Finally, I got this call from some guy's mother. She said her son had the dog, and she promised to call back with more information, but I never heard from her again. So I went to the police and tried to get his address. They wouldn't give it to me, so I hired a private detective to find out where the thief lived. I went to his house about five the next morning and made a big thing about getting out of my car and trying to look as big and black as possible. Three hours later the guy calls, real scared, and says, 'I've got your dog.' It took a lot of money and effort, but Phoebe was worth it. We call her Patty Hearst now."

I kissed Patty good-bye and promised to bring her daughter Sophie over to say hello. Not that Sophie was interested in a family reunion. Not long ago she ran into her twin sister, Gertrude, at Blanche's house. Gertrude, Paul's first champion, was there having puppies, but Sophie was about as pleased to see her sister as she is to have her nails clipped, an activity she regards as a torture worthy of an intervention from Amnesty International.

"If you call Lorene, don't tell her about the kidnapping," Paul cautioned. "She's kind of fussy."

"Fussy" was putting it mildly. Lorene has been obsessed with pugs since 1964, when she started breeding them. "My mom and dad raised and showed Boston terriers," she told me when I phoned. "But as soon as I saw a pug, I was bit by the pug bug. At one point, I had twenty. I love how soft they are. And the sleepy smell that they emit from their ears and their neck area when they're sleeping on my pillow."

Lorene completely understood why I preferred ebony pugs to their fawn sisters. "The black ones are more possessive," she said. "And they're more enthusiastic. If you want to do something with them, they're with you. Fawn people can't understand it, but everything about the fawns is intensified in the blacks. It can be a black with a fawn mother and fawn sisters and brothers who just happened to turn out black. Still, that pug knows he's better. It's not bloodline. It's color."

Suddenly her voice grew stern. "What's scary is that pugs are becoming so popular. And pugs are not for everybody. They require a lot of care. They're sweet, but they're stubborn and very gullible. They trust anybody. They'll get in anybody's car. Pugs need people who will understand that and protect them from themselves and from life."

I knew I was in trouble when I began to speculate as to whether I was worthy.

For the next two hours, Lorene interrogated me like a senator checking out a Supreme Court nominee. First, I had to assure her that I only planned to have two pugs.

"I don't think people should keep a lot of dogs," Lorene declared, and I envisioned with horror how Blanche, who has scores of dogs, would respond to that. "They won't be able to meet their emotional needs. The amount of time you spend with pugs makes a big difference in how they relate to humans."

Funny, I spend all day with Sophie and all it has accomplished is to teach her the most effective way to annoy me.

Next, I had to pledge that I wasn't pregnant and didn't intend to become so for two years. "An infant would interfere with the pug's emotional needs," Lorene explained. It pained me to guarantee that the puppy was in no danger of an anxiety complex. Three years earlier, I had been diagnosed with breast cancer. Then, not long before I began shopping for a new puppy, I'd had a localized recurrence and been forced to undergo a mastectomy and reconstructive surgery. While my treatment was successful and my doctors optimistic, given the hormonal nature of the disease, pregnancy was a risky venture that they didn't advise.

Lorene also had to be assured that I worked at home (God forbid the dog would be a latchkey pup) and that my previous pugs had gone peacefully to the Great Sofa Cushion in the Sky (not "accidentally" struck by a four iron or run over in the driveway). I later learned that she refused to give her own children pugs on the grounds that they weren't responsible enough. After an hour, Lorene conceded that I was "probably" a safe bet. "I have a little black female who will be old enough to travel in four weeks," she said.

I explained about needing a Type B personality.

"The puppy is used to being bossed around by Daphne, her litter mate, so she will have no trouble being second banana," Lorene assured me.

It sounded perfect. I agreed to send a substantial check. She agreed to send baby pictures. I thanked her profusely.

But the conversation wasn't over yet.

"You have to come and get her," Lorene said.

This posed certain logistical problems. I live in Venice Beach, California. Lorene lived two thousand miles away in Lansing, Michigan. There was no way I was going to fly there to pick up a puppy. It was kind of nice to know that I had limits. (Though if she had lived in Paris, I would have gone in a trice.)

Lorene refused to air-freight her. The puppy, who I planned to name Clara Bella, was only permitted to fly if she was in the cabin, under my seat. "That's nonsense," said Blanche, who ships dogs all over the country by Delta Dash.

That would have been the end of it, but Fate was determined to bring Clara and me together. I found out that Lorene and I were going to be in Manhattan within days of each other. She was leaving the city on a Sunday, and I was arriving the following Tuesday for meetings with magazine editors and my book publisher. But a few days later, Lorene called and said it was all arranged. Monday, she'd park the pug in Manhattan with Judy, her friend and fellow breeder. Judy would keep the puppy until Friday, so she wouldn't interfere with my meetings. Clara and I would spend the weekend together bonding, and on Sunday we'd fly home. All I had to do was pay fifty dollars to the airline to reserve cabin space under my seat.

"I'm surprised Lorene doesn't require her to have her own seat in first class," Duke said.

No sooner had I borrowed a Vuitton pet carrier than I received an urgent call from Lorene. She and Clara were ready to hit the highway. But there had been a small change in plan. Judy had to leave town unexpectedly, so instead of keeping Clara until Friday, she would drop her off at my hotel on Wednesday morning. She hoped I didn't mind. Mind? I had reservations at the San Carlos, a small hotel on the East Side, where I always stayed and got a special rate. They didn't take pets. I could hide Clara for a night, especially since she wasn't allowed to walk on the street because she hadn't had her shots. But five days was pushing my luck.

"Switch hotels," Lorene said. As if it was easy to find a Manhattan hotel across the street from my publisher where a junior suite went for well under two hundred dollars.

"Switch breeders," Duke said. As if it was easy to find a female black pug of excellent heritage who was ready to take Bess's place.

Instead, I called the late Herb Goldstein, a friend of Mother's and one of the owners of the Hotel San Carlos, and threw myself on his mercy. He graciously permitted me to keep Clara in my room. I not so graciously failed to mention that she was nine weeks old and, to the best of my knowledge, not housebroken.

Packing was a logistical nightmare, as I had to anticipate both the puppy's needs and my own. The wardrobe requirements for a business trip to Manhattan are far more taxing than the dress code for a writer working from her home on Venice Beach. The person monitoring the X-ray machine at the airport beheld a bizarre juxtaposition of business suits, silk blouses, Dispoz-a-Scoops—my pooper-scooper of choice—rawhide chips, and Nature's Miracle, a liquid with magic enzymes that supposedly remove pet odors and stains. Certainly when it opened midflight and leaked all over my new black cashmere sweater, it left scarcely a trace.

On the big morning, I tipped the maid lavishly, covered the bathroom floor with *The New York Times,* and waited anxiously, like I was expecting a baby. Labor dragged on and on. Clara was two hours late. I was about to cancel lunch with Loretta, my agent, when the phone rang. "Some woman is honking for you on the street," said Gabriel at the front desk.

I dashed downstairs. Given Lorene's paranoia, I expected to be questioned extensively and maybe asked for fingerprints, just in case she decided to press charges against me for pug abuse in the future. Instead, I was waved over to a dented gray Honda parked in a red zone on Fiftieth Street. "I'm late for a hair appointment," the driver hollered. Through the window, she passed me a ventilated black nylon bag and a sack of Puppy Chow.

"The pug is submissively wetting," she added, "and she has a little diarrhea." Then the light changed and she sped away.

I stood frozen on Fiftieth Street like a drug courier, holding a squirming bag. I got through the lobby and into the elevator before she began to whimper. Safe in my room, I unzipped the bag and out climbed Clara Bella, a sad-looking, bat-eared creature about as large as my size five-and-a-half sneaker. She had a white skunklike stripe on her loosely curled tail, which was closer in shape to a question mark than the breed-standard double corkscrew. This was unsettling because the puppy had been billed as "show quality." But Lorene was somewhere on the highway between New York and Michigan and couldn't be reached.

I called Duke. "I bought a skunk," I wailed. (A couple of weeks later Lorene would assure me that age would tighten the curl and the skunk stripe was the result of Clara having sat in some bleach. She was half right. The skunk stripe disappeared. The question-mark tail remained.)

Sensing that I was less than overwhelmed, the Lilliputian Clara chirped with rapturous delight at my mere existence and washed my cheek with exuberant kisses. It would be the last time that she displayed such enthusiasm for me, whom she quickly pegged as a patsy, but I naïvely believed it was love at first sight. The elated puppy sprang into my lap and chewed my bangs until they frizzed unbecomingly. All I could do was giggle and caress her.

And thus my indentureship commenced.

The Origin of Species

$\mathcal{D}$r. Pangloss looked up from his doodle pad and shook his head. "But why do you find pugs so appealing?" he asked, discreetly flicking a half dozen of Clara's discarded black hairs from his beige corduroy chair and choking back an allergic sneeze.

I was mystified that he could ask such a question, though I'm aware that pugs provoke a bipolar reaction—either "Aren't they cute?" or "Damn, those dogs are butt-ugly." I gave him my stock rejoinder: "Pugs are living proof that God has a sense of humor." Why else would he create a comic-looking beast that doesn't hunt or herd or go to ground, or even fetch, unless what it's fetching is pizza? *The New York Times* once referred to the breed as "virtually untrainable," and as near as I can tell, its raison d'être is to divert human beings. As *The Encyclopedia of the Dogs* by Bruce Fogle states in the "Key Facts About the Pug" section: "Date of origin: Antiquity. First use: Companion. Use Today: Companion."

"So, you admire their sense of entitlement," Pangloss said briskly, like I was missing his point. "Anything else?"

It's hard to analyze a love affair that is grounded in gut instinct and chemistry as opposed to rational thought, but ever conscientious—a trait Pangloss claims is my greatest weakness—I tried. "There hasn't been a day that my pugs haven't made me smile, and that's more than I can say for most people I know," I said. "And unlike human beings, they're consistent. You always know what to expect with a pug."

"Good, good," said Pangloss. "Now we're getting somewhere."

I sat in silence for a moment or two and listened to Clara purr and snort. Waves of love washed over me. "This is embarrassing to admit," I said haltingly. "But for twenty years pugs have been my family. Some women divide their lives by their jobs or their boyfriends. I divide my life by pugs."

Pangloss stopped coloring in his latest prop, a hand-lettered poster of a ladder listing states of mind, starting from Shame (at the bottom) to Enlightenment (at the top). "You're kidding," he said.

Oh, would that that were the case.

I was nineteen before I saw a pug in the flesh, though I had been exposed to them on an intellectual level without being aware of what I'd seen. As a child, my favorite book was Kay Thompson's *Eloise*, about the precocious little girl who lived in a penthouse at the Plaza Hotel. Eloise shared the penthouse with Weenie, a pug or, as she described him, "a dog that looked like a cat." Sometimes Eloise put sunglasses on Weenie and scratched his back with a wire hanger, which the pampered Weenie tolerated with good grace. Kay Thompson lived in Rome with her equally spoiled pug, Fenice. He sported a jaunty scarf around his midriff and subsisted on a diet of green Chuckles. According to an article in *Vanity*

Fair, Thompson's "devotion to the pug was such that she reportedly sawed the legs off her grand piano in order to move it into her bedroom at the top of a spiral staircase, where she would play songs for him."

I also watched the sixties cartoon show *Johnny Quest,* in which a pug named Bandit played a minor role. But the official *coup de foudre* came when I returned home to Baltimore from Northwestern University for Thanksgiving vacation and landed in the midst of a family free-fire zone.

My parents were a few months away from what would be a marathon, no-blow-too-low divorce—and this was before such splits were commonplace. You could have cut the domestic tension with an electric knife, which as I recall, Mother found an unorthodox use for. Dad and my brother, Bobby, were sitting in the small, grass-papered den watching college football games. Outside in the hall, Mother gleefully switched the electric knife on and off to create static during key plays.

Having been trapped at O'Hare for seven hours, due to inclement weather, in order to make it home for this antipodal Norman Rockwellian event, I was feeling kind of sorry for myself. (Fortunately, I didn't know that this was the last time my family would gather in my lifetime or I'd have eaten all the Sara Lee brownies in the fridge.) Suddenly, sensing my distress—or more likely sensing a born chump—a diminutive tan furball with a black mask trotted bandy-legged down my parents' hall and plopped into my lap. She stared at me with bulgy unblinking brown eyes and licked off my lipstick with her unsettlingly long, rough, pink tongue. (I later learned that the tongue, a quarter of an inch too long, had kept her out of the show ring.) I was paralyzed by her cuteness and heartened by the display of affection. "She likes me," I marveled, not realizing that like most of her breed she was not blessed with the charism of discernment. Her name was Maggie May, she was an eight-month-old pug, and she belonged to my sister, Laurie. Otherwise, I would have stolen her on the spot.

Laurie had grown lonely with her older siblings away at college and had begged our parents for a puppy. "Mother researched every dog on the planet," my sister recalled. "After months of dragging me to dog shows, she finally decided that the perfect dog for me was a cairn terrier, like Toto. We went to Marjorie Shriver, a breeder in Towson, to buy the cairn. She also bred pugs. We picked out a cairn, but the pug kept getting in my face. It was such a goofy little thing. We even put money down on the cairn, but it wasn't old enough to leave. We got in the car, and I kept talking about the pug. So we turned around and went and got her." (Years later, Mrs. Shriver would tell me that she had to give up on the cairns, because "pugs are so bossy and so egotistical that the terriers suffered.")

Maggie was an enchanting soul who warbled arias like Maria Callas if you squealed at her at a high pitch, and she enjoyed being towed around the swimming pool while reclining regally on a raft. Not that Maggie was flawless; like all pugs, she enjoyed an outsized sense of self-worth. This had become apparent a few weeks earlier when my parents bought a second dog named Bobbin, a bichon frise.

My childhood home was separated from a highway-access road by a wide field. My parents couldn't understand why they kept finding Bobbin on the road. "One day we watched, and we saw Maggie lead her out into the field, then nudge her toward the road, then trot back, leaving the other dog stranded," Laurie said. "Maggie needed to be the center of attention, and if anyone else was, well, then their days were numbered. She was Clara's true predecessor."

I returned to Northwestern with pugs on the brain. When I

was supposed to be studying for finals in the library, I found myself researching the origin of the species.

A crash course, Pug 101: The breed has a longer history than any dog except the greyhound. It even has a motto: *Multum in parvo,* which is Latin for "a lot of dog in a small space." Pugs originated in China, the ancestral home of all short-faced dogs. First spotted in a town called Lo-Chiang, in the district of Sichuan, the primordial pugs were known as *Lo-Chiang-sze* or *Lo-sze.* The precise date remains a mystery—estimates range from 700 B.C. to A.D. 200—partly because between 255 and 205 B.C. the first emperor, Ch'in Shih, whose tomb outside Xi'an is graced by the amazing terra-cotta army, destroyed so much literary material.

(I found plenty of evidence of pug habitation when Duke and I visited Xi'an a few years ago. We were strolling near the Great Mosque when we came upon a marketplace where vendors were selling intriguing bric-a-brac—photographs of the Dowager Empress, Red Army compasses, cigarette lighters with a miniature enamel portrait of Chairman Mao that played "The East Is Rising" when you pushed a button. On a whim, I showed a vendor a photo of Clara. She trilled something in Mandarin, and within minutes, I was inundated with pug-shaped curios: combination locks, bronze chops, figurines, and bookends. I am not a pug-icon collector, but Blanche is, and she would never forgive me if I passed up the treasure trove.)

Chinese records dating from the end of the first century mention a puglike dog called pai, which means a short-legged, short-headed creature whose habitat was under the table. Not on the table, as my husband insists. Duke believes pugs were originally bred out of a meat breed from dogs who were spared from the cooking pot by their winsome appearance. Nei, a friend who grew up in Beijing, concurred. "Too cute to eat," he said.

Bred by eunuchs, these dogs became the favorites of emperors. According to pug historian Susan Graham Weall (*The Pug*, 1965), the emperor Ling Ti (A.D. 168–190) gave his favorite pug the official hat and belt of the Chin Hsien grade— the highest literary rank. "Other small dogs were given the title K'ai Fu and Yi Tung, which approximated to that of Viceroy and Imperial Guardian," Ms. Weall wrote. Bitches were granted ranks equivalent to the wives of such officials, and the small dogs were fed the best of meat and rice, slept on fine carpets, and were guarded by soldiers.

As China began trading, first via the Silk Road and later by sea, pugs captivated the world. During the Sung dynasty (969–1153), Lo-szes, also known as Foo dogs, were given as gifts to Japanese dignitaries. Pugs made an appearance in Lhasa, Tibet, where they were dubbed *lags k'yi*, or hand dogs. Local legend states that if a human lays his hand upon a freshly hatched eagle, it will be transformed into a pug. (If a pug goes near an eagle, it will be transformed into a sizable vet bill.)

Portuguese explorer Vasco de Gama opened the sea route to China in 1498. Soon after, pugs arrived in Europe courtesy of Portuguese sailors, who were no doubt aware of the impact a luscious little lapdog could have on their girlfriends. Even before formal trade between Holland and China began in 1604, pugs left an indelible mark on the Netherlands. On September 11, 1572, a pug named Pompey saved the life of William the Silent, prince of Orange, during the Battle of Hermigny. The Spanish commander, the duke of Alva, led six hundred musketeers on a surprise night raid on the rebel Dutch. The prince slept unaware that his men were being slaughtered until the brave—or, more likely, merely in the mood for a midnight snack—little Pompey awoke and scratched his master's face. Prince William escaped unharmed, and today his effigy in Delft Cathedral has a statue of Pompey at his feet.

By the seventeenth century, pugs were chewing the satin slippers of bluebloods all over Europe. When William the Silent's great-grandson, William III, and his bride, Mary, daughter of England's King James II, ascended the British throne in 1688, their pugs, known in Holland as *happa-honds* or Dutch mastiffs, replaced King Charles spaniels as court favorites. Bedecked with orange ribbons to show their support for the House of Orange, the pugs became the perfect grace note for ladies of fashion. The painter William Hogarth immortalized his leggy pug, Trump, in his *Self-Portrait,* which today hangs in the Tate Gallery. In Spain, Goya painted a portrait of a pug in traditional collar and bells along with the marquesa de Pontejos. It now hangs in the National Gallery of Art in Washington.

Meanwhile, in Central Europe, china and porcelain factories, most notably Meissen, were churning out litters of pug figurines. The managing director of the Meissen factory, Count Bruhl, had pugs, and they served as models. The elector of Saxony, a Grand Master of Freemasons, was one of Meissen's best customers. When the pope excommunicated the German Freemasons in 1736, they clandestinely continued their activities as Mopsorden, or the Order of the Pug. The pug became their mascot.

In 1761 George III married a passionate pugophile, Princess Charlotte of Meclenburg-Strelitz, and a portrait of king and pug can be seen at Hampton Court. Another avid pug fancier was the empress Josephine, whose birthday, June 23, Clara shares. Josephine was never sans pugs, even during the revolution, when she was imprisoned in Les Carmes, a Carmelite monastery. (Note for trivia buffs: her cell mate was Madame Tussaud.) Her favorite, Fortuné, carried messages in his collar between his mistress and Napoleon.

Frederic Masson noted in his 1899 book *Josephine, Empress and Queen,* that "Josephine's fondness for Fortuné nearly led to a quarrel with Napoleon on their wedding night. Pointing to Josephine's dog, lying on the sofa, he said, 'Do you see that gentleman: he is my rival. He was in possession of Madame's bed when I married her. I wished to remove him: it was quite useless to think of it. I was told that I must either sleep elsewhere or consent to share my bed. That annoyed me considerably, but I had to make up my mind. I gave way. The favourite was less accommodating. I bear proofs on my leg of what I say.' " Fortuné was later killed by the cook's bulldog, but Josephine promptly got several more pugs.

This is not to suggest the pug was universally beloved. In 1804, a miscreant named Taplin disparaged it in *The Sportsman's Cabinet: A Correct Delineation of the Canine Race.* "In the whole catalogue of the canine species there is not one of less utility or possessing less powers of attraction than the pug-dog," he wrote. It is theorized that these harsh words were responsible for a downslide in pug popularity. The ever-resiliant pug rebounded, and by the 1870s, a dog historian noted, "The Pug market is overstocked and everywhere in town and country these animals swarm." The pug can be found on antique advertising geegaws and postcards. Queen Victoria had a gaggle of pugs: Olga, Pedro, Venus, Minka, Fatima, Mops, Topsy, Duchess, and Boscow, who is buried at

Frogmore House Gardens. In 1897 Premier Black Gin, a pug owned by Alexandra, princess of Wales, was in the Parade of Champions at the London Kennel Association Show.

Over the years, the crown of creation acquired a wide variety of pompous names: the Lutheran dog (because by saving William the Silent, the little pug allowed the Reformation to continue in Europe), Camuses (French for flat-nosed), Mopschund (from the German verb *mopen,* "to mope," which well describes the pug's melancholy expression), and Carlin, after a famous eighteenth-century French actor who played the part of the harlequin.

For Duke's last birthday I bought him the *Oxford English Dictionary* on CD-ROM. Upon hooking it up, he immediately looked up the etymology of the word *pug*. I had always heard that *pug* evolved from the Latin *pugnus,* which means "fist," which the pug's face rather resembles. But per the *O.E.D.,* the word first appeared in the English language in the sixteenth century and was used as an endearment for a human being. A hundred years later *pug* described a pet monkey, a mistress, and a small demon or imp. It was not until the 1700s that definition number seven came into the language: "a dwarf breed of dog, resembling a bull dog in miniature; on account of its affectionate nature much kept as a pet."

Duke instructed the software to look up any phrases with *pug* in it, and his eyes twinkled when he came to the following: "Pug slut," he read gleefully, "the female of pug dog."

Clara was maintaining a vigil under his chair, hoping a few crumbs of the pretzel he was eating would fall her way. She looked up and smiled, her pink tongue protruding from her lips. "Clara, are you a pug slut?" he cooed in a voice he's never used with me. She tilted her head to her most flattering angle and raised her eyebrows coquettishly.

Luckily, twenty years ago, I couldn't foresee that one day I would be sharing my husband's affections with a winsome but conniving pug. Or else my life might have been a lot drearier.

Fast-forward two years. I graduated from college and moved to California. Temporarily estranged from my parents, who seemed to be putting more energy and ingenuity into their divorce than they had in their marriage, I shared a garden apartment three blocks from UCLA with Richard, my then-boyfriend and now ex-husband. While on a trip to New York, we spied a soignée older woman sitting in the shoe department of Bergdorf Goodman, with a black and a fawn pug lounging at her feet. Automatically, I fell to the ground and began romping with her dogs, a behavior that I would subsequently find extremely annoying when strangers did it to me. Their owner bore the intrusion with good grace and even referred me to a couple of kennels where I too might acquire such an attractive brace. A photographer came over and asked if he could take a picture. "Sure," I said, and posed with pugs in lap.

Later, Richard cackled. "He didn't want your picture. Didn't you know? That was the actress Sylvia Sidney."

Who knew? I only had eyes for the pugs.

On our way back to Los Angeles, Richard and I stopped in Chicago to visit some college friends. We were in the suburbs, looking at dollhouse furniture—miniatures being the second-most addictive substance in my life after pugs. Bored, Richard wandered into a newsstand and idly flipped through a copy of *Dog Fancy*. He dragged me out of the dollhouse store, whooping, "There's a pug farm nearby. C'mon, let's go." We searched for an hour until we finally noticed a bronze pug figurine on the mailbox. A sign read, WELCOME TO CJ'S KENNEL. I ran out of the car, knocked on the door, and explained I was in the market for a pair of puppies.

The duenna was out, but an acolyte led us to an adjacent barn configured with a half dozen indoor runs, delineated like swim lanes. In the center a majestic fawn pug stood motionless on a little podium like a chubby French king. "That's Gold Rush," the acolyte said proudly. "He's a champion."

A black puppy in a cage reached out and tapped my shoulder. When I pet her, she cheeped like a monkey. I was told that this was Gold Rush's prodigal daughter, Bruce. She had been recently returned by a dissatisfied buyer.

"Bruce? Are you sure she's a girl?"

The acolyte shrugged. Never mind, I thought. I'll call her Bess. The acolyte opened the cage. Bruce, who had long shapely legs, sprang into my arms and greeted me with joyous and stinky abandon. In the space of thirty seconds, she peed on me, drooled on me, licked me until I reeked of pug saliva. She must have imprinted me in her psyche like a gosling does with the mother goose because for the next fourteen years Bess revered me with a most unpuglike devotion. (Bess's adoration was largely responsible for my preference for black pugs, though I've never had one since who held me in such esteem.) On that first meeting she screeched like no animal I'd ever heard—my vet would later christen her "the pug that screams like a human being." I imagined her imploring, "Get me out of this dump before I suffer permanent gender damage."

That evening I called the breeder and arranged to purchase Bruce and an unseen fawn puppy that the breeder explained was "the pick of the litter from one of my dogs out in Iowa." Either the breeder was less than frank or the Iowa kennel was in the middle of a nuclear-waste dump. In any case, a week later the puppies arrived by air freight. Bruce, whom I immediately rechristened Bess, bolted out of her Sky Kennel and into my arms. The apple-headed, splay-footed fawn puppy, whom I named Stella, paid no attention to me whatsoever until dinnertime, when she trotted eagerly to her dish. (For the next fourteen years she ignored me unless I was holding a doughnut.)

At the time I had no way of knowing that Bess and Stella would see me through marriage, divorce, dating, remarriage, my first book, and breast cancer (I would visualize little pugs tearing through my bloodstream, eating malignant cells the way they wolfed down dinner scraps) or that they would become my emotional anchor and keep me physically fit and sane. But as I watched Bess and Stella scurry across the wood floors and skid to a stop, I knew I wouldn't be lonely again, and I was deeply grateful.

So grateful that when the pugs turned my life upside down forty-eight hours after their arrival, I couldn't complain. Everyone in our apartment building had cats, and Richard and I had been told that all we needed to have a pet was a hundred-dollar security deposit. The day after the pugs arrived, I ran into the landlord and blithely handed him a check. He handed it back, along with an ultimatum. "Move out in thirty days, or get rid of those dogs."

"Maybe we should send them back," Richard said practically, "before we get too attached to them."

I sent him to the grocery store to pick up kibble and cardboard boxes and cheerfully began to pack. At the time, I believed that giving up our apartment was the biggest sacrifice I'd make to keep a pug happy. But that was back when I still thought of my pugs as pets.

Before Clara.

The Glimmer of Intelligence

*M*other maintains that she was the first person to recognize that Clara was special. The first time she said it, and she's said it a million times since, I felt obliged to point out that the obstinate Sophie was better-looking. Sophie is such a living manifestation of the American Kennel Club standard—cobby, muscular body, massive head, double-curled tail—that Blanche, a tough judge of pug flesh, cannot see her without muttering, "She could have been a contender." Unspoken is the accusation, "If you hadn't been so stupid as to have had Sophie spayed," an operation that disqualified her from the show ring under American Kennel Club rules.

"Don't get me wrong," Mother said tactfully. "Sophie is a nice dog. But Clara is Miss Personality."

She made this proclamation a couple of days after I'd taken possession of the squirming black bag. We—Mother, the squirming bag, and I—were in Saks Fifth Avenue, waiting for the aggressively chic Escada-clad Personal Shopper to stop scratching Clara's belly and produce a suitable dress for me to wear to my sister Laurie's wedding. The bride had informed me that as her matron of honor I could choose anything I liked.

Just so long as it was ankle-length, off-white, and in the spirit of Caroline Kennedy's wedding gown.

Having come to New York expressly to meet my publisher and visit magazine editors, I was not really in the mood to try on frocks. But Mother, who is to shopping what Tiger Woods is to golf, insisted. "It's a shame not to take advantage of the stores in the city." Mother doesn't believe there are stores in Los Angeles, a place she regards as a nicely landscaped wasteland because it's not on Eastern standard time and the news anchors spend an inordinate amount of time talking about the weather. She would pick me up at the Hotel San Carlos at ten o'clock sharp.

Clara was not invited to join our shopping expedition, nor had I any intention of taking her along. I'd been warned that her paws could not touch the fabled sidewalks of New York because she didn't have all her shots and could thus contract a virulent and no doubt expensive puppy disease. I was also cognizant that a baby pug should be confined to a small space until she has mastered housebreaking. I planned to leave her in the bathroom of my junior suite, which after only a day of pug occupancy resembled an annex to the Beekman Pet Emporium two blocks away on Second Avenue.

In less than twenty-four hours I'd accumulated more gear for Clara than I'd bought for Bess and Stella in fourteen years. Amenities included several copies of *The New York Times* (the newspaper of record did a better job covering the bathroom floor than the tabloids), Wee Wee Pads (high-priced wads of paper scientifically impregnated with a scent that was supposed to attract the puppy but in fact repelled her), a hideous doughnut-shaped bed made of chartreuse shag carpet (a parting gift from her breeder), a Dan Quayle rubber squeak toy (mea culpa, I couldn't resist), and a shocking-pink feeding bowl filled with organic lamb-and-rice puppy kibble. She was also the recipient of a dozen minibagels from the Doggy Bakery (a welcome gift from Loretta, my agent), rawhide lollipops (a gift from Mother), and a stuffed white rabbit in red coveralls, which Lorene, the breeder, had given Clara to keep her from pining for her litter mates back in Michigan (a total waste of money; Clara never looked back).

Clara was not a material girl, and these accoutrements didn't turn a hair on her jet-black head. Five minutes after her arrival, while I was on the phone with Duke wailing about her skunk stripe, she inspected our junior suite like Leona Helmsley checking to see if the chocolate mints on the pillows were lined up at right angles. Clara noticed the spacious queen-sized bed, the plush carpet, and the cozy loveseat in my sitting room. She beheld the cold hard floor—tile, not even marble—in her tiny bathroom. And she realized that the Human had put her own comfort over the pug's—a serious error that must be corrected at once so the Human would not make this mistake again.

It was impossible to reason with her. Clara emerged from that nylon bag fully formed, like Venus rose from the scallop shell. If I went into the galley kitchen to fetch an apple, she trailed me and announced that she too might be in the mood for a little fruit. (She grew so fond of apples—particularly the high-priced Fujis—that Duke later nicknamed her the Fruit Bat.) When I stretched out on the loveseat to watch yet another made-for-television-ratings figure-skating competition—Monistat's Battle of the Has-Beens?—Clara stood on her hind legs and remonstrated until I lifted her onto my lap (she rooted for Oksana Baiul, whom she resembles). Loretta met Clara an hour after she arrived and with tremendous amusement watched her carry squeak toys out of the bathroom and deposit them on the sitting room floor. "She's busy," Loretta observed. "She has an agenda. I only hope you're on it."

Our first night together I insisted that Clara sleep alone. She protested; I resisted. She pushed open the bathroom door and appeared at my bedside, cooing like a wounded dove. She prodded me with her paw and gave me the "I'm madly in love with you, how can you reject me?" stare. I remained firm. I said, "You're a dog, Clara," and carried the indignant beast back to her quarters. A minute later she escaped again. This time Clara took a long running start in the sitting room, used my suitcase as a launching pad, and catapulted onto the bed. She crept over to the vacant pillow—as if I didn't realize she was there—artfully arranged herself so her tail was in my face, and snored delicately. I was so dazzled by her problem-solving ability that I let her stay. Clara didn't stir until our nine o'clock wake-up call. Then she stretched languidly, jumped down from the bed, trotted into the bathroom, anointed the Home section of *The New York Times*, and returned to bed.

On the day of the great shopping expedition, Gabriel at the front desk called at nine-fifteen. Mother was waiting outside. I sighed with exasperation. She is habitually forty-five minutes early. I am habitually only five minutes early, which by her reckoning makes me habitually forty minutes late. Three minutes later Gabriel called again. "Hurry up, Mom is double-parked." A native New Yorker, Mom drives around the city in her Town Car the way she once cruised around the Baltimore suburbs where I grew up. I hastily poured some kibble into

Clara's dish, figuring I could make a getaway while she was eating.

Clara did not fall for the ruse. She carefully memorized the sequence of events: Human puts on coat. Picks up purse. Runs around like a crazy person looking for her sunglasses (it's overcast in Manhattan, but Human has lived in Los Angeles for twenty years and is phobic about glare). Swears because she can't find her keys. Eventually locates keys in the bottom of her purse, where she had looked not five minutes earlier. Tries to distract pug with a bowl of nasty-looking brown pellets.

Clara concluded: Keys mean abandonment. As soon as the door opened, she dashed through my feet and sped down the hall to the elevator.

"What a precious little puppy," a chambermaid gushed.

I picked her up and said, "Bad dog, Clara."

She squealed like a pig being slaughtered.

"Oh, no, don't hurt the precious little puppy," cried the maid.

"She's doing it for effect," I muttered, for the first of what would be many times. I carried Precious back to our room. She uncurled her tail and trembled. She furrowed her brow. She sat on my shoe. "See you later," I said, and locked the door.

Halfway down the corridor, I heard her whimper like Camille. Had I been home, I would have kept walking. Such is an advantage of home ownership. But I was in a hotel, dependent on the kindness of a tenderhearted owner who wouldn't be nearly so tenderhearted if another guest complained.

I unlocked the door. I stated the obvious. "You want to come."

"Duh," thought Clara.

I unzipped her black bag.

"Sucker," thought Clara. She gave me a patronizing smile, displaying two crooked jack-o'-lantern teeth, and scampered into the bag. She snuggled on her blanket and remained silent as I carried her through the lobby.

Mother's eyes narrowed as I climbed into the front seat. "Where did you get that purse?" she asked. "It's too big for you."

I partially unzipped the bag, and Clara's head popped out like a periscope. She peered at the leather bucket seats. She reasoned, "What the hell am I doing in this hot bag?" She climbed out and made a nest on the armrest.

"I don't think it's smart to bring her," said Mother.

"You're right," I agreed. "But she wants to come."

Clara flared her mushroom nostrils, fixed Mother in her crosshairs, and attempted to bend Mother's will—a task I've never managed in my lifetime. I watched with fascination as Clara willfully turned up the volume of her own cuteness. She extended her front paws and stretched languidly. Her lips parted ever so slightly to reveal a glimpse of rosebud-pink tongue. Her entire being became smaller and squarer.

Mother shrugged, started the car, and cut in front of a bus. "You were just like that when you were a little girl," she said. "I used to take you everywhere."

She miraculously found a parking space on the street a block from Saks. I said, "Clara, get in the bag," and after a quick deliberation as to whether this action was in her own best interest, the pug made a dramatic leap. As we rode the escalator to the fifth floor, she peeped through the mesh ventilation panels at all the luckless shoppers who would never get a chance to stroke her glossy black coat. She sent a telepathic entreaty to Mother, who was rapidly settling into her role as doting grandmother.

"Clara is too warm," Mother said. She partially unzipped the bag, and the periscope emerged. Once we reached the Fifth Avenue Club, the plush lounge where customers who patronize the store's Personal Shoppers get to try on clothes, Mother declared that Clara preferred to sit on the comfy chintz couch.

I was not enthusiastic. I recalled the day that I picked Sophie up from Paul Winfield. She was five months old. I'd brought along a portable Sky Kennel and carefully placed the puppy inside it so she wouldn't feel insecure on the long drive home. Duke had asked me to stop by his office with the new member of the family. I carried Sophie's box into his office and opened the kennel door. Sophie refused to come out.

"She's scared," Duke said in his gentlest voice. He whispered sweet nothings into her cage, but Sophie wouldn't budge. Now that I know Sophie, I realize it wasn't fear, just obstinacy.

Back at Saks, I expressed concern that Clara might experience similar stranger anxiety.

"Don't be ridiculous," Mother said, and released the puppy like Elsa the lioness in *Born Free*. Clara admired herself in the three-way mirror, then gracefully arranged herself on a thousand-dollar Armani skirt that a previous customer had discarded in a corner of the dressing room. When the Personal Shopper appeared, wearing so much costume jewelry she clanked, Clara sashayed over to greet her and sat demurely on her shoe. She widened her Bette Davis eyes until the Shopper got the message and picked her up. Clara licked off half a pound of Clinique foundation and shed at least five dozen black hairs, but the Shopper didn't mind. Instead, she rounded up a half dozen of her immaculately dressed colleagues. Clara worked the crowded dressing room like Clinton on the campaign trail, occasionally raking her needle claws on a pair of seventy-dollar Wolford stockings.

Mother had a revelation. "She doesn't behave like a dog," she whispered. "I've had dogs all my life, and that isn't what she is. She's a little person walking on all fours."

Initially, I suspected that Mother was laying it on so thick because she believed that Clara was the closest thing to a grandchild she was likely to get from me. But the longer I spent with Clara, the more I realized what Mother had seen immediately: Clara had powers. Still, for fifteen years I'd prided myself on treating my pets like dogs, not people, and I didn't intend to make an exception.

"Clara, would you like a glass of water?" asked the Shopper.

"No, thank you," I said. Water, an unhousebroken puppy, and ivory carpet were not a good mix.

"Bottled water would be lovely," Mother said imperiously. "Clara's a little parched." Frankly, I was surprised she didn't suggest we stop by Rumpelmayer's so Clara could have an egg cream.

As if on cue, Clara panted dramatically, her rosebud tongue unfurled to twice its original size. The Personal Shopper hastily fetched a cut-crystal goblet and a bottle of Evian. From the way Clara attacked it, you would have thought the sneaky bitch had been stranded in the Sahara for a month with a leaky canteen.

"Poor dear was thirsty," the Shopper said reproachfully.

I disliked having my parenting skills questioned by a total stranger. "She had water before we left."

Mother lowered her voice. "She was born to act. Like Shirley Temple, who at age four was an international star."

Mother was born to be a stage mother. I was a washout, but with Clara, she finally had her opportunity. She glanced at her watch, realized we were—gasp!—only an hour early for our next appointment, at Barneys, and dragged the pug away from the admiring throngs. She whispered to Clara, "Always leave them wanting more." To avoid having the pug suffer from loneliness on the ride down the escalator, Mother handed me the Sherpa Bag while she cradled Clara in her arms. The sight of the tiny black puppy pressed against Mother's white mink attracted the eye of nearly every shopper in the store.

That escalator ride taught Clara a valuable lesson: A pug gets more attention at eye level. Henceforth she would refuse to stand on an escalator; she automatically assumes the paws-locked position and makes me hold her aloft. She did, however, master elevators and revolving doors.

I never did find a dress, but by morning's end, Clara was the toast of Barneys, Bloomingdale's, Henri Bendel, and Bergdorf Goodman. Mother suggested that we take her "someplace special" for lunch, but I passed. Though Jacqueline Susann wrote that poodles used to be regularly checked at "21," I didn't think my mother's favorite haunts, Le Cirque and the Friars Club, were pug-friendly, so I brought her back to the Hotel San Carlos.

By the time we got to the lobby, I suspected the puppy's entire inside was one big bladder. Like the Queen of England, she never let a call of nature come between her and her public. When Gabriel at the front desk refused to turn over my room key until he'd met Clara—or, as he called her, because he was Spanish, Clarita—she sat placidly on the reception counter and allowed herself to be stroked by the doorman, the bellboy, and several of our fellow guests. She waited until we were back in our room, then she trotted into the bathroom, squatted gracefully on *The New York Times,* and returned to her command post on the sofa. She looked up at me eagerly as if to ask, "So, where are we going next?"

I wound up taking her to all my meetings, and she did my career a world of good. Normally, when I'm in New York I call on various publications to solicit assignments. Editors aren't thrilled to see a freelance writer, and before Clara, my average meeting lasted at most twenty minutes. But when I entered a magazine office with the world's most ingratiating puppy riding shotgun in my shoulder bag, the dynamic improved considerably. By the second meeting, Clara had worked out a fail-safe sales pitch. I gave my name to the gatekeeper, and ever so subtly the periscope rose from the bag and surveyed the situation. If she wasn't noticed immediately, she sneezed delicately or snorted. "What on earth do you have in that bag?" the gatekeeper would ask, and the pug would give her a conspiratorial wink, as if to say, "How clever of you to notice."

Invariably, she'd be invited to come out of her bag. She emerged slowly, like Gypsy Rose Lee fingering a glove. She wobbled a little, like a newborn colt, to elicit sympathy, then made a beeline for the most powerful person in the room. I felt like Shari Lewis with Lamb Chop. Instead of promoting myself as a writer, I found myself providing color commentary for Clara's performance. "Yes, black pugs are rare." "No, she doesn't have breathing problems." "Yes, the Duke and Duchess of Windsor kept pugs too." In fact, they were bathed every day in Miss Dior perfume. Clara shares the Duke's birthday, but she's not proud of it. ("Nazi sympathizer," Clara says.)

I couldn't complain, even though Clara came away from these encounters with all sorts of souvenirs: bottled water, string cheese, squeak toys, a traveling feeding dish, even half a pastrami on rye, at places that didn't even offer me a Diet Coke. (This is the biggest difference between doing business on the East and West coasts. On the latter you are always served refreshments, even if you're about to be fired.) I was beholdened to Clara for her professional support. It was impossible for a snooty women's magazine editor to intimidate me or price my clothes when she was crawling on the floor with the pug. When I smuggled Clara into *The New York Times,* an editor at the Travel section insisted on carrying her over to meet an editor at the magazine who had heretofore failed to respond to any of my letters or calls. Clara was given a couple of copies of the paper (she favored the Home section) as a parting gift. I even got an assignment.

Her greatest triumph came at my publisher's office. My first book was about to come out, and I had gone to New York to meet my then-editor, David. He is not a pug person and seemed taken aback when exclamations of "Isn't she cute?" began ringing down the hall. (Then again, the man who was David's boss, publishing lord S. I. Newhouse, had a pug named Nero who every year was given a birthday party—complete with caviar and twenty pug guests—by the writer Alexandra Penney. Nero died, but his successor, Cicero, is similarly feted.) A sales meeting was in progress, and Clara was passed around the conference table with great reverence, like she was the author of the megaseller *Midnight in the Garden of Good and Evil.* She even got to meet Peter Gethers, whose famous cat, Norton, travels in a similar Sherpa Bag. "We may have to send Clara on tour with you," David said, and the buoyant pug kissed his nose, much to his chagrin.

By the end of her first visit to Manhattan, Clara had gotten me more assignments than my agent. "She's in control," said Loretta, who would later express regret that she had failed to sign Clara as a client at this time. "She's the cutest puppy in the world, and she has an attitude."

Mother drove us to the airport and made me promise to bring Clara back to New York at Christmastime so the pug could see the tree at Rockefeller Center. I was surprised she didn't offer to take her skating.

Our flight home was uneventful. Clara stayed in her bag, stowed under the seat in front of me, until the pilot turned off the FASTEN SEAT BELT sign. Then she mewed imploringly to be let out. I explained that it was against airline regulations. She assured me that she understood the need for stealth. (Clara would prove to be an accomplished sneak.) She snored quietly in my lap, hidden under a blanket, and only made her presence known when the stewardess came around with lunch. Clara awoke instantly and fired up her begging program. She put her paws on the armrest and stared at the meal cart. She savored the aroma of the prefabricated food. She licked her lips hopefully. (She may have been the first passenger in years to express eagerness for an airline meal.)

"Would Clara like a little steak?" the flight attendant asked. Actually, Clara would. She also ate my roll and half my fruit plate, and she drank water from a plastic cup. Somewhere over Denver I stuffed her back into her bag and carried her into the bathroom. I set the Home section of *The New York Times* on the floor, and she did her business. I was walking back to my seat when the stewardess asked, "Would Clara like to meet the pilot?" Actually, Clara would, and she returned from the cockpit with a set of American Airlines wings.

"At least they didn't let her fly the plane," Duke later said.

The stewardess allowed Clara to remain in my lap until we approached Los Angeles. Then she apologetically asked me to put her under the seat for landing. Clara darted into her bag without a protest.

Having conquered the sky, Mother, the publishing industry, and me, Clara felt pretty cocky when we landed at Los Angeles International Airport. Duke met us at the gate, took one look at her, and exclaimed, "She's the cutest thing I've ever seen." That was when I realized our future roles were cast: I'd be playing Margo Channing to Clara's Eve Harrington.

Only one hurdle remained.

How was Eve going to deal with Sophie?

Over the Top

On our way back from the airport, Duke and I were stopped at a light when he pointed to the car in front of us. A fluffy white Pomeranian, no bigger than the infant Clara, was sprawled out on the rear deck gazing out the window. "Maybe you can teach Clara to do that," Duke said.

"That dog's mother must be out of her mind," I snapped. "If she accelerates too abruptly, her pooch will go flying."

"Report her to the ASPCA," Duke suggested.

I wouldn't be surprised if I could.

Clara had the good fortune to arrive when the entire nation was in the throes of pet dementia. The pet's—or for the politically correct, the companion animal's—position in society had drastically improved in the fifteen years since I got Bess and Stella. My previous pugs led what seemed to me to be an enviable life. Okay, so they didn't dine off porcelain bowls like the Duchess of Windsor's pugs. But they spent their days snoozing under my desk (pugs are prodigious sleepers) in a house at the beach with a fenced-in yard and sofas that weren't off-limits. Bess and Stella promenaded daily on the second biggest attraction in Southern California after Disneyland, the Venice boardwalk, where cars are not permitted and droves of tourists clustered around to take their pictures and stroke their glossy coats.

I considered Bess and Stella to be pampered—dare I say spoiled? Then the stalwart Sophie arrived and it gradually dawned on me that I had fallen behind the curve. At seven months, Sophie contracted ear mites. Naturally, I didn't notice her affliction until late Friday afternoon, when it was too late to drive across town and give Dr. Shekel, my vet of over fifteen years, a hundred dollars for a magical elixir. (Dogs, like cars and household appliances, seldom break down during routine business hours.) Rather than spend an entire weekend with her incessant scratching and agonized yipping, I took her to a nearby animal clinic. The vet made me fill out an extensive questionnaire so she could analyze the quality of our relationship. One question read: "Do you think of your (fill in the species) as A) Just an animal? B) Your pet? or C) A member of the family?"

In truth, I thought of Sophie as "D) Bane of my existence," but I checked "B." The doctor looked at me like I was O. J. Simpson. "My Yorkie is like my daughter," she said coldly.

That's when it hit me: The role of Pet Owner had changed. It was no longer okay to feed them whatever supermarket chow was on special: I had to drive out of my way to a deluxe pet boutique or warehouse-sized superstore to purchase high-ticket, scientifically blended (what motivates a scientist to go into dog-food research?) premium brands like Science Diet, Iams, or Clara's personal favorite, Nutro Max Mini Naturally Preserved Kibble. According to the package, a big selling point of this recipe is—I kid you not—low stool volume. Allow me to quote from the label: "Firm, low-volume stools mean faster, easier cleanup, and a cleaner, more hygienic environment for your dog and family."

Pity the copywriter who had to come up with that. (Then again, she probably got a raise.)

Bookstores devoted entire sections to improving my relationship with my animals. Either the books were written by a dog who enjoyed a life my pugs could only dream about—for example, Peter Mayle's shaggy Boy, who lives in Provence—or else they were disapproving manuals along the lines of *Smart Pet, Stupid Master*. They operated on the same guilt-giving principal as New Age self-help books and women's magazines: No matter what the problem, it was my fault. I was lax because I refused to brush my dogs' teeth, consult a behavioral psychologist if they chewed my shoes, or take them to a dog park for maximum socialization. No longer could I reward a pug with rawhide treats; I had to prove my love with ceramic bowls hand-painted with their names, copper repoussé sculptures of them created from their photographs, gold lamé bow ties, and doggy life jackets. I was even expected to throw birthday parties and send "Sorry to Hear You Got Fixed" greeting cards.

It was not enough to own a dog: I had to be its mother.

I can hear you snickering that this is an isolated phenomenon peculiar to Southern California, ground zero for all outlandish things. Well, think again. I recently read that a Thai businessman spent twenty thousand dollars on the wedding of his two Siamese cats. A pet hotel in Japan offers volcanic hot-sand therapy. (And no doubt, sells treatment to combat the volcanic hot-sand fleas.) A Manhattan attorney specializes in disputes between pet owners and landlords. Harrods offers $16,000 four-poster beds decorated with gold leaf, ostrich feathers, and satin, and Neiman Marcus offers a $9,400 neo-classical pet mansion. The swank mail order catalog In the Company of Dogs sells blue-and-white porcelain dishes, fisherman knit sweaters, damask beds, even a dining table with a walnut finish and turned spindle legs. The catalog is the brainchild of Bill Rauhauser, former CFO of F.A.O. Schwarz, and his designer wife, Ann Counts—the parents of Nicholas and Alexander, two borzois. "We started it because two members of our family have four legs and we couldn't find the type of quality product that mirrored our lifestyle and what we wanted to have for our four-legged family members," Counts told me.

Rauhauser added, "For example, we wanted a handsome wood-surfaced dining table with a water-resistant finish so they could eat dinner in a healthy way that also fit in with our kitchen decor. It had a sense of style and it had a value, and it also had the quality we were looking for in our personal possessions."

The market for such finery is vast. *Harper's* Index estimated that a million dogs had been named as beneficiaries in wills. The Pet Industry Joint Advisory Council, located in Washington, D.C., reported that in 1996 there were 58.2 million dogs in America and 66.12 million cats, whose owners shelled out $18.5 billion in 1995 on products, foods, and services. (That's up $168.50 billion from 1993.) A 1996–1997 annual survey made by the American Pet Products Manufacturers Association (APPMA) estimated that slightly less than 58 million U.S. households have pets. In 1996, 66 percent of all pet owners gave Snoopy or Fido a Christmas present, 25 percent gave birthday presents, and 4 percent sent valentines.

And to think that in over twenty years of pug ownership, I'd never dressed a dog up for Halloween.

I would have guessed that the obsessive behavior is due to the fact that more people live alone and want to show their appreciation for their furry roommates. But Doug Poindexter, executive vice president of World Wide Pet Supply Association in Arcadia, California, claims it triggers back to the fitness movement. "In the last ten years, as the human side of existence began to take better care of themselves they also took better care of their animals," Mr. Poindexter said. "The human self-care worked its way down the evolutionary ladder and brought on the explosion on premium dog food, vitamins, dressing, and all the other things just followed that."

"More and more people are deciding not to have children," added psychologist Barbara Cadow, a clinical associate at the University of Southern California. "That wasn't an option years ago. But nowadays, people make that decision freely. Then they find that there's a hole in their life. And the lucky pets fill it."

Take the spectacularly fortunate Schuylor and Berni, an Old English sheepdog and a Lhasa apso who belong to my friends James and Codette. "The only difference between them and children is we don't have to put away for college," Codette says. "We don't have to buy them a car or clothing. Though I do. They have raincoats and sweaters."

Schuylor and Berni get top billing on the phone-machine message and go everywhere, even to Vegas, where their companion humans found a hotel that welcomed the seventy-pound Schuylor (talk about a casino doing anything to get you in). "I even took them to the Blessing of the Animals," Codette says. "Shortly after Schuylor was blessed he ran away and someone called us and said they found him. I don't know if there's a correlation."

I do. To have a relationship with an animal companion is to

be in touch with a higher form of love. You have to accept it for what it is. You can't try to make a gerbil into a parakeet. And in exchange, "You come home from work in a bad mood, you don't want to hear your wife talk about her problems," says my stepfather, Paul, whose heart belonged to Tommy, a West Highland terrier, who recently passed away. "But a dog doesn't argue. He's just glad to see you." Paul showed his appreciation by holding a cool compress to Tommy's forehead when the weather got really hot.

Still, there's a fine line between being an indulgent Pet Owner and a Pet Parent, though nobody agrees about exactly where the line should be drawn. Blanche, who used to run a chichi Woodland Hills grooming shop, explains the difference this way. "An owner brings the dog in, says she wants a regular kennel clip on her poodle, asks what time the dog will be ready, leaves, comes back at the appointed hour, pays, goes home, and in six weeks, I see her again. But the parent walks in clutching the dog to her breast. She asks if the dog will be in the crate all day, she tells you to be careful of the feet, the eyes, the ears, and she wants a special Continental clip with a little rounded topknot and the toenails polished. Then she asks when the dog will be ready, you say three hours, and she starts to whine, and she goes on whining until you say, one hour. Then she returns, looks at her dog as if you have been beating it, and cries, 'Poor poopsy, poor poopsy.' "

I considered myself to be an owner because my pugs didn't have a personal trainer or a four-figure doghouse designed by an architect. And I didn't consider myself to be their mom. But my husband disagreed. "You've done everything for that puppy except find a Montessori school," Duke said, referring to Clara. "I think you're close to the danger zone."

So is he, according to my friend Gamma Rae's definition of

a Pet Parent: "anyone who has ever made up songs about their pet." Right after he met Clara, my husband startled me by singing a chorus of "Pugolina" to the tune of "Thumbelina." (The bridge went, "Though you're no bigger than my shoe, than my shoe, oh, Pugolina, don't be blue. Scratch and dig! Run and yelp! Bite and chew!") Duke claimed that his behavior was perfectly natural. "It wasn't for the dog, it was for you," he argued. "The dog doesn't understand the lyrics." (I wouldn't bet on that.)

I suppose that all Pet Owners (except perhaps the owner of the psychotic Doberman behind the barbed wire in the junk-yard) are Pet Parents to some degree. The question is degree. Hovering close to the edge is my sister, Laurie, who has three cats, Gigi, George, and Gypsy. When she and her husband moved from Chicago to Dallas, she bent over backward to ease the felines' transition. "I read books on the psychological problems they'd face," Laurie confessed. "I gave them bottled water to minimize digestive upsets. I even bought *Video Cat-nip*, a tape of birds and squirrels, to keep them entertained. We still don't have doctors, and they have a staff of vets and a house sitter. They have someone who lives with them when we go out of town."

By any definition, Melody, an insurance agent and self-described "supermom" to her shih tzus, Betty and Barney, is far over the red line. "I live for their poop!" she exclaimed when I ran into her at Petco, the animal kingdom's answer to IKEA. "They have a nanny who comes in twice a day, and sweaters for when it gets cold. They even have their own stroller. I take them out in it as much as possible."

I delicately inquired if her dogs had some kind of disability such as hip dysplasia. It was as if I had suggested her children had lice. "They're too little to walk long distances," she said indignantly, and when I mentioned that pugs are about the same size and have no trouble, she assured me her shih tzus were "extremely athletic." (I've yet to meet a Pet Parent who described any aspect about his or her creature as unexceptional.) "The stroller allows me to spend more time with them," she claimed.

This logic does not surprise Matthew Margolis, owner of the National Institute for Dog Training. "Pet Parents literally treat their animals like a child, even to the point of talking to it like a child or making excuses," he says. "Like, they say, 'He only goes to the bathroom because he's angry,' or 'I'm not giving him enough attention and that's why he doesn't listen.' They forget that dogs are not people in dog's clothing."

My husband has threatened to commit me if he ever comes home and finds the pugs in a party dress or a cowboy outfit. But Marie Wang, who used to manage Posh Pets, an animal-fashion house on the Venice boardwalk that specialized in such apparel, never had trouble finding customers. "If it's summer, parents need sunglasses and a visor," she said. "If it's winter, they need a biker jacket or a sweater or a raincoat. We've even had people inquire about lingerie."

Wang agreed teddies and chemises were a little over the top, but she didn't see anything odd about making bridal gowns and tuxedoes for parents who want to include their animals in their wedding. "We make sure the trim on the tuxedo matches the decorations," she said.

Her boss, designer Gwen Zeller, has outfitted cats, iguanas, llamas, horses, goats, and pigs, but her most unusual request came from the mother of a black Labrador retriever named Nickie. "She was having a Bark Mitzvah for her dog when it turned thirteen in dog years," Zeller recalled. The woman planned a religious service followed by a party for

twenty dog guests and their owners. "We made the Bark Mitzvah dog a yarmulke and a Western-style suit, and the other
dogs got custom-designed monogrammed hats."

Cat owners need not feel superior. Recently Gamma Rae
offered this explanation as to why her cat, Beltane, liked to
play with thumbtacks: "She's fascinated by the manifestation
of contrast." Gamma Rae is so daft she intends to become a
Pet Grandparent soon, when she has her cat bred. "The wonderful thing about being a Pet Parent is that it opens your eyes
to a whole other world."

Moreover, it's an almost entirely positive experience. Pets,
unlike people, are easy to please. I can bring home a six-inch
stuffed whale with a squeaker inside, and Sophie's entertained
for hours. This no doubt accounts for why in 1996 three quarters of all dog owners didn't think twice about purchasing
shampoos, I.D. tags, dog deodorants, pooper-scoopers, auto
seat belts, bows and ribbons, automatic feeding devices,
breath-control products, colognes, pet doors, and stain re-
movers.

"A lot of therapists advise clients to get an animal," psychologist Cadow says. She has patients whose "kids" are bun-
nies and ferrets, but dogs are particularly beneficial because
you have to take them out. "There's a whole community based
on having the dog. Walking the dog. Taking it to the dog park.
We need those connections." I'm not sure I really needed to
become the Hollywood correspondent for *Pug Talk* magazine.
But if I were a baker, I suppose I'd try my hand at dog cookies.

People who don't have companion animals can't imagine
how great a hold they have on your heart. Thanks to the pugs,
I always had a compelling reason to get out of bed every morning and even though I work alone, I never lacked for compan-
ionship. Sometimes my grip on reality slipped; I wondered

where the three sixes are hidden under Sophie's fur. But most of the time I was in control.

Unlike Claire, who worries about her Samoyeds constantly. "I read somewhere that people were kidnapping pedigreed dogs and putting them in a pen with killer dogs and making them fight for their life," she said. "That's honestly my worst fear. They're so sheltered. My husband and I won't even have an argument in front of them, for God's sake."

Margolis, the animal trainer, sees the range of human emotions at his "Betty Ford Treatment Center for Dogs," the three-week rehabilitation camp for chronic shoe eaters, barkers, and social delinquents that he runs in Monterey Park. "You can't believe the separation anxiety people feel when they drop off their animal," he said. "They cry hysterically. They ask, 'Will he hate me? Will he forget me? Will he think I'm a bad parent?' On Saturdays, visiting day, they come filled with guilt, bearing gifts. A lady brought three shopping bags. One was filled with blankets and pillows. One was toys—squeakies, chewies. And the final bag had three barbecued chickens. She sat on my patio and set it all up."

Just listening to these stories made me hang my head in shame. While my husband and I took Bess, Stella, and later Sophie along on weekend trips to Desert Hot Springs or Santa Barbara, on longer jaunts I left them in good hands, kissed them good-bye, and didn't look back. This backfired on me only once in the past, before I met Blanche, when I went on a three-week trip to Ecuador and left the pugs with my irritating neighbor Danielle, the dog nanny.

I returned to the canine version of the movie *The Hand That Rocks the Cradle: The Hand That Holds the Leash.* Bess looked so much younger I suspected she had been given sheep-cell injections. Sophie greeted me with cool disdain.

All my neighbors remarked how much happier my dogs seemed with Danielle, and I soon learned why. She walked each pug separately, scheduled play dates with other dogs in the neighborhood, and served up a round-the-clock smorgasbord of treats.

"Maybe you could sue her for alienation of pug affection," Duke said.

I got over my resentment in about three seconds. I looked on the bright side. They had had a good time. Jealousy was beneath me; I was not a Pet Parent. The pugs were dogs. Darling dogs, willful dogs, lovable to be sure, but I was a Human. I was in charge.

Then along came Clara, and all bets were off.

Alpha Meets Super Alpha

On the day her world fell apart, Sophie was sixteen months old and had been with us for almost a year, plenty of time for us to determine that she was a less-than-satisfying beast. Granted, she was beautiful and, for a pug, quite athletic: she ran through puddles with joyous abandon and enjoyed a good game of fetch. (Though true to her contrary nature, she refused to bring the squeak toy back to me and would stop a foot away from my outstretched hand, look up defiantly, and make me wrench the saliva-drenched object from her teeth.) Sophie had a repertoire of attention-getting behaviors that could be used by the CIA instead of thumbscrews to break spies during interrogation. My astrologer friend, Gamma Rae Orion, checked her chart, and blames her personality on the fact that Sophie, born May 28, 1991, is a Gemini with her moon in Sagittarius. "Geminis, they are annoying," Gamma Rae said. "It's the frenetic sign of the zodiac. Her moon in Sag means that she can't settle down, she has lots of nervous energy and a short attention span, and she's emotionally shallow."

I don't put much stock in astrology—I prefer my hocus-pocus undiluted by quasi-astronomical facts—but I had to admit that, as usual, Gamma Rae was on target. In addition to Sophie's aforementioned compulsion to wake me at four in the morning, there was her patented Crippling Maneuver, in which she'd hurl her muscular eighteen-pound body into the back of my knees. When walking on the boardwalk, she charged under the wheels of skateboards (big dogs chase cars, little dogs aim lower in the vehicular evolutionary chain), sniffed the grass endlessly as if reading her E-mail, and lay down without warning so I lurched backward like I was on the wrong end of a bungee cord. These habits were minor annoyances compared with her constant delight in the sound of her own voice.

Sophie barked at anything—a dog barking three thousand miles away, a plant swaying in a breeze, a magazine subscription card falling to the floor, the rug shifting, if I stood up, if I sat down. And once she started, she kept going, like the Energizer Bunny. Outside, her particular enemy was a neighbor named Magnolia, who as far as I know never did anything to earn the pug's enmity, though she regularly vexed people on our block by pruning our jacaranda trees and bougainvillea vines without first asking permission. Magnolia could be fifty feet away and Sophie freaked out.

"She doesn't like me," Magnolia would laugh, oddly pleased to be Sophie's enemy.

"She hates you," I would respond, not to be unkind, but because it made her smile. Once Magnolia cut her hair and we ran into her on the boardwalk. For an instant, Sophie didn't recognize her and trotted over to be petted. Magnolia bent down and Sophie recoiled in horror—"Oh, no, it's you!"—and started hollering as if Freddy Krueger had come to call.

"I love that she doesn't hide her feelings," Magnolia said.

Inside, Sophie's nemesis was a trio of Burmese marionettes that hung from my office ceiling. The puppets had been in the same place since Sophie arrived, but every afternoon at three o'clock she noticed them anew and kept them at bay with angry "Woof woof woofs!" until six o'clock, when Duke came home and told her to shut up. Maybe the light hit the puppets at a strange angle, maybe Sophie was getting a message from the Pug Planet to attack, or maybe the puppets were talking back to her. This was not a passing fancy. It got to a point where I'd be talking to editors on the phone, the hellish woof woofs would commence, and they would say knowingly, "Oh, it's puppet time."

My sister, who originally gave me Sophie as a birthday present and was thus predisposed to like her, spent a weekend with us and expressed surprise that no one had shot the pug. "The first time she barks you make the mistake of thinking, 'Oh, there must be a problem,' " Laurie said, "but then you realize there's no rhyme or reason. She's like the boy who cried wolf—the dog who cried *ruff*. She just likes to bark her little face off."

I considered a psychiatric intervention. Maybe she was schizophrenic and kept hearing imaginary voices in her head that she needed to speak to all the time.

Curiously, Sophie seldom conversed with other dogs—unless she saw them or any other animal on television, in which case she charged the screen, howled furiously, and ran behind the set to drive the intruder away. (We once rented the Glenn Close version of *101 Dalmations* and had to turn it off after five minutes because Sophie had a psychotic episode.) Live members of her species rarely appeared on her radar screen. She passed dozens of dogs on the Venice boardwalk, but she only had eyes for Henri—a mindless auburn-haired Pomeranian who lived in the apartment building across the street.

The skittish hairball weighed no more than five pounds (of which no more than three ounces could have possibly contained brain material), and he humped my leg frantically when I tried to pet him. Henri belonged to the equally brainless Danielle, who introduced herself as "Henri's mama," in the breathless bogus French accent she inherited from her second suicidal husband (she had three, which seemed more than coincidence). Danielle wore earrings with silver letters that spelled DOG MOM, and all her waking hours were devoted to providing Henri with quality time. She regarded me with disdain, much in the same way that stay-at-home moms view their working counterparts.

She drove me nuts. At nine o'clock each morning, she knocked on my door and asked, in her breathy Franglish, if Madame Sophia could come out and play. Since our house has a fenced-in yard and her apartment did not, Danielle felt it was in our puppies' best interest to have play dates on our lawn. The first time, out of sheer politeness, I sat on the front steps with her and tried to engage her in conversation. But after twenty minutes of, "Is Sophie fixed?" and "Have you tried Science Diet?" my brain short-circuited. I stood up and called, "Sophie, come!" in my most authoritative voice. Sophie gave me her fuck-you stare and resumed digging up the hydrangea bush. Danielle clucked disapprovingly as I forcibly scooped the pug up and carried her into the house.

"Zey need zeir socialization," Danielle scolded.

"Sorry," I said. "I'm on deadline." Big mistake.

Danielle sensed a window of opportunity and flung it open. "I vill be happy to vatch zem play," she twittered.

Who was I to deny my pug pleasure?

Danielle promised to put Sophie back in the house when she and Henri finally wearied of uprooting the beds of impatiens and gorging on the avocados that dropped from our tree. Six hours later, when puppet time came and went without a yip, I went outside to investigate. Danielle had spread a blanket out on the grass and was planted there like a lawn ornament. She was serving Sophie and Henri Milk-Bones and chew sticks on teal plastic plates. Why Sophie needed treats when her black muzzle was topped by the avocado equivalent of a milk moustache was beyond me. "She looks like Kermit the Frog," I complained.

"Avocados make zee coat shiny," said Danielle.

I figured my neighbor would lose interest in the doggy day care center within a week, but I overestimated her requirements for intellectual stimulation. In the days that followed she came to regard our lawn as her private office. I half expected her to have Dog Nanny business cards printed up with our address. I looked on the bright side. Sophie got bored sleeping under my desk while I wrote and took it as a personal challenge to distract me. And Danielle was convenient, and what's more, she was free. If work took me away from home, she took the pug for a walk. Still, as weeks passed, and then months, each day bringing more chew toys or, worse, another neighbor's puppy or, worse still, a sparkling bon mot from Danielle such as, "For every one flea on your dog, another ninety-nine are busy hatching," I realized the nanny had to go.

It was worth twice what I paid for Clara to replace Henri as the object of Sophie's affections.

Sensitive to Sophie's feelings, I went inside to greet her while Duke waited outside with the wee surprise. Sophie was overjoyed to see me—her only endearing quality is her unswerving devotion. She exhibited all her most exasperating behavior: she sprang at the back of my knees, raked her claws on my stockings, and tugged at my skirt with her teeth like the dog in the old Coppertone ad that pulled down the little girl's swimsuit. When I bent over to pick her up, she squirmed frantically like a greased pig and sneezed triumphantly in my face. It was at this point, as I wiped pug mucus from my white silk blouse, that the unfavorable comparisons to Clara began.

I noted: When I picked up the featherweight Clara, she purred like a kitten, then put her paws around my neck as if to give me a hug.

After five minutes, Sophie lost interest in me and began scratching her rump on the corner of an antique dresser. Duke brought Clara inside and set her down on the floor. Side by side, she and Sophie made an attractive brace. "Are they related?" Duke asked. (I had no way of knowing that I would be subsequently asked this question an average of eight times a day. Bess and Stella were different colors, so their genetic connection didn't come up, but with Clara and Sophie it does—incessantly. My husband would later come up with the perfect retort: "One's ours, one's adopted.") Technically, they are first cousins. Sophie's mother, Phoebe, is the sister of Clara's mother, Cubby.

"They look like twelve- and fourteen-point type in the same font," Duke said.

Sophie ignored the puppy, much the way she ignores her own reflection in the mirror. Clara put up with the slight for a couple of minutes, then she sank her sharp baby teeth into Sophie's velvet button ear. Sophie chased her through the house, and they had a picturesque pug-of-war with Duke's bathrobe belt. The muscular Sophie, being at the time ten pounds heavier, had the advantage, but Clara showed no signs of being intimidated.

"See?" I exclaimed. "They're getting along."

"Maybe I was wrong," Duke conceded.

Alas, he was right. Sophie played with Clara for an hour, and then she whined by the front door, clearly expecting that Danielle would come and take the puppy home. Meanwhile, Clara trotted around the house, noting the location of the water dish, the dinner table (she would earn a black belt in begging), the sofa. It wasn't until Sophie saw me put newspaper down in the small bathroom off our bedroom—the same bathroom where Sophie slept before graduating to a cozy bed in front of the heater in a corner of our bedroom—that she realized the interloper was here to stay. From then on, Sophie regarded Clara not like Jo regarded Meg, but more like Remus viewed Romulus.

I had specifically asked Lorene for a laid-back pug who could be beta to Sophie's alpha, but Clara had no intention of playing second fiddle. She was cagey enough to let Sophie believe she was Top Dog—she graciously allowed Sophie to take away her chew toys, and when Clara peed and Sophie promptly anointed the same spot to hide Clara's scent and show her dominance the way wolves do, Clara didn't object. It was clear in her own mind that she had the Humans in her back pocket. My friend Jon, who would become her most devoted fan, christened her Super Alpha, and after that, the Divine Miss C.

Sophie never had a chance. Despite her great beauty, she could not compete with her cunning eight-pound sister. We expected that in time the bitsy Clara would fill out and lose her obscene cuteness, but months passed and she remained pocket-sized. Lorene, I later learned, bred her pugs to be small so as better to fit on your lap. Certainly, it made for greater portability—Clara enjoyed being carried so much that Duke suggested I graft a handle on her back.

But it wasn't just a matter of looks. From earliest puppy-hood, Clara had the ability to determine what was in her own best interest and act accordingly. She dispatched Danielle posthaste. The morning after Clara arrived, the Dog Nanny appeared on schedule, Henri tucked under her arm, eager to take charge of the charismatic puppy. Clara swiftly calculated that there was no advantage to spending her days on the front lawn munching a rawhide flip chip. When Sophie ran over to greet Henri, Clara grabbed Sophie's tail and chased her around the yard. Sophie, like all pugs, prefers her own kind to any other breed, and she cut Henri dead. The scorned Pomeranian foolishly attempted to mount the diminutive Clara. She let forth a high-pitched cry and flung herself in my lap, shaking dramatically.

"I'm afraid Henri is too manly for Clara," I said to Danielle.

"He's just being friendly," she sniffed. "Give him another chance." I did. He mounted Clara again. She bit him with her sharp teeth.

I thought Danielle would have Clara arrested for assault and battery. She grabbed Henri and kissed his wounds, murmuring, "My *petit chien.*" Without so much as an *au revoir,* she turned on her heels and slammed the front gate behind her. I felt sorry for removing her raison d'être, but fortunately, a tenant in her building brought home a two-month-old poodle and Danielle transferred her attentions to him. Sophie didn't miss her nanny. She was too busy defending her turf.

Sometime in the early hours of their relationship, Clara and Sophie held a summit meeting. Like the Allies at Yalta dividing Europe, they split up the attention-getting behavior. The ingratiating Clara chose most of the winning traits: she came instantly when called, sensed a vacant lap from the opposite side of the house and rushed to the sofa to fill it, and tailed us like a bodyguard, afraid of being left behind. "The Daffodil is such a needy little creature," said Duke, who found her enchanting.

By contrast, the closed-minded Sophie became even more so. Henceforth, she regarded any command as a suggestion that could be safely ignored. Her barking escalated to the point where I looked longingly at a Rechargeable Anti-Bark Collar, which according to the catalog copy issued a warning beep, then a mild electric shock at the first vibration from the dog's throat. "It has seven programmable stimulation levels," I said wistfully.

"The thing that drives me crazy is that Sophie knows she goes for a walk every night." Duke sighed. "She likes to go for a walk, but every night she falls asleep under your desk and refuses to come out. She makes me crawl under the desk and drag her out to take her on her walk. There's a cushion under your desk, which smells a lot like pug, a smell that I have become all too familiar with."

I spent an equal amount of time saying, "Dammit, Sophie!" as I said, "Good dog, Clara!" so neither was ignored. Granted, I am regularly accused of favoring Miss C, and all I can say is guilty as charged. I defy anyone to spend a day with the pugs and not arrive at the same conclusion.

Sophie celebrated Clara's arrival by forgetting everything she knew about housebreaking, which wasn't all that much. I'd been trying to train her for almost a year, and I wouldn't characterize it as a stunning success. At first I blamed my difficulty on society's ridiculous new permissiveness toward animals. With Bess and Stella, I achieved rapid and long-lasting results with the rub-their-noses-in-it-and-scold-them method. I could count on one hand the number of lapses they had over fourteen years, most of which were my fault because I worked overtime and came home late. But by the time I got Sophie, I risked being reported to PETA if I so much as raised my voice. Animal behaviorists maintained that unless you catch a dog in the act, it has no idea of why you are angry. And any attempt to punish the animal will interfere with the bonding process.

Instead, animal trainers advance theories on housebreaking, much the way pediatricians advocate potty-training techniques. Matthew Margolis, author of *Good Dog, Bad Dog*, runs the largest dog-training facility in the world and has trained dogs for Elizabeth Taylor, Kenny Rogers, and Robert Wagner. He answers the phone, "Woof!" When I interviewed him for *Pug Talk*, I asked him what to do about Sophie. He recommended that I pick up all the newspapers in my house, feed and water Sophie on a strict schedule, neutralize all odors, and put a puppy pen outside, where I should leave her all day until she got the idea she was supposed to go outside.

I tried. Sophie whimpered and barked for hours. When I finally brought her inside, she ran to the living room carpet about to explode and promptly did so.

"You have to confine her," Margolis said. "So she cries and moans. You can't run your life around her. You can't be her baby-sitter."

"Actually, she thinks I'm her maid," I said.

"You can't give her the run of the house. The key is that if she's in the house and she hasn't gone to the bathroom outside, then you keep her with you or you confine her in a crate."

I tried, honest I did. But when I kept her with me, she invariably waited until I was on an important business call before she circled nervously and sank into a squat. And as for the crate, contrary to conventional wisdom that stated that a dog would never mess her den, Sophie regularly did.

Margolis suggested that perhaps I wasn't firm enough. "Training does one thing. It says to the dog, 'This is what I expect from you. Do this and I'll give you love and affection. This is in your best interest.' That way you're both on the same wavelength versus 'Come'—dog doesn't come. 'Stop that!'—dog doesn't listen."

I followed his advice, and for a few weeks it looked like Sophie was housebroken.

To celebrate, we took her to San Francisco. For five hours, we walked around the city. Sophie caused a near-riot on Union Street, where gay hairdressers, furniture designers, antique dealers, and artists ran after her shouting, "Too cute, too cute." We ended our day with a stroll through Golden Gate Park. For five hours, Sophie sniffed and sniffed, but she never did empty her bladder. She waited until we returned to our room at the Marriott at Fisherman's Wharf, and then she squatted on a throw pillow.

Anna Marie Wilson, editor in chief of *Pug Talk*, attributed Sophie's balkiness to having spent the first five months of her life at Paul Winfield's house, where housebreaking was not a serious requirement. For Sophie's sake, I would like to blame her learning difficulties on her age or my methodology. However, my experience with Clara proved otherwise.

Once Clara was vaccinated and immune from the myriad virulent dog viruses that could result in instant death, I put a piece of soiled newspaper in the yard and explained the situation: "If you want to go shopping in Beverly Hills, you've got to give up *The New York Times* and use the grass."

Clara looked pensive, no doubt determining if Beverly Hills was worth such a sacrifice. Meanwhile, Sophie wool-gathered in the yard, shredding bougainvillea, scratching her back against the bark of the jacaranda tree, and chewing grass (which she invariably threw up the instant she came inside). "Dammit, Sophie, hurry up," I begged.

Clara made a note: The Moron is annoying the Human.

She pranced over to a blooming mound of impatiens and squatted daintily. She received more praise than I've received in my entire writing career, and a sliver of Monterey Jack cheese. Whether it was the positive feedback or the cheese that did it—I'd put money on the cheese—by the end of the week Clara was more or less housebroken. If nature called, she trotted over to the door and scratched it with her paw until I let her out. This is not to suggest that she is perfect—quite the contrary. But she lapses only when she feels the need to discipline me. How do I know this? I picked up on the subtle clues. The first time I went to Saks Fifth Avenue without her, I came home and found a steaming mound on my pillow. This wasn't something she could have done by accident. Clara had to pry open the bedroom door, use the antique trunk at the foot of the bed as a springboard, then climb up a mound of pillows to arch her back and leave her foul-smelling protest.

"I've never known a dog to go on furniture," Duke said. He tried to scold her, but the thin-skinned, high-strung Clara takes criticism about as well as the film director James Cameron. Raise your voice or look crossly at her and she flops on her back and submissively wets. Duke calls it the stinkbomb defense. Still, as long as I obeyed Clara, she behaved flawlessly, and not once in her entire life has she erred in a store, a hotel room, or on the set of a television show, though she has left a message at my publisher's office when she felt I wasn't being treated well. What's more, having listened to me say, "Dammit, Sophie, hurry up," over and over, she concluded that "Hurry up" was a command that meant "Go now!" I can take her on foreign turf and tell her "Hurry up," and she does.

On the other hand, Clara felt the leash was déclassé—perhaps because she spent her formative weeks being carried in the Sherpa Bag. Or perhaps she simply decided it was demeaning to be dragged around like a child's pull toy. It was kind of strange because when we were in New York, I had purchased a lightweight lead and choke chain and Clara had willingly trotted around our hotel room by my side. I guess she was just trying to make a good first impression. Back at home, I slipped a lightweight nylon choke over Clara's head and clipped on Sophie's leash, figuring she'd be a good example. Sophie sauntered between my legs, braiding me in her leash like I was a maypole. Clara assumed the paws-locked position and refused to budge. I coaxed. I pulled. I jerked. She foamed at the mouth and yelped. Neighbors called out "You're hurting the puppy," and cowed, I picked her up and carried her back home. I was mystified. Leash training had never been an issue before. In the past, I had had a few awkward minutes when Bess, Stella, or Sophie resisted and I had to drag them a couple feet, but they got the idea.

My husband, who fancies himself to be Gunther Goebel Williams, the famous lion tamer, insisted I just had to be firm. He dragged Clara outside, down our walk street, toward the Venice boardwalk. She rolled and tumbled like a stuffed animal, foaming at the mouth. "She just won't walk on a lead," Duke marveled, as if discovering it anew. (Men refuse to believe the existence of any problem, even a burnt-out lightbulb, until they experience it themselves.) He dragged her forcibly, and Clara pulled at the choke until she cut off her air supply and went into a convulsion. The neighbors threatened to call the ASPCA.

"Maybe she's into autoerotic strangulation," Duke said as he sheepishly carried her home. Clara located her Sherpa Bag in my closet and pulled it out by the handle. She looked up hopefully.

For once, I stood firm.

The owner of Dog Stars, a preposterously snooty, over-priced pet boutique near my home, maintained that Clara was resisting because I forced her to wear a five-dollar training lead.

"She'd be proud to walk in this," said Dog Stars, showing me a forty-two-dollar faux zebra collar with a matching sixty-dollar leash.

When it became obvious that my guilt wasn't sufficient to overcome my inherent cheapness, she changed tactics. "You can't expect her to work for nothing," Dog Stars sneered, and recommended that I invest in a salami-shaped training bait called Roll Over Sausage, which I would come to suspect contains heroin.

I knelt down on the sidewalk—a Venice Beach sidewalk—and held a bit of this substance in front of Clara's nose. She froze. I slipped a piece between her crooked teeth, and Clara begrudgingly took a halting step and opened her mouth ex-pectantly. It took half an hour and a pound of sausage to go the fifty yards between the house and the beach. Neighbors yelled, "You go, girl!" and Clara, gratified by the attention, picked up speed. When we finally reached the boardwalk, she styled like a circus acrobat who has just performed a triple somersault on the flying trapeze. A dozen tourists clustered around the tiny puppy and petted her. I fielded the usual stupid pug questions: "No, she's not a shar-pei." "Yes, pugs usually come in tan." "No, I don't curl her tail."

Clara had a revelation: Leash equals instant adoration.

Just as I was congratulating myself, a pair of Dobermans in thick chain collars with spikes sauntered by. The diminutive Clara made a kamikaze vertical leap for the larger Dobie's throat and began barking hysterically. I picked her up and said, "No, Clara," but empowered by the safety of my arms, she let forth a truly horrifying scream, a cross between a car alarm and a stuck pig.

"Let me at him, let me at him," cheered a boardwalk huckster twisting balloons into animals.

"Poor thing is afraid," said one of the kids from the drug-rehabilitation center.

Ah, would that that were the case. Unlike *Good Dog, Carl,* the gentle rottweiler in Alexandra Day's children's books, who takes the baby for a ride on his back and even gives the child a bath, Bad Dog, Clara turned out to have an aggressive streak. In the days that followed, the Napoleonic pug attacked German shepherds, pit bulls, giant mastiffs, wolf hybrids— any dog large enough to rip her to shreds. Yorkies, toy poodles, Malteses could safely pass without incident. Duke came home from the evening walk incredulous. "She drove on a giant husky," he said. "The husky rolled her, and she lay on her back and peed in the air. Then she drove on a Russian wolfhound."

Cowboy Joe, a rope twirler who offers biblical counseling in exchange for a small contribution, gave Clara a nickname that endures to this day: the Meanest Dog on the Boardwalk Per Pound.

And what of Sophie, who heretofore had never displayed

aggression toward anything larger than a skateboard? Within a week, she learned to follow the fearless Clara into combat, her voice trumpeting loudly as the pair of them challenged Great Danes, collies, giant schnauzers, and even standard poodles.

Obviously, I had to take action before they got into trouble.

Unfortunately, trouble came before I figured out what to do.

The Things I Do for Pugs

$\mathcal{S}$even years ago, I got an intriguing call from Anna Marie Wilson, of Dallas. "I'm the editor of *Pug Talk* magazine," she began, and I was flummoxed. Thirteen years a pug slave and I'd never heard of this publication, though I should have realized its existence was inevitable. Every other subculture in America—from dollhouse-miniature collectors to orchid growers to readers of "Adam West Remembers Batman"—has a club, Web site, and/or a magazine.

"How did you get my name?" I stammered.

"One of our readers sent in an article you wrote for the *Los Angeles Times*. About pug discrimination. Do you know what I'm referring to?"

Of course. "Ugly Dogs and the Women Who Love Them." I wrote it because I was tired of would-be wits asking if Bess and Stella walked into a wall, or were run over by a truck or hit in the head with a shovel. I realize that people have definite ideas about what a dog should be and pugs are an acquired taste. Still, even my own husband complained they weren't real dogs because they didn't have a snout.

"Would you give us permission to reprint?" asked Anna Marie. "We can't pay very much . . ."

I was struggling to digest the pug-magazine concept, so I changed the subject. "How many pugs do you have?"

"Not a one," she said. "I have poodles. I've been offered pugs in all directions, but I don't want one. If you think I'm going to get stuck in that morass of pug politics . . ."

An image floated to mind. Pugs on Larry King accusing each other of accepting illicit campaign contributions or having sex with a subordinate puppy. "Then how did you get the magazine?"

Anna Marie sighed ruefully. "It was willed to me by my friend Mimi. Mimi's husband, Jack, had founded *Pug Talk* back in 1967 or 1968, I forget which year."

"*Pug Talk* is thirty years old?"

"I'm afraid so." Anna Marie chuckled. "Jack and Mimi had a printing press in their home and they turned out a decent-looking magazine, but then Jack had a heart attack in 1971. Mimi had thirteen or fourteen pugs, their house was turned over to the pugs, and she kept *Pug Talk* going until she had a stroke. Her whole family lived in Canada, so she went back there for treatment and I kept the magazine going while she was away because I wanted her to have something to come back to. She died in Canada in the middle of the winter. The ground was frozen so solid they couldn't bury her until spring of the next year."

It was a weird story. But then, I've never been able to resist a bizarre experience.

Anna Marie continued. "Her family went through her possessions and found an old will. I kept hoping that they didn't find all of it. They asked me if I wanted *Pug Talk*, and I said,

'No, I don't want the damn magazine.' The next thing I knew they had given it to me for a dollar and other considerations. I don't know how it developed. It just grew like Topsy."

"What's the circulation?"

"Around three thousand."

"You're kidding."

"I wish I were. About your article . . ."

I couldn't resist. "Take it."

"What do you want in exchange?" asked Anna Marie.

"A lifetime subscription." Such breathtaking negotiating skills are why my agent, Loretta, cringes whenever I report that I made a deal.

A few days later, I opened my mailbox and pulled out a surprisingly thick and slick publication with a winsome fawn pug on the cover and a banner headline that proclaimed THE BROOD BITCH ISSUE. I scanned the whelping announcements. A centerfold of an ebony champion stretched out on a bearskin wearing only a tasteful strand of pearls. Photos of amateurs— called "Love Pugs" to distinguish them from the professionals—bedecked in space helmets, sombreros, and hula skirts. Vitriolic letters blasting a breeder who while in the show ring allegedly jabs her dogs in the belly with her thumb—"the strongest in the business"—to give it an even top line. My favorites were the full-page obituaries. I beheld a tribute to the geriatric, rheumy-eyed "Pugsmimmon 1982–1994—At the end of the voyage may you find a soft bed to sleep in, a veteran's class to strut your stuff in, and no nail clippers. Thanks for the memories." I also noted the valediction to a human judge who had gone "to the great show ring in the sky."

When I regained my composure, I called Anna Marie and congratulated her on an excellent publication. (*Pug Talk* has twice been named Best Breed Publication by the Dog Writers

Association of America.) In time, I learned that Anna Marie—whom I have still never met even though I've spoken to her on the phone for hours—is the daughter of a textbook publisher. She edited her father's books, once wrote a squib for *Reader's Digest*, has a master's in Spanish, and was chief clerk for a justice of the court. What her résumé modestly didn't include was the persuasive Southern charm that somehow convinced me to put my professional credibility on the line to make her magazine the publication of record for celebrity pug news.

As fate would have it, my association with *Pug Talk* came at the precise moment when the breed was making yet another comeback. In 1977, when I first got Bess and Stella, 6,066 pugs were registered with the American Kennel Club. By 1987 registered pugs numbered 10,400, and by 1996 their ranks had swelled to 18,398. They'd been out of fashion in the seventies and early eighties, so out of fashion that when I took Bess and Stella out in public they were regularly mistaken for Pekingese or pit-bull pups. The rare few who could identify the breed were either fellow enthusiasts or else they had an elderly relative whose pug choked to death on a chicken bone. But all that was about to change.

One day my sister woke me up at six-thirty in the morning. "You've got to see *The Adventures of Milo and Otis*," Laurie said urgently. Was she out of her mind? The only thing I want to see at that hour is my pillow. "It's a movie about a pug," she explained.

I sat up abruptly and squealed, "A pug is starring in a movie!" Not that this was the first time the beasts have graced the silver screen. Pugs can be seen swarming over Jack Lemmon in *The Great Race* and have also appeared in *Tom Jones, The Summer House, The Great Gatsby,* and David Lynch's *Dune,* where a neofeudal future pug is the pet of Duke Leto

Atreides (played by Juergen Prochnow). But these roles were just walk-ons—*The Adventures of Milo and Otis,* a live-action film written and directed by Masanori Hata, is like the pug version of *Gone With the Wind.*

The film, a top-grossing hit in Japan, was shot over four years on Hokkaido, Japan's northern island, where Hata has a private menagerie of almost three hundred animals, many of which are in the film. There are no humans in *Milo and Otis,* just the voice of narrator Dudley Moore, who tells the tale of Milo, a kitten with no street smarts who runs away from his farm and gets carried off by a rushing river. He is accompanied and later rescued by his friend Otis, an athletic fawn pug. Duke couldn't imagine the self-serving pug coming to anyone's rescue. "Unless maybe the cat was being attacked by a giant glazed doughnut," he conceded. But during the course of the movie, Otis did a half pike with a twist into the river, fought a bear, rode a turtle, and traipsed through the snow unprotected by a hand-knitted sweater or even booties.

Anna Marie was unimpressed. "I've heard rumors that the pug was mistreated during filming," she said. "Do you think you could check it out?"

Why not? I called Columbia Pictures and asked to speak to Baskin, the film's publicist. "What publication are you representing?" asked Baskin's gatekeeper in the bored, hectoring tone Hollywood gatekeepers use to ascertain your importance.

"Pug Talk," I said with not quite the same confidence with which I say, *"The New York Times."* I was willing to bet the next words I'd hear were, "He's in a meeting."

"Pug Talk?" hooted the gatekeeper.

"Think of it as the *Vanity Fair* of the pug world."

He put me through at once.

At that point I formulated what would become my standard *Pug Talk* pitch. It began, "This is probably the strangest request you've had all day."

"I doubt it," said Baskin.

"*Pug Talk* readers wanted to know if Otis was mistreated during the course of making the film."

"*Pug Talk*? You're a reporter for *Pug Talk*?"

I hastily reeled off other journalistic credentials.

"Send me a copy," he said, when he stopped cackling. "I'll see what I can do."

I messengered over the latest "Stud Dog" issue, featuring manly pugs with tasteful erections and spiked collars, and waited for his reaction.

If I had been calling for an assignment that would have furthered my career, I would probably have waited months. But *Pug Talk* has a miraculous effect on people. A few hours later, Baskin called back. "The American Humane Society put its stamp of approval on the film," he said. "The animal actors, including thirty pugs and kittens, were shot in their natural environment reacting to situations created by the director and the crew."

I thanked him profusely. Baskin saw a placement opportunity. "Would you like to interview the director?" the publicist asked. "He's in Japan, but we can set something up by fax, seeing as it's for *Pug Talk*." To my astonishment, Columbia Pictures arranged for a translator, and within twenty-four hours I had my first exclusive. I asked the hard-hitting questions: "Was Otis in danger during his fight with the bear?"

"I found the bear when he was still a very small cub in his parents' den after having been orphaned by hunters," director Hata wrote back. "I took the orphaned cub home and raised him with the pug that was to play Otis. The two animals were together morning, noon, and night, and so they came to be like brothers."

"That pug looks like he was scared to death," Anna Marie snorted. But she was pleased, and in exchange she gave me the best title I have gleaned in fifteen years of journalism: *Pug Talk*'s Hollywood correspondent. She even sent me official stationery illustrated with a pug on a director's chair. It is not quite as intimidating as lawyer's stationery, but nobody forgets it.

It is dangerous to express appreciation to a writer, because it happens so infrequently the writer gets flustered and loses her will.

"I read in *People* magazine that Paula Abdul has pugs," Anna Marie said, and *Pug Talk*'s Hollywood correspondent was on the case. Ms. Abdul was in the middle of a cross-country tour to promote her second album, *Spellbound,* but when her publicist heard that *Pug Talk* was calling, he accepted immediately on her behalf. Thus I was able to inform readers that the rock star's pugs were named Little Ricky, Fat Fred, and Puggy Sue. Their favorite food was chicken. Little Ricky shared Ms. Abdul's bed and her vocal lessons. "He sings with me, especially the high notes," she revealed.

I asked what the essence of Pugness was, and Ms. Abdul said, "Pugs are the most unique-looking dogs. People say I look like my dog."

Frankly, I feel this is every pug owner's big fear, but I kept silent.

She continued, "The most interesting thing is that my pugs take on whatever mood I'm in. If I'm upset, they're upset. If I have a stomachache, my dogs vomit. If I'm sick and I want to lie in bed, they sleep all day. It's very strange."

She did voice a complaint about the breed: "Pugs do smell," said Ms. Abdul. "They have a very incredible stench about them, and only a pug owner can handle it."

This tiny criticism brought indignant letters from outraged readers, which delighted Anna Marie so much she sent me a pug watch.

My favorite interview was with Leon Wieseltier, the literary editor of *The New Republic,* the famous and prestigious journal of opinion published in Washington, D.C. Wieseltier's pug, Stuffy, formally known as Stuff Smith, after the well-known jazz musician, was disparaged in an article about *The New Republic* that appeared in *Vanity Fair.* Author Marjorie Williams had noted, "Leon Wieseltier's frowning pug dog, Stuffy, stands like a bad omen in the doorway that leads from the reception area back to the magazine's offices—a fitting herald for the antagonisms that seethe within the corridors beyond." It seemed like a cheap dig at Stuffy, a comely black pug whose graying kisser once graced the cover of his Human's magazine, and I was pleased when the staff of *The New Republic* sent an irate letter to *Vanity Fair* on the pug's behalf. It read in part: "We are outraged at the suggestion that Stuffy, the wise black pug who greets visitors to our office, is 'a bad omen.' He is an omen only of friendship and well-being and he is a much-loved mascot. We know better than to demand a retraction or an apology on his behalf. But the tawdriness of your attack on Stuffy is plain to all."

I called Leon Wieseltier to get the lowdown, and he gave me my pithiest pug quote to date. He said, "I once thought all of God's creatures could be located on a spectrum with the pug at the high end and Gore Vidal on the low end."

On the other hand, Clara's most treasured *Pug Talk* memory came after Disney released the animated musical *Poca-*

hontas, which featured a pug named Percy, the spoiled pet of the villain Governor Ratcliffe. (To the best of my knowledge the crown of creation was not involved in that particular chapter of American history—the first pug immigrated after the Civil War, and the breed wasn't accepted by the American Kennel Club until 1885.) Percy—part of a troupe of sidekick animals providing a grace note to the action—was carried aboard ship on a fluffy pink cushion and later lounged in a hip bath, shower cap on his head, eating cherries. As for the scene when he donned an Indian headdress—oh, be still my heart. The animator had characterized the beast perfectly—from the authentically buglike walk to his enormous sense of entitlement.

I made a groveling phone call to a Disney publicist and begged to be allowed to interview the genius responsible for the first animated pug since Bandit in *Johnny Quest.* Thus, Clara and I were invited to visit the Disney Animation Studio in Burbank to meet Chris Buck, the supervising animator of Percy. The directions were appropriately Disney-esque. "Turn right at the building with the giant sorcerer's hat."

Clara wasn't permitted to roam free around the corporate Magic Kingdom, so I was advised to sneak her in. She rode like a maharani in her Sherpa Bag until we reached Chris Buck's office. Then, sensing that finally she was about to meet a person who could truly appreciate her every nuance, she sprang out of the bag like a stripper popping out of a cake. Buck showed Clara to her own rolling chair, and she became, well, animated. He couldn't keep his eyes off her. I felt like I was interrupting Wyeth and Helga.

"What made you decide to put a pug in the film?" I asked.

"It was set in that era where nobility carried pugs," he said. "The pug was the choice dog of royalty, as far as I know."

Actually, Pocahontas lived between 1595 and 1617, and William and Mary didn't bring pugs to England until 1688. So it is unlikely that the English nobility under James I carried pugs, though their Dutch counterparts certainly did. But I didn't want to seem petty. "Did the pug have to compete with a King Charles spaniel to get the part?"

"We didn't consider another dog," he said. "The pug was just perfect for the villain's hands and arms. At the beginning, he actually had a much bigger part. Percy was going to get lost in the woods, and then he was going to end up in the Indian village and the Indians were going to take care of him for a while. Then perhaps another animal would get him in touch with his own animal roots. The pug was going to go through this whole change from being a very stuffy little animal of royalty to being stuck in the woods, going through hell. He was going to howl in the woods and start to be a dog."

"But the pug is not a dog," I said. "My husband has lived with pugs for ten years, and he still can't get over how different they are. For instance, the pug has no objection to being carried, which he thinks is highly unnatural. I carry Clara everywhere. You saw how willingly she sat in her bag."

"I was shocked. I heard you were bringing her, but I didn't expect her to be in a bag."

Clara opened her mouth wide and yawned. The animator ran a thoughtful finger across her jawline. "When the pug opens the mouth, it's quite large," he said. "They have a huge mouth, but we cheated that to get more of a muzzle. Percy's a little bulldoggy in the mouth. One thing I was adamant about was getting the pug belly. At one point they wanted to sharpen it, but it's a nice rounded belly. Not fat. Gently rounded. It's very appealing."

Clara rolled over and presented her delectable tummy for

scratching. Buck gave her a gentle pat. That was all the encouragement she needed. She flew through the air from her chair to his knee, put her paws on his shoulders, and licked him. "Your dog doesn't like attention too much," he exclaimed.

"She's incredibly needy, like Judy Garland in the drug years," I said. I wanted to get back to the business of pug animation, but he was smitten. Thoughtfully, he uncurled Clara's tail and studied it as she curled it back up. "I actually did drawings of the pug tail movement," he confessed.

I loved the scene when Percy was sad and his tail went straight. My old pug Bess once had a stroke and her tail wouldn't curl for a week despite Dr. Shekel's four hundred dollars' worth of medication and tests. It broke my heart. The curled tail is Pugness personified. "Get it up, Bess," I pleaded, feeling like a woman in the midst of a bad sexual experience. Eventually, Bess's tail twisted into a loose ringlet, though her double corkscrew never returned.

"We didn't realize the pug used his tail to express moods," Buck said. "We just figured it was a great animation device. Every time an animated character gets shocked, everything stands straight. With Percy, you'll notice that anytime he gets rubbed or hit or upset, the tail uncurls. It might just go for a few frames, but the tail will straighten and then curl back up. When Percy gets scared, the ears go down."

As if to demonstrate, Clara flattened first her left ear and then her right. She flashed the jack-o'-lantern smile.

"I can't get over her tooth. Look how dear she is."

The conniving pug wasn't being sweet, she was merely auditioning. But who was I to come between her and the main chance?

Of course, in pursuing pug celebrities I've had some notable failures. I saw an opportunity for a major coup when Norman Mailer's *Harlot's Ghost* came out. In all his publicity pictures, Mr. Mailer posed with Huey, a virile fawn pug. I resolved to get an interview. It happened that a Random House publicist knew Mr. Mailer and obligingly sent over my letter along with a list of questions. Alas, Mr. Mailer wrote back and confessed that he couldn't supply any interesting answers because the pug belonged to his son. The closest encounter he'd had with Huey was during the photo shoot. He suggested that I try the playwright John Guare, who had two darling black pugs named Rose and Louise.

I looked on the bright side. Someday Norman Mailer's autograph would be worth money. I managed to track down John Guare's address through a friend of a friend of a friend (four degrees of separation), but he didn't respond to my interview request.

Ah, well, maybe someday . . .

An Eye for an Eye

W̲ithin a month of her arrival Clara was bored and frustrated. She wanted to be my constant companion, the way she was in New York, but she was thwarted by my refusal to play favorites. This surprised Clara, because to her, although Sophie looked like a pug, it was obvious she was many rungs lower on the evolutionary ladder. "I can just see Clara at Vassar, strumming a guitar and writing poetry," Duke said. "Most pugs are not bright, but she is a smart little dog by any standards." As for Sophie, he rolled his eyes and said, "Syracuse on a field-hockey scholarship—if we're lucky."

I was caught in a bind. I preferred Clara's company but didn't want to hurt Sophie's feelings by leaving her behind. Sophie had single-handedly gotten me through the pain of Bess's and Stella's deaths, and what's more, she adored me. Sophie would lie in wait in the bathroom while I took a shower so when I emerged she could dry my legs with her tongue. (Admittedly, this display of devotion was more revolting than touching.) I tried spending quality time with each pug separately, but it left me hardly any time to see my girlfriends. Besides, running errands with Sophie was as stress-free as an IRS audit. She yapped impatiently at the video store when I was looking for a movie. She deliberately slipped off her collar when we were crossing a busy street. And if an unenlightened store manager made me hold her while I was shopping, carrying the eighteen-pounder was a drag.

"People shouldn't compare children," I said to Loretta, my agent.

"But they do," she said briskly. "That's why there's therapy."

Clara tried to make things easier. If the pugs were eating breakfast and I picked up my keys, then she shoved her dish in Sophie's direction and stealthily left the house. She vaulted into the passenger seat and positioned her face in front of the air-conditioning vent. The instant I reached the freeway on-ramp, she took a nap, awaking only when the car came to a complete stop in front of our destination. It didn't matter what destination. Clara's strong suit was her adaptability. She allowed me to push her around Staples in a shopping cart. At the nail salon she sat on my lap, paws on the manicuring table, not voicing a complaint, even when Debbie the nail technician painted her claws Ponce de Lilac. And afterward, when we returned home from an expedition, Clara crawled into her bed and feigned sleep, reasoning that Sophie wouldn't realize she'd ever left the house.

But Sophie sniffed her and knew the truth, and her hostility mounted. The madder she got about Clara, the more devoted to me she became. I soon felt like a savory soup bone. If I sat between them on the sofa—right hand scratching Sophie, left rubbing Clara's belly—a hellish cacophany filled the air. Clara made a Michael Jordan–like vertical leap and sank her teeth in the scruff of Sophie's neck. Then the pair rose on their hind legs like bears and swatted each other with their tiny paws. Sophie, having at the time an eight-pound advantage, always won and triumphantly mounted Clara, crowing. Clara waited until Sophie lost interest and dismounted, then she charged again and the battle began anew with the bizarre pug battle cries ringing out.

"I'd love to get those sounds on my answering machine," said Duke. At his suggestion, I taped a pug fight for the radio-station sound engineer who collected strange noises.

"Could you make them fight in the studio so I could sample it in the computer?" the engineer asked hopefully.

I didn't think it was wise to encourage them. Though I confess that once, and only once, I deliberately set them off to entertain my friend Marian. She doubled over laughing. "I wonder what they're saying," she asked. " 'Get out of my face!' 'No, you get out of my face!' 'I'm the better pug.' 'No, I'm the better pug.' I can't imagine what makes them do that."

"Pure, unadulterated hatred," I suggested.

Marian looked at me like I was staging Saturday-night cockfights. "It's terrible," she said sternly. "They're supposed to love each other. And you're supposed to foster good feelings."

I consulted Dr. Pangloss. Clara came along just to make sure the decision went her way. Her performance was impressive. She cheered up a depressed patient who was leaving. She loped into Pangloss's study, placed her dainty dime-sized paw on his shoe, and gave him the pick-me-up-now stare. Once convinced of his admiration, she jumped off his lap, sprung onto mine, and took another nap, waking only when I poured a glass of water, at which point she tapped my arm, licked her lips, and sipped daintily from a Styrofoam cup. Sophie in the

same situation yapped furiously at his stone statue of the ele-
phant-headed Hindu god, Ganesha, chased her tail for half an
hour, and sharpened her claws on an antique kilim.

Pangloss, like Clara, couldn't understand why I was con-
flicted. "They're like Ego and Id," he declared. "Leave Ego at
home. She might be relieved to have Id out of the way."

He had a point. At home, the pugs were engaged in a turf
war. Sophie claimed the cushion under my desk; Clara took
the high ground: atop the living room sofa or, better still, on
the pillows on our bed. (Pugs have a comfort-seeking gene that
is truly mind-boggling. If you put a pug in an empty room with
three socks, it will push the socks together to form a cushion.)
The only neutral territory was the kitchen and the dining
room. Sophie patrolled under the table, waiting for a scrap of
salmon or turkey to fall to the floor. Clara stood on her hind
legs, front paws on the edge of my chair, gazing up at me like
Dondi, the cartoon urchin, now and then belting out an insis-
tent, low-pitched yap.

"Don't feed her from the table," Duke lectured, but Clara
wore me down.

The truce ended when we cleared the table and set the
dirty plates on the floor for the pugs to prerinse. Sophie snowplowed Clara away with her massive head. Undaunted, Clara
vaulted onto a dining room chair and picked tuna from the remains of a Niçoise salad. "This is wrong," Duke said, pulling
her off the chair by the scruff of her neck. Clara shrieked like
he was beating her, and he never did it again.

The inevitable tragedy occurred on a muggy fall afternoon.
The pugs and I were ambling down Main Street in Santa Monica when the owner of a vintage-clothing store waved me inside. After weeks of searching, I'd located a matron-of-honor
dress for my sister's wedding, and it was ready for a final fit-

ting. Clara posed fetchingly on a Victorian loveseat while I tried on the cream-colored antique silk dress. Sophie wandered around the store sniffing velvet pillows, chewing on the end of a lacy veil, barking at herself in the mirror. A young mother pushing a three-year-old in a stroller spotted the pugs through the window and decided to give her daughter a zoology lesson. (Another irksome thing people do all the time when you have pugs.)

"Bowwows," Mama said, pointing to the pugs. She released her daughter from the stroller for a better look. The little girl toddled over to Sophie and uncurled her tail. Sophie endured the assault with good grace.

"Are they friendly?" asked her mother, after the fact.

"To everyone but each other," I said. As a rule pugs are great with kids; it's one of the breed's selling points.

Meagan—or was it Emily?—bent down and hugged Clara like she was a stuffed Paddington Bear. Clara gently licked her nose. The child kissed her on the lips and then turned to her mother and lisped, "Bowwow has a boo-boo."

"What's wrong with puppy's eye?" Mama translated.

"Nothing," I said defensively, but then I looked closer.

Clara was holding her eye shut, and injured, she seemed even smaller than usual. Sophie beamed beatifically. I yanked off the maid-of-honor dress, pulled on my clothes, and looked at my watch, cursing. It was five-thirty. Dr. Shekel closed at six. I didn't have enough time to walk the pugs home and drive across town in rush-hour traffic. Then I remembered that a friend who is so gaga about her pets that she has written large checks for doggy acupuncture and kitty chemotherapy once recommended the Total Dog Cat Rabbit and Ferret Clinic, only five minutes away.

The clinic looked like a nursery school, with giant primary-colored cardboard cutouts of barnyard friends and a fenced-in play area where two kittens and a teacup poodle were playing ball. An overmuscled youth with a tattoo of an iguana on his forearm offered me a brochure advertising pet fitness training. I passed. The doctor, who couldn't have been more than thirty, had mahogany-tinted braids that fell to her waist. She wore spandex leggings and a threadbare lab coat with a giant button that read HAVE YOU SOCIALIZED YOUR PET TODAY? She introduced herself as Dr. Pammy, which struck me as a bad sign.

"Wow," she said cheerfully. "This is one unhappy cornea." As if on cue, Clara began shaking. Dr. Pammy glowered at Sophie. "Were they in a fight?"

I wanted to give Sophie the benefit of the doubt. It could have been a cactus . . . or a cat . . . "They spar from time to time," I confessed.

"Keep them apart," said Dr. Pammy. She knelt down and chirped at the pugs, "I know you'll miss each other, but it's for your own good." She handed me a tube of ointment and a bill for seventy-five dollars.

"No drops?" I asked. I'd never had a pug eye problem before that didn't require drops. For years, Stella was on some magical forty-dollar-a-gram solution that according to Dr. Shekel had been originally designed for racehorses.

"This is better," said Dr. Pammy, and I thanked her and left.

I never saw her again, though for the next three years she sent me guilt-inducing letters inspired by the same direct-mail marketing technique pioneered by Publishers Clearing House: "Dear Margo, Your pug, Clara, can't tell you that she's feeling bad, but Margo, doesn't Clara deserve the very best health care?"

Clara did, which was why I took action, two days later when her eye looked worse. I rushed her to Dr. Shekel, who has made so much money treating my pugs' ailments that he could send quintuplets through Stanford. Dr. Shekel put orange drops in Clara's eye, peered through an instrument, and shook his head. "This doesn't look good," he said laconically. Then, as is his wont, he handed me the scope so I could see for myself.

"No, thanks," I said for perhaps the three hundredth time. I'm sure that Dr. Shekel has patients who enjoy looking at tapeworms, mites, and ripped corneas. But it's not for me.

"What are you going to do?" I wailed. The vet was taken aback. Usually, when he delivers a diagnosis, I respond with a breezy "Okay, how much?"

Shekel patted my arm and offered Clara a doggy vitamin, which she accepted politely and later threw up in my car. "I have to operate," he said sotto voce.

I've heard these words from doctors before, and not once, even when my own life was at stake, did I respond as viscerally as I did upon hearing that my tiny puppy would go under the knife. I felt a rush of love and an atavistic compulsion to protect Clara from harm. Dr. Shekel had spayed all my pugs, cleaned their teeth under anesthesia, removed tumors, and had even put Bess to sleep. In eighteen years I had never questioned his judgment. But this was Clara. The sunshine of my life.

"What kind of operation?" I pressed.

"I have to sew her eye shut to give it a chance to heal."

Without conscious thought or effort I began to channel the

spirit of Mother, a medical groupie who will only go to a doctor if he is the chief of his specialty at a world-famous teaching hospital. "How many of these operations have you done?" (A question I never asked my own doctors.)

Shekel looked hurt. "A bunch."

"What was the end result?"

He shrugged. "They all lost their sight."

I didn't like those odds. Mother's voice grew louder: "I'm getting a second opinion from a specialist." My rational mind snickered, "Doggy eye doctor?" I pictured an eye chart with bones and fire hydrants instead of *E*'s.

To my astonishment, Dr. Shekel consulted a directory and wrote down the phone numbers of three veterinary ophthalmologists.

"Do you want me to call?" he asked.

I shook my head. The telephone is to me what razors were to Sweeney Todd. Once, while in a limousine going from Baltimore to Philadelphia, we passed a harbor. The driver pointed out the docked AT&T fleet—sparkling white ships that crossed the Atlantic laying telephone cables. Given my phone bills, I was surprised a ship wasn't named after me.

Dr. Shekel watched spellbound, as I dialed, rapid-fire. The first ophthalmologist was out of town, the second was a hundred miles away in Sun Valley. The third required me to navigate through a ridiculously detailed voice mail menu— "Press one for Acupuncture, two for Chemotherapy, three for Boarding Reservations, four for the Pharmacy, five for Aromatherapy, six for Physical Therapy . . ." I lost patience at "nine for Nail Clipping" and punched the *0*. A surly operator came on and informed me that Dr. Blinkmeister, the ophthalmologist, was semiretired and only saw patients on Tuesdays.

She transferred me to Scheduling, and I was forced to spend five minutes listening to a recording describing the breeding patterns of a flea.

Eventually, a human came back on the line. "Dr. Blinkmeister has an opening in six weeks. Do you wish to make an appointment?"

I did not. It was Tuesday, and her office, located in what Dr. Shekel enviously described as a fancy-schmancy medical center, was up the street. I scooped the invalid up in my arms, all the while murmuring, "Don't worry, darling, Mommy's here."

"Keep her away from Sophie," Shekel warned as I carried the patient to the car.

Fancy Schmancy Medical Center was so sophisticated that all that was missing was a support group so the puppies and kitties could commiserate about being flea-dipped and spayed. The ultramodern building was all white and chrome, and the air smelled like Lysol and lavender. The imposing five-foot-high counter guarded a computer system that NASA would envy. I stood on tiptoe and yelled, "Help, it's an emergency!"

"Shh," said the receptionist in a white lab coat. "Patients are trying to sleep." She thrust a clipboard into my hands and ordered me to sign in.

I was oddly reassured to notice she had the nonexistent people skills that is the hallmark of human beings who work in the animal-care industry. "I don't have an appointment," I explained, "but I have to see Dr. Blinkmeister."

"She's booked."

"Please," I begged. "My pug will go blind."

"Other doggies have problems too," she said.

"Who cares?" (Mother would be so proud.)

Sensing I needed help, I set the invalid down on the counter. She scooted over to the receptionist and shrank her being until she seemed minuscule and pathetic. The receptionist morphed into another person—a human being—before my eyes. "Oh, sweetheart, what happened?" she cooed. Clara lay her head on the receptionist's arm and whimpered.

"Wait here," she said. "I'll squeeze you in."

It took two hours, which was about how long I needed to make up answers to fill in the blanks of the extensive medical-history form. Did Clara's mother, Cubby, have mange? Did her paternal grandfather have breathing problems? Did her sisters have difficulty whelping?

Clara bravely forced down a couple dozen complimentary Milk-Bones to keep up her strength. Finally, an orderly in green scrubs and a shower cap escorted us in to see Dr. Blinkmeister. She looked like the meanest teacher in elementary school. "Hi, precious," she whispered, kissing Clara on the top of her head. She glowered at me like a social worker whose child has suspicious bruises. "Why did you let it go so long?" she asked.

I explained about the ointment.

"Ointment's no good," Blinkmeister snapped. She shone a light in Clara's eye and muttered something under her breath about a dreadful pet owner who didn't deserve to have a dog. She turned off the lights, donned a pair of goggles, and inspected the eye again. It was all I could do to keep from bursting into tears. "Can you save the eye without surgery?"

"Don't know," she said. She barked out an order, and the orderly fetched a clear plastic cone, which she called an Elizabethan collar. She fastened it around Clara's tiny head. The pug looked like a satellite dish or an Anne Geddes photograph of an infant dressed as a giant sunflower.

Blinkmeister wrote prescriptions for five different kinds of eyedrops, each of which had to be administered every two hours. "Don't put them in all at once," she added. "Wait fifteen minutes between drops."

"Does she need drops in the middle of the night too?"

"Round the clock," she said, scowling. "Unless you want her to go blind?"

I recoiled in horror. "How long does she need the medicine?"

Her scowl escalated to a glare. "At least a week. Then we'll see how she's doing. Do you have a problem with that?"

Actually, I did. It was Tuesday. My sister was getting married on Sunday. We were flying to Chicago on Friday night.

"Cancel the trip," the specialist said.

I doubted my sister would postpone her wedding until I nursed the pug back to health. Nor did I think that Blanche, who was scheduled to watch the pugs, would appreciate being saddled with the eyedrop routine. "Don't worry," I promised. "I'll take good care of her."

"It's important she gets all the drops on schedule," warned the doctor. "And whatever you do, don't let her near another dog."

Clara may have looked pitiful in her plastic collar, but deep down, she was exhilarated. I had come to my senses. I appreciated her true worth. Under doctors' orders to keep her away from Sophie, I was no longer troubled by guilt. I moved the perpetrator's bed out of the master bathroom into my office. Clara stretched out like a goddess in front of our bedroom heater. As I catered to her every whim, I was reminded of a poem that Winston Churchill composed when his daughter's pug was ailing. It began:

> *Oh, what is the matter with poor Puggy-wug?*
> *Pet him and kiss him and give him a hug . . .*

Inspired, I found myself making up my own doggerel—or rather, puggerel.

> *Blow half my income on a rare bug-eye drug,*
> *Don't flinch when she vomits on the new Turkish rug*
> *Lug her around when she lies like a slug,*
> *That is the way to revive Puggy-wug.*

Of course, Puggy-wug made the most of her misfortune. When the gluttonous pug gamely used her cone to scoop kibble, my softhearted husband fried her a burger and hand-fed it to her bit by bit. And while the eyedrops meant sleep deprivation for me, for Clara it guaranteed a constant stream of attention. Curiously, once Sophie was forbidden to see her rival, she seemed to miss her. She charged the closed door with her head, like a battering ram. Duke dropped her off at Blanche's to get her out of the way.

Having never been apart from Clara, naturally I wanted to take her with us to Chicago, but Duke sensibly pointed out that her cone wouldn't fit in her Sherpa Bag. Blanche suggested the safest place to leave her was the Fancy Schmancy Animal Center. And wouldn't you know it? They had a vacancy in the intensive-care ward, reserved for pets requiring medication. It cost about as much as our Chicago hotel, but Clara would receive round-the-clock medical care. I was concerned because she had to spend three days in a cage. "Clara's resourceful," Duke assured me. "She won't suffer."

On my way to drop her off, I stopped at Dr. Shekel's office

to pick up proof that her inoculations were up to date. What I was thinking was, "It's a good thing I didn't listen to you." He inspected Clara's eye and smiled. "It's a good thing I sent you to a specialist," he said.

I've never known a man who didn't take credit for a woman's bright idea, so I kept my mouth shut. The important thing was Clara was better.

I called the hospital from the airport to check up on the patient. (Press forty-three for Intensive Care.) "What kind of dog?" asked the chief nurse, who had a phone voice modeled after Nurse Ratched in *One Flew Over the Cuckoo's Nest*.

"The little black pug with the bad eye."

Her voice warmed like a cup of coffee zapped in a microwave. "Oh! Clara!" she gushed. "She's adorable. We're all playing with her."

Sunday night we drove straight from the airport to the hospital. Every doctor and nurse was Clara's slave. Her cage was filled with toys and treats that I hadn't bought her, and her eye had improved enough that we could dispense with the humiliating cone. Her eyedrop routine was cut back to a more manageable five times a day, and after a few more weeks of vigilance Clara was back to normal. To this day, her left eye has a small scar and looks blue when photographed.

As for Sophie, this story has a tragic ending, though it didn't manifest itself for some time. She was thrilled to return from exile at Blanche's house, where she was treated like a private in boot camp. After a week surrounded by scores of pugs, Sophie was relieved to only have to deal with one rival. Once assured that she had me in her back pocket, Clara became more accepting. That isn't to say the pugs liked each other, quite the contrary, but an accommodation was reached.

Or so I thought. Three years later, Clara—or a cactus or a cat—got revenge. Late one Friday night, of course, I realized that Sophie's beautiful right eye was cloudy. I immediately began the round-the-clock eyedrop routine and rushed her to the hospital. This time I was not so lucky. Sophie required emergency surgery. Blinkmeister was able to save the eye, but when Sophie returned, her beauty, her biggest advantage in life, was flawed. She looked like the Crypt Keeper and to this day has only limited vision in her bad eye.

Did Clara get revenge?

You be the judge.

Camp Blanche

The first time I called Blanche Roberts, I thought she was terribly rude. She answered the phone with a terse, "What do you want?" which I came to realize was by her standards fairly polite. I've sat in her living room and heard her tell callers, "Do not ever bother me again," in the same stern tone she scolds pupils when she teaches school. "How else am I supposed to get rid of idiots who call me at seven o'clock in the morning expecting me to give them a puppy?" Blanche grumbled.

How else indeed, I agreed, unwilling to rile her.

In fairness, once Blanche realized that I wasn't a puppy mooch or, worse, a spy for the spiteful rival breeder whom she had reason to believe was spreading rumors that her latest Best in Show had mange, she warmed up a few degrees. When asked if I could interview her for *Pug Talk*, she was almost gracious. "You might as well come over," she groaned. Either I made a decent impression or she wanted to make sure the article was flattering, because at the end of our first meeting she offered to keep the pugs when we traveled, an offer I could not refuse. Clara might prefer the Four Seasons Hotel, where thanks to their Pet Recognition Program, shortly after check-in a room-service waiter appears, bearing a silver tray with dog biscuits, bottled water, and a different squeaky toy from the one she received on her last visit. But Blanche charges only five dollars a day, and in exchange I get peace of mind and an excuse to visit. Our friendship is as old as Clara, a pug who Blanche considers to be "delicately boned," her euphemism for a mutant pygmy.

Blanche lives forty miles away, in a remote corner of the San Fernando Valley. In deference to the otherworldliness of the destination, I take the scenic route: up the Pacific Coast Highway, through Topanga Canyon on a winding one-lane road that cuts through the Santa Monica Mountains. Her home is the kind of architectural hybrid peculiar to Southern California: part ranch, part English Tudor, with a heavily latticed antebellumish verandah out back that overlooks a tennis court and—courtesy of the previous owner, a rock musician—a guitar-shaped swimming pool. (Blanche trains her puppies to swim over to the steps in case they fall in.) She shares the sprawling pile with her husband, Quentin, a dear man (though he'd be happier if he never saw a pug again), and their youngest daughter, Jennifer, who grew up amidst so many pugs it's a wonder she ever figured out she's human.

At last count Blanche has produced eighty champions and seven All Breed Best of Show winners. She judges all over the United States and in Taiwan and Japan, where a champion with good bloodlines can be sold for tens of thousands of dollars. (Quentin threatens to Delta Dash a few to Tokyo whenever Blanche goes out of town.) She shows under the name of Blaque Kennels. "A combination of Blanche and Quentin," she explained. "When I first got into pugs twenty-five years ago, I tried to get him interested. I figured if his name was on it, it would appeal to his ego. He wasn't fooled. He prefers golf."

Blanche is simultaneously the most and least pug-obsessed pug person I know. On the one hand, her home is like a theme park. Even before you enter, you tread on bronze pug bas reliefs embedded in the circular driveway. Life-sized pug sculptures guard the massive oak front door, which boasts a brass pug-head knocker, and a silkscreened bitch looks at you from the welcome mat. Inside, it's more of the same. Lots more.

The focal point of her living room is the Pug Wall of Glory, a twenty-foot expanse of built-in floor-to-ceiling bookcases filled with more than a thousand pug tchotchkes, each carefully fastened down with a sticky wax that is marketed in Los Angeles as Earthquake Putty. The cumulative effect is right out of the Twilight Zone: Dresden pugs, Royal Doulton pugs, Staffordshire pugs, whimsically posed Meissen pugs in all sizes with trademark beauty marks and blue enameled collars punctuated with golden bells. Pugs from China, from Taiwan, even a garishly painted puglike something from Mexico, which I found in a market in Cuernavaca. Beer steins with pugs, Toby jugs with pugs, mugs with pugs, amber meerschaum pipes, silver cigarette cases, thimbles with pugs. Hundred-year-old Viennese bronzes of skiing pugs and pugs sitting on an easy chair reading *The New York Times*. Pug bookends, pug piggy banks, pug doorstops, even a pug pocket-watch stand with a hook on the nose and bulging flashlight eyes so you can tell time in the dark. On the sofa, needle-pointed pug pillows, of course, and on the wall, old advertisements, illustrations, and paintings ... Come Christmas, the tree is festooned with pug ornaments and topped with a pug angel.

To give you an idea of the scope of her collection, not long ago I took Blanche as my date to a press party given by Sotheby's to preview the contents of the Duke and Duchess of Windsor's Paris villa, to be sold at auction. (The owner of the property, Mohamed Al Fayed, is the father of the doomed Dodi, who died with Diana, Princess of Wales.) The Duke and Duchess, the foremost pug parents of their day, kept a bevy of pugs, and it was said that the Duke always fretted that his wife would learn of another pug show, for fear she'd buy more. I was atwitter because the nonrefundable $120 three-volume cata-log, which I stupidly purchased two days before the publicist invited me to the party and gave me one for free, was filled with the Duchess's pug collectibles—a silver paper knife "ter-minating in the cast head of a pug dog," a pair of gilded letter openers "in the form of pug heads," collars engraved with the names of the Windsors' dogs—Peter, Disraeli, Davey, Trooper, Gen Sengh, Minoroo—a nineteenth-century porcelain scent bottle in the shape of a pug, even bed linens embroidered with the word PUGS, topped by an embroidered coronet.

If I were a collector or just wanted to blow a few hundred dollars, I would have bid on the Porthault cotton bath mat with the pug appliqué. But I'd just wind up passing it along to Blanche, and she didn't want it. Or so she said.

"It's not the best collection I've ever seen," Blanche sniffed, though she later conceded that some of the pictures were charming.

The portrait of the Duke of Windsor with Dizzy? The photograph of the Duchess with five pugs on the steps in front of her house?

"No, the watercolors of Pookie and Trooper," she said impatiently. "I don't give a damn about the Duke and Duchess." (The pug portraits fetched $18,400 at auction. Eleven pug-shaped pillows brought in a staggering $37,375.)

The preview party was disappointing, since the only pug on display was a Dresden figurine with a chipped ear. "Hell, I've got a better one in my collection," Blanche said. We passed a set of the Duke's old golf clubs. Being a royal groupie and a longtime subscriber to *Majesty* magazine, I was able to tell her that the Duke regularly violated country-club laws and took a pug out with him when he golfed. Once he was walking down the fairway and noticed his pug was lurching behind him, overcome with heat prostration. To his credit, the Duke, who was not known for his good judgment, interrupted his game and rushed the pug to the hospital.

"I heard the pug died," said Blanche.

Here's what I love about Blanche: She isn't gaga. She has no trouble resisting the machinations of a breed that has been successfully manipulating human beings for thousands of years. To avoid witnessing an indecorous display of sentimentality when I drop Clara and Sophie off for an extended stay, she wrenches them from my hands the moment I arrive and whisks them away to what Blanche calls "the Guest Quarters" and I call "the Prison," on the side of her house.

The first time, when I attempted to follow her and kiss them good-bye, she barked, "Go see the puppies." Tail between my legs, I slunked over to the spare bedroom earmarked as the nursery. Only new mothers and their offspring are permitted in Blanche's house; the rest are exiled to the backyard barracks. In the nursery, where, incidentally, Blanche mid-whelped Sophie, five three-week-old puppies the size of hamsters gleefully shredded their soiled newspapers, while their mother, weary from nursing, snored in a playpen shrouded with Laura Ashley sheets. The instant the tinies spied a Human—a slave!—they instinctively darted to the gate, leaping like koi, competing for my affection. In the beginning, when I climbed over the gate to cavort with them, Blanche made clucking noises about my giving them viruses. Now she just shakes her streaked-blond head tolerantly and smiles at my weakness.

I cannot see a pug puppy without becoming entranced. "Cute puppy," I trilled as it snatched my sunglasses, or chewed on my hair.

"Yes, she has a nice arch of the back and a good top line," Blanche called from the kitchen, where decked out in an apron decorated with a pug chorus line doing the cancan, she was warming gruel. "Those puppies were sired by a frozen semen shipment from a Swedish dog."

I didn't want to think about the mechanics of this. "They ship sperm?"

"All the time," she said. "It goes through Customs."

Blanche herded me outdoors to show off the pugs' new digs, built after the earthquake buckled the foundation on the old kennel. It reminds me of those spiffy horse farms owned by millionaires in Kentucky. The entrance to the thirty-five-by-thirteen-foot barracks, also English Tudor ranch, is marked by a pair of heart-stoppingly hideous pug topiaries. I counted seventeen champions sunbathing in the adjacent 140-foot-by-15-foot-run. Five older puppies cavorted on the tennis courts. As soon as Blanche opened the kennel door, she yelled, "Puppy, puppy, puppy, puppy," and one by one her pugs barreled through the pet door—*thwack, thwack, thwack, thwack*—like a never-ending succession of clowns emerging from a teeny car. One by one, they peed on the kennel's new concrete floor.

"I see they have a lot of respect for their new dwelling."

Blanche shrugged. "They go outside, and then they come in here to pee. They haven't made the connection between here and outside. The floor has a sealer they use in fish markets, so no odors can get in. I just hose it down with bleach and water."

Her annual bleach bill must run to four figures. Six latecomers squeezed through the pet door and sprayed the freshly painted walls. Blanche didn't flinch. "The walls are covered with a clear Mylar sheeting," she explained. "I wanted all washable surfaces."

She designed the kennel with the same attention to detail that recently compelled her to commission a backdrop of fifes and drums for a pug specialty—a competition for pugs only—in Boston with a "Let Freedom Ring" theme. (She tried to dress the handlers up in Revolutionary War uniforms but ran into a snafu with the local costume supplier.) "What I had in mind no one else had in mind," she said, speaking of her kennel. Twenty-one of what Blanche calls "beds" and I call "wire cages with scraps of sheepskin" are set up off the ground on custom-built shelves that are bolted in so they won't tumble in a temblor. When the pugs are what Blanche calls "tucked in for the night" and I call "incarcerated," they look like banks of televisions at appliance stores.

"You'll notice the kennel is air-conditioned and heated," Blanche said, like Jacqueline Kennedy giving her White House tour. "Over here is the dishwasher, and my washer and dryer, so I don't have to go back in the house to wash the towels and bedding. And I have my own little water heater. And of course, a monitoring system so I can hear them. I have a receiver inside."

That must be charming—listening to the collective snores, wheezes, snuffling, and liquid sucking sounds.

"I need a dog that makes me laugh. They do."

The pugs' kitchen is nicer than the one in my house. The ash-wood cabinets are custom-made, the Kohler sink has deluxe three-hundred-dollar faucets and a garbage disposal. Blanche's brother-in-law Bill scavenged the lot from a new house that was destroyed in the earthquake. On the kitchen table is a color television. ("Their favorite show is *I Love Lucy*," Blanche informed me.) And in the corner, a refrigerator covered with pug refrigerator magnets is crammed with serums and bacon drippings. "Grease is good for their coats," said Blanche.

This did not surprise me. When Clara and Sophie return from a visit with Blanche they are gigantic, like Macy's Thanksgiving Day Parade balloons. Speaking of Thanksgiving, Duke and I have a standing invitation to Blanche's traditional holiday feast. I'm a fanatic about eating healthy. The first year, I walked into Blanche's kitchen and watched with ill-concealed dismay as she casually dropped a pound of butter into every pot and pan on the stove. I christened it the "I Hate Your Heart Thanksgiving." She invited us back anyway.

Though her approach to human nutrition contradicts all modern-day health warnings, her quest for the perfect dog food rivals Galahad's for the Grail. Last year she guilt-tripped me into giving up the all-natural, low-output Nutro Max, which I can easily find in any pet store, in favor of another scientifically blended brand that is only sold by a distributor fifteen miles away. Dutifully, I dragged home a fifty-pound sack that took up all the storage space in the kitchen and attracted every ant for miles. And what was my reward for my diligence? Two weeks later Blanche decided the chow made her bitches sterile and insisted that I switch brands.

Blanche likes to believe that she has control over her

pack. "They go in the same bed every night," she says. "I have them arranged, girl, boy, girl, boy. That way there are fewer arguments. Boys argue over food, over anything, if someone is sitting the wrong way. See, look at that boy." She pointed to Starkeeper, a young whiz in the show ring, who was humping Firefox, an older, wiser male who must have weighed twenty-five pounds. Firefox snarled, but Starkeeper continued his amorous advance. As lovers, pugs don't have the raw natural beauty of say, two horses mating. A pug humping looks like an eighty-year-old man impersonating Elvis. The fight ended with both pugs peeing copiously.

"Tell me the truth," I asked. "Are any of these dogs house-broken?"

Blanche rolled her eyes like I was being petty. "No, Margo," she declared. "They're not housebroken. I can't expect it. It would be insane to demand anything of these dogs. Can you understand? People who keep the dogs in the house always have to concern themselves with housebreaking. I don't think about it. My pugs never think about it."

"But what do you do when you travel to shows?"

"They won't go in a crate."

This is one of the big lies: A dog will not mess his crate.

"They don't," Blanche insisted. "They keep their beds clean."

I sniggered. "Okay, let's say for argument's sake that lie is true. They have to go somewhere."

She swept a furball from the counter. "Well, if it's not concrete, they won't go." (This is in contrast to Clara and Sophie, who will only go on manicured lawns, or ivy in a pinch.)

"So what do you do? Let them run around the hotel parking lot?"

"Okay," she conceded. "Sometimes they make a little mistake. Are you happy?"

"I'm just trying to get the facts straight."

Blanche wiped her hands on her A PUG FOR ALL SEASONS T-shirt and grimaced. "The problem is when you have more than one or two pugs, then you don't know who did it and you have to punish everyone and it takes too much time. I don't care where they pee, it doesn't concern me. These dogs never do anything wrong. They never get scolded. They're happy out here with each other."

I've yet to meet a pug who prefers its own kind to a human lap. But maybe this is how they would be in the wild. "Do they have a pack mentality?"

Blanche laughed nervously. "Well, there was the chicken incident."

"Will this explain why Sophie cackled like a rooster after her last stay?"

"No," said Blanche, "though there are roosters down the street. The people next door had a chicken named Irma. Irma was, like, seventeen years old, which is highly unusual for a chicken. She used to sit on the fence overlooking the run and cackle at the pugs. Irma must have fallen off the fence at some point. I was on the phone, and Jennifer came to get me. She said, 'Mom, there are feathers in the back door.' I said, 'I'll be out in a minute,' but of course she kept after me. So I came out, and sure enough, there were Irma feathers everywhere. I went next door. The husband was there, and I didn't know him very well. I said, 'I think that Irma is dead.' He said, 'Why don't you put her in a box and bring her over and we'll bury her?' "

I shook with silent laughter as she went on. "I didn't know

what to say, so I came back over here and I got a bag. I figured I'd put Irma's remains, whatever they were, in a bag and put some stones in it. As I was putting one of the claws in the bag, Barbara, the wife, came over. I felt like I had just robbed a bank or something. She said, 'Oh, the pugs ate her.' I said, 'Yes Barbara, they ate her.' "

"Your pugs killed a chicken?"

"I'm sure what happened was that Irma fell off the fence. The pugs wanted to play at first. Then someone got the first bite. It became a game. Then it became a meal. It wasn't good."

"What did they do next? Bring down a flock of sheep?"

"Nothing," said Blanche. "I swear."

She walked me out to the car and hurried me past the guest house where Sophie and Clara were locked up. "Don't worry about them," she admonished. "They'll have fun."

I knew she was lying because whenever I pick them up, they race to my car and even Sophie jumps in, which is not only uncharacteristic but difficult, considering she's five pounds heavier from the bacon grease. But as I saw it, the greatest advantage to having pugs rather than children is that I can leave them with Blanche if we want to go away.

"Pugs don't hold a grudge," added Blanche. "It doesn't matter what happened yesterday or this morning. You are everything. You don't get that with kids."

"I've always been afraid that if I had a child, I would treat it like a pug."

"It would be a lucky child," Blanche said.

Somewhere deep in the bottom of my soul, a seed took root.

Behavior Modification

⸺ ⟨ೡ⟩ ⸺

*A*fter the eye incident I decided the rambunctious pugs needed a course in obedience training. Marjorie, the Venice Beach Canine Connection, recommended Your Best Friend Academy, run by Faith Mantooth. Marjorie's dog, Ralph, a lovable golden retriever–Great Dane mix only slightly smaller than a Jeep Cherokee, had recently graduated from a six-week course taught by Faith in nearby Penmar Park. "Faith is amazing," Marjorie said as Ralph came on command and sat motionless at her feet. "She uses all positive feedback."

I loathe group activities—Duke says my epitaph will read, "She was not a joiner" so I wasn't keen on dragging Sophie and Clara to the park, at night, to be educated along with a pack of unruly puppies. Especially since the incorrigible Clara showed no signs of forsaking her mission to rid the world of behemoth Akitas, Great Pyrenees, Neopolitan mastiffs, and any other four-legged creature larger than she. (Clara once saw a Shetland pony at the Santa Monica Farmer's Market and charged.) Faith was willing to come to the house and tutor them privately, and her methods sounded promising. "I don't yell at the dog or jerk it around," she said. "And I don't believe in saying no."

Lucky thing. Pugs think that "No" means "Wait until my back is turned." "What do you believe in?" I asked.

"Hot dogs," Faith said with such fervor I suspected she was the Oscar Meyer heiress. "All-beef hot dogs. Dogs never get them, and they adore them."

I expected a heavyset martinet like Barbara Woodhouse, the famous British dog trainer in Wellingtons who need only bellow, "Walkies," and the most hardened cur turns into Rin Tin Tin. Faith turned out to be a tall, slim, honey-blonde kitted out in short shorts. Picture a cross between Geena Davis in *The Accidental Tourist* and Daisy on *The Dukes of Hazzard*, and you've got the idea. Duke took a look and heeled. As for Clara and Sophie, they gave her their traditional greeting, excitedly raking their claws on her long, tanned, shapely legs. "Sit," she said calmly, raising up a cupped hand like she was bowling. Clara clawed at her shins. Sophie untied her shoelaces with her teeth. "Whoops," said Faith. She waited until Clara sat down. "Good sit," she said, slipping her a sliver of hot dog.

Clara had a religious experience.

"When they see something coming up over their head, the body inclines down to a sit position," Faith explained. "At first the dog doesn't know about the food treat, and it's a good way to show them what you want without pushing them around."

Actually, the ever-ravenous Clara picked up on the food part in about three seconds. "Sit," said Faith. Clara sprang in the air toward the hot dog like a salmon.

"Whoops," Faith said again and again until the salivating beast sat impatiently at her feet. "Good sit." Clara almost tore off Faith's finger lunging for the wiener. "Gentle," Faith said, and as I watched with incredulity, Clara delicately slurped the treat with her tongue. Faith passed me the Ziploc bag filled with hot dogs and told me to try with Sophie.

"Sit," I said. Sophie yawned, closed her owl eyes, and curled up on the kitchen floor for a nap. "Sit," I repeated.

The trainer issued a firm correction on the spot. "You should only say a command once, or the dog will think you don't mean it," Faith said. She snatched the hot dog from me and held it in front of Sophie. "Sit," she said. Sophie languidly stretched, then slowly inched her butt down into a sitting position and took the bait. Faith gave me another chance. "Sophie, sit," I said. Sophie sat, albeit five feet away. "Good dog." I smiled and gave her a reward.

The trainer looked like she wanted to swat me with a rolled-up newspaper. "You want her to sit right at your feet, between your legs," she said, "and after she sits, say, 'Good sit,' not 'Good dog,' so she knows what she did."

"I'm sorry," I said meekly and made another attempt. Sophie meandered out of the kitchen to see if any interesting breakfast scraps were lurking underneath the dining room table.

"Your hand was in the wrong position," Faith snapped.

There's something amiss with a positive-feedback system where the human is criticized constantly.

For her next trick, the dog trainer put a piece of hot dog between her teeth. "Watch," she said to Clara, who was already staring at her the way motorists gawk at a crash scene. Faith spat out the hot dog, and it flew across the kitchen floor. "Get it!" she ordered Clara. Clara dove across the tile. Sophie tackled her and growled. Clara was about to launch a counterattack when Faith intervened.

"Sit," she said. The intellectual Clara wavered for a moment, discerning if there was anything in it for her. She sat, reluctantly, the first time she ever walked away from a fight. Faith spat another hot dog in her direction. "You should practice this a lot," she told me. "It's for attention training."

Hot dogs are a substance I would only put in my mouth if I had been stranded in the forest for several weeks and had run out of poisonous mushrooms. "Can I do it with grapes? She loves grapes."

"I'm sure Clara would rather have hot dogs," Faith said. "You want to make training a treat for her so she looks forward to it."

Funny, most of the other dog manuals maintained I had to show the dog who was boss. I had just finished reading *The Dog Who Loved Too Much*, by Nicholas Dodman, a professor of behavioral pharmacology at the Tufts University School of Veterinary Medicine. He believes that dogs (mind you, he didn't say pugs) do not feel a compulsive need to be number one; they can be quite low in the social hierarchy as long as they know where they stand. In fact, he argued a dog would be relieved to know someone else was in charge.

Faith spewed another round of hot dogs at the pugs. "There are a million ways to train a dog, and I'm not saying the other ways don't work, but I do know this way is more humane. And you're being honest with your animal. You're asking them to do something. You're showing them how. And you're rewarding them. It lends itself to the dog wanting to repeat the behavior."

I wouldn't bet on that. Back in the good old days, when a dog owner didn't require a personal coach, I trained Bess and Stella with Milk-Bones. They learned how to sit, shake, lie down, and roll over. But they wouldn't do a damn thing unless I had a treat in my hand.

Faith cited some psychological experiment in which rats

that were rewarded intermittently worked harder than the control-group rats that were rewarded all the time. "They'll always have the hope that there will be something for them and they'll obey," she said. "Though I was at Sea World the other day, and they wouldn't dream of not rewarding Shamu, the killer whale, with a big pail of fish every time."

"What about obeying out of love of their master?"

The dog trainer gave an exasperated sigh. "If you go to work enough times and you don't get paid, you're going to stop going, no matter how much you love your job. Eventually, a dog is going to look at you and say, 'Why should I do this? What's in it for me?' "

Clara sat in front of me and looked me straight in the eye. "See, she wants to please you," Faith said.

Clara wanted another hot dog. I was holding the baggie. End of story.

"If she wanted to please you too much, then you wouldn't enjoy her," Faith said. "She cultivates an air of defiance to amuse you."

Professor Dodman might have argued that Clara simply had a problem with dominance. In his book, he observed that one way a dog raises his status is by climbing on top of something like a bed, chair, or sofa—three areas of the house that Clara claimed as her own. I didn't have the heart to rebuke her, since I'd behave similarly, if I were only nine inches high. Dodman might also blame my puppy's inflated ego on my habit of showering her with affection. "This is not a problem if the dog is not dominant," he wrote, "but can undermine the authority of owners who find themselves losing control. Dogs that are petted for nothing have much less incentive to work for a reward."

"One of the hardest things about training pugs is to keep

them on the ground," Faith agreed. "They're small, and they want to be on top of you all the time. But the pug should know her place is to sit on the floor."

For thousands of years the pugs' place has been on the sofa, and no amount of hot dogs was going to reverse that.

The trainer ordered me to work with each pug separately for a half hour in the morning and a half hour at night and to practice with them together for an additional half hour. What was my leisure time compared to their schooling? I worked like a dog. (Just not my dogs.) By the end of the week, Clara sat on command. Sophie sat too, though never exactly where she was supposed to, and only for an instant, after which she lay down. Duke, who habitually leaves repetitive drudge work to me, interrupted the training sessions to point out that I was giving the wrong hand signal or using the wrong tone of voice. Sometimes he'd just help himself to a hot dog.

"Off," I snapped, and he backed away.

Unbeknownst to me, he was training the pugs too. Training them to be real dogs, like his fantasy pets, border collies, which drag home dead animals and herd things. Each evening, when my husband took the pugs down to the board-walk, he set them free. When a neighbor whose Alaskan mala-mute was terrorized by the free-range Clara told me what was going on, I was appalled. It was dark, the pugs are jet black, and at night the boardwalk is inhabited by less than savory citizens—it was only a matter of time before the pugs vanished into thin air. "Don't worry," Duke said. "They behave much better off lead."

Fool that I was, I believed him. On a glorious Monday morning, when the warm breeze smelled like the sea and rising yeast from the bakery a few blocks away, the girls and I strolled down Ocean Park Promenade in Santa Monica. I decided to give them a pop quiz. Off leash Clara stayed close, straying only when she came upon a discarded pizza crust, and even then, when I kept walking, she skittered after me like a bug and swiftly caught up. Sophie stopped to sniff the trash cans, which are placed along the esplanade every five feet. "Sophie, come!" I called. She gave me her patented screw-you glare and darted down to the beach, where a dog's presence can result in an eighty-dollar fine (ironically given by police on horseback). I chased her to the surf, forcibly halted her excavation of a maggoty cheeseburger, and hauled her back to the promenade. "This is your last chance," I cautioned, like a mother threatening a toddler with time-out.

For a few yards Sophie heeled, and then her soft button ears pricked up. In the distance I saw a three-ton sweeper slowly advancing. "Pugs, sit," I ordered. Clara sat. I clipped on her leash. Sophie sat for a nanosecond, then sprinted off on a suicidal five-hundred-yard dash toward the sweeper's wheels. I raced after her, waving my arms, screaming, "Sophie, come!" but she continued her death charge. Luckily, the driver saw me and slammed on the brakes before the pug was flattened like a cartoon character.

"You probably gave her the wrong command," Duke said later.

While I persevered with the low-profile home-schooling, endlessly exhorting the pugs to lie down and stay, my husband opted for a high-profile field trip: hiking in the Santa Monica Mountains. Clara courageously followed him along the trail, occasionally looking back to make sure I was bringing up the rear. Sophie scampered backward, planting her face an inch from the toe of my boots, all the while howling at the dirt that flew up as I walked—a maddening and inexplicable pastime that she picked up on the sands of Santa Barbara's dog-friendly Arroyo Burro Beach. Neither pug ventured off the trail, which Duke took as evidence that they were heeling and I took as proof that like me, they were daunted by the posted rattlesnake warnings. We came to a shallow stream. Duke crossed on a path of slippery rocks. Clara and Sophie assumed the paws-locked position. I bent down to pick them up. "Leave them alone," Duke commanded. "They're dogs. They'll come."

"Not in my lifetime."

"Honey," he said. "Trust me."

I reluctantly crossed and waited on the bank. Duke stood on a rock midstream and commanded Sophie to ford the stream. The water was at most two inches deep, but Sophie lay in the mud on the opposite bank and glared defiantly. I made a move to go get her.

"Stay," my husband said. "She has to learn to obey."

For ten minutes I sat on the bank. Finally Duke waded across and prodded Sophie into the stream with the tip of his sneaker.

I recited Faith's credo. "You want to build your relationship with the dog with voice and hand commands. If you're manhandling it, then you're not getting communication."

"Good dog," Duke exclaimed as Sophie galloped through the water. For me it was a Pyrrhic victory. Sophie did cross the raging waters, but she developed a skin allergy from the mud, sand, and algae.

As for Clara, she hunkered on the bank, shivering, and made herself look tiny and square. When Duke tried to nudge her into the water, she squawked and ran away.

"Get her. Now!" I ordered, and for a change, my husband obeyed.

"That's the voice you should use when you're training them," Duke said. He waded across and scooped Clara up in his arms. "Daffodil," he murmured, "you're so manipulative."

Did Clara thank me for intervening? Hell no, she licked his face gratefully.

Loyalty was not Clara's strong point. You would think that since I spent the day with her, fed her, walked her, chauffeured her, scooped her poop, and home-schooled her, I would be the center of her universe. Instead, she worshipped Duke. Anna Marie voiced the opinion that Clara's diffidence toward me was due to the fact that she was certain she had me in her back pocket, while my husband represented a continual challenge. All I knew was that when the back gate slammed at seven o'clock and Duke returned from work, Clara abandoned me instantly and sprinted to the door to hail the conquering hero. For the remainder of the evening she held a vigil on his lap, and if I hugged him or attempted to converse, she butted me away with her microscopic head.

"Honey," Duke said, laughing and cuddling my rival, "you're coming between us."

I was reminded of a Spanish expression that my housekeeper, Lupe, taught me: *"Al que hace mas se le toma en cuenta menos."* "The more you do, the less they value you." I looked on the bright side. Clara's infidelity gave Sophie the chance to spend the entire evening on my lap. (Unlike Clara, who lived to snuggle, Sophie used her quality time to rip magazines or chew my needlepoint canvas.)

All told, I invested close to three hundred dollars, not including the hot dogs, in the pugs' education. In exchange, I received a constant stream of negative feedback and the pugs each gained a couple of pounds. True, they also gained a rudimentary understanding of "Sit," "Down," "Stay," "Off,"

"Come," and "Heel," but I wouldn't call them obedience-trained. I'd call them greedy. I expected that Clara, being smarter, would be a model student, but in truth, both pugs were equally mercenary. If I had food, they performed; if not, I was out of luck. I took to carrying plastic bags filled with sliced hot dogs in my pockets, so I could order Clara to sit when a bearlike Newfoundland passed and hopefully forestall an attack. In the weeks to follow, Clara ripped holes in all my jackets, looking to reward herself.

The pugs did display a natural affinity for parlor tricks, which Clara in particular realized were valuable for generating human attention. Faith insisted they learn perhaps the quintessential Los Angeles command—"Park!" When given this order, the pugs were supposed to trot around my back and plant themselves on my left side in preparation to heel. It seemed like a waste of time, since the only way they heeled was if I stooped over and held a hot dog in front of their noses—an uncomfortable position to sustain on a long walk. Clara used "Park" to great advantage. Whenever she felt she was being slighted she skipped around me like a square dancer do-si-do-ing, and she was always rewarded with a hug. When she "parked" on the Venice boardwalk, she drew a delighted crowd, who occasionally threw quarters. If I failed as a writer, I could set up shop between the chainsaw juggler, tarot readers, and the masseurs who crack your neck even though they have no chiropractic training.

Faith, who was never satisfied, suggested that I teach them a variation of "Park," in which they run around me in the opposite direction. "The command for that is 'Get in.' "

"Get real."

"You can teach them all kinds of tricks," said Faith. "The key is to catch a dog in a natural behavior and give a word to it. For instance, if you have a dog who shakes after a bath, then when it's shaking say, 'Shimmy!' After the sixteenth time, she'll do it on command."

I passed on shimmying, but I taught the loquacious Sophie to speak and got Clara to flop on her back and play dead when I said, "Bang." Both pugs also can dance on their hind legs and shake hands if there's something in it for them.

"If they shake with one paw, change hands, so they'll do it with the other one too," Faith said.

I did not consider it necessary for the pugs to be ambidextrous. I don't have lofty ambitions for them, unlike another pug owner I know, Elaine Garvey, whose fawn dogs, Oliver and Django, earned their Agility Excellent titles and compete in agility trials. I was aghast to learn that five-year-old Oliver and four-year-old Django clambered up and down six-foot-three-inch A-frames, slalomed through weave poles, and barreled over jumps. "What did you use as a training reward?" I asked. "Beef Wellington?"

"My dogs, they work for green beans," Garvey said.

And to think it took four packages of hot dogs for Clara to lie down.

"One time we were at a night show and, it being dinnertime, I thought I'd use that advantage to get Oliver revved up," Garvey said. "I brought his dinner, and right before it was his turn I took it out and showed it to him. I said, 'Oliver, here's your dinner,' and then I took it away. We got to the start line, and he was pumped. He did three obstacles out of thirteen, and then he left to get his dinner. He found his way through this huge crowd, and off he went."

That was the only thing she said that made sense to me. Garvey graciously invited Clara and Sophie to attend an agility-training session. For a moment I thought it might be amusing to watch Clara cross a teeterboard, but then my sense of self-preservation reasserted itself. No doubt in the course of instructing the pugs to weave through a line of poles they would receive dozens of compliments and my training methods would continually come under attack. In fact, during my last lesson with the critical Faith, I suggested she consider giving the hardworking human a word of praise.

"I'm a perfectionist," Faith admitted. "I went into dog training because I prefer animals to people." Still, I must have made an impression because on the final lesson, when Sophie performed a flawless sit/stay, Faith turned to me and said, "Good Margo, good job."

But was it really? I spent close to a hundred hours teaching Clara a dozen tricks. In the same amount of time, listening to cassettes in my car, I learned how to speak basic Spanish. Armed with her legerdemains, her preternatural social skills, and her passion for the spotlight, the pompous little Clara could upstage me in almost any endeavor. Meanwhile, I could instruct the guy at the car wash, *"Por favor, use la aspiradora bien. Hay mucho pelo de perro."* ("Please vacuum well, there's a lot of dog hair.") The pug and I did share a blind spot. For all our combined knowledge, there was one fact neither of us truly understood.

Clara was not a person.

Around Town

All my other pugs—even the cranky Sophie—settled into a predictable routine. They ate—*anything!*—They slept—*constantly!*—demanding only the occasional belly scratch, a brisk walk, and a few crumbs from my morning bagel. Clara was not that easily satisfied. She wanted at least half of my bagel (she preferred sesame or whole wheat) and cooped most of what I considered to be my life. As soon as Duke (her golden boy, even though he did hardly anything for her except take her on an evening walk and let her warm his lap when he was watching the Lakers) left for work, the shameless coquette suddenly remembered I existed. She cantered over, ears bobbing, tail wagging, and clawed my shins until I lifted her up to eye level. Then she coolly looked me over like a politician regards her advance person and asked, "So, what's on the schedule today?"

If my response was an unsatisfactory "I have a meeting downtown at the *Los Angeles Times,* but you're staying home," Clara booted up her fail-safe software program, GuiltMaster. Cocked her head from side to side. Snorted disbelievingly. Danced around in merry circles as I dressed. Sometimes she simply walked out the door and waited by the gate. If I picked her up and bodily tossed her back into the house, then she darted out and shadowed me like a CIA operative. Several times she found ways to slip into the car and hide in the backseat until I cleared the driveway, at which point her craving to sit in the front near the air-conditioning vent outweighed her fear of making her presence known. The first time she barreled over the armrest and shocked me when I was driving, I nearly totaled the car. After that, I kept an extra leash in the glove compartment.

Gamma Rae blamed it all on the stars. Clara, born June 23, 1992, is a Cancer with a moon in Aries. "She has a quick, shrewd mind, an ability to use self-assertion to good effect, an individualistic approach to life, and an original magnetic style," said Gamma Rae. "Her weakness is an oversensitivity to criticism and a sort of divine discontent."

I doubted it was Mars in Taurus that made Clara indomitable, but I was certain that every day she pushed the envelope a bit further. She tagged along when I got my hair cut at Umberto, the twelve-thousand-square-foot Beverly Hills beauty shrine. Clarina, *la bella Clarina,* looked *tutto Italiano* as her nails clickety-clacked along the tumbled marble floors, past the faux Pompeian frescoes over the reception desk, into the shampoo room, where trompe l'oeil wood beams crisscross the ceilings. Unfortunately, Umberto made me check her in the cloakroom due to unenlightened Beverly Hills health regulations, but Clarina didn't seem to mind. When I left her she was sucking up to the coat checker, a bored young Latina who had nothing to do all day but take your coat, hand you a number, and hope when you returned that you'd give her a tip. She was delighted to play with the pug; after all, no one in Los

Angeles has much in the way of coats to check. A pug was good for at least a couple of dollars.

I settled into Umberto's chair and said what I always say: "Don't cut it too short." Umberto ignored me; he didn't become the owner of *le grand salon* by letting his clients tell him how to cut their hair. "I can't believe you brought an animal in here," muttered Umberto, who hates pets. He introduced me to a high-ranking entertainment-industry attorney, getting highlights in the next station. "She's nuts about her damn animals too."

The attorney jumped at the chance to brag about her unparalleled devotion to her pets—Miles, a golden retriever, a couple of Arabian horses, and a Persian cat named Gretchen. "No one is a better mommy than me," she exclaimed, and I rolled my eyes. "I hire a sitter to keep the horses company when I'm at work," the attorney said. "Miles has regular appointments with a therapist. And I'm looking into getting Gretchen stuffed."

That got my attention. "Excuse me," I said. "Why would you stuff your cat?"

"You're both sick," Umberto said. To show his contempt he snipped an extra inch off my bangs.

"Whenever I take a shower Gretchen sits on the edge of the tub and watches me," the attorney explained. "She's getting on in years, and I've decided that when she finally crosses the rainbow bridge I'm going to stuff her and put her in the bathroom in her favorite spot."

For a moment I actually contemplated stuffing Clara and putting her in the passenger seat of my car. Then I came to my senses. The odds are far greater that she will stuff me. And where will I be displayed, I wondered. Probably on the sofa, so she'll always have a free lap. (Clara's lap instincts are highly evolved. She can hear a lap forming from clear across the house.)

When Umberto was through, I collected Clara from the cloakroom. She was holding court. Stylists, manicurists, facialists, waxers, makeup artists, and their work-in-progress clients circled her, stroking her glossy black coat and straightening her pink collar. A colorist offered to touch up the white patch on her chest, but I passed. Clara was reluctant to leave but acquiesced when she learned we were going to Saks. Clara loves Saks because all the gay shoe salesmen appreciate an adorable pug and there's a pet boutique on the ground floor with Versace leashes and a four-hundred-dollar iron four-poster bed that she feels she deserves. As usual, Clara made a detour to the bed and stretched out on the mattress, which drew choruses of "Too cute for words" from other shoppers. A salesperson pointedly reminded me that Christmas was coming, but I refused to succumb.

Nevertheless, it was depressingly clear that the pug was more popular than me. For a while, I took a Saturday job as a miniature contractor at Petite Designs, a dollhouse boutique owned by my friend Susan. The only condition of my employment was that I bring Clara along. While I labored in the back of the store carefully cutting teeny shingles or painting the trim on itsy-bitsy windows, Baby Suck Up remained in front, schmoozing with the customers. She liked it best when there was a class in progress because invariably the group took a break from their microlandscaping or quilting and went over to the nearby McDonald's to pick up lunch. Clara sat worshipfully at their feet waiting for the french fry or cheeseburger that inevitably came her way. I knew things were out of hand when Susan called in the middle of the week to ask, "Do you think Clara would like a chicken sandwich for lunch on Saturday, or would she prefer turkey?" (For the record, she didn't order lunch for me.) Susan's mother, Jackie, even stitched a needlepoint collar for Clara out of silk embroidery floss.

But I didn't begrudge the pug attention. My life was sunnier with Clara along. The ultimate social lubricant, she kept me in touch with joy, and even experiences that I dreaded were transformed by her presence. Much less enjoyable than dollhouse duty were visits to Dr. Morris D. Zoom, my oncologist at the so-called best hospital in the West. Life would be merrily rolling along, and then suddenly it would be time for a checkup and I had to put my future on hold and worry about my mortality. I felt like an overdue library book that had to be checked out for another ninety days. I'd sit in the waiting room, thoughtfully stocked with riveting periodicals like *Marrow Monthly*, exchanging terrified glances with ashen-faced patients. A grim-faced volunteer rolled a cart stacked with cheery brochures like *Everything You Want to Know About Lymphoma* or *Brain Cancer Made Simple*. She stopped in front of me and asked, "Is there anything you'd like?"

"Do you have *People*?" I asked.

Zoom, a brilliant physician, didn't really comprehend that these visits were stressful. He'd say, "Any problems?" I'd say, "Just a little nervous," and he'd shake his head and ask, "Why?" I'd be lying half naked on the examining table praying he wouldn't find any suspicious lumps, and meanwhile he'd be discussing his philosophy on the demise of musical theater.

By contrast, when the vivacious Clara poked her head out of her bag, the entire waiting room perked up. She was like Princess Diana paying an impromptu visit to the sick. She shook hands, even though I didn't have hot dogs; she parked;

she even stood on her hind legs and did a fandango. Zoom was
so unnerved by her presence that he interrupted his riff about
how Nathan Lane's performance in *A Funny Thing Happened
on the Way to the Forum* couldn't compare with Zero Mostel's
and burst into a chorus of "Springtime for Hitler," from his favorite movie, *The Producers.* He even told me I was doing
okay.

Clara could warm the heart of the most misanthropic
human. I took her to my friend Jon's town house. Jon lives in an
area of Los Angeles so pristine that it reminds me of Switzer-
land and spends most of his days in his home office contemplating further enhancements to his incredibly sophisticated
computer system. His house is devoid of any color except
black, white, and steel; his books are arranged by subject, and
he has invested more in filing cabinets than Elizabeth Taylor
has in diamonds. He is so meticulous that when he offers me a
glass of iced tea and hands me a spoon and a packet of Sweet'n
Low, I have a panic attack. I am afraid that I will put the spoon
in the wrong slot of his dishwasher. ("If one utensil is out of
place, I wouldn't care," he recently assured me in an attempt
to seem less anal. "I've tried to figure out the optimum posi-
tioning, but I'm handicapped by lack of knowledge about what
happens after I close the dishwasher door.")

Clara had no such inhibitions. She zipped into Jon's office, braced her front paws on his ergonomic chair, and stared
at his lap.

"What does she want?" he asked.

"She sees a vacant lap."

Jon hoisted her on his knee; she rested her head on his
keyboard. To my astonishment, he didn't even cringe when he
noticed a stray black pug hair on his mouse pad. Such was her
conquest, he later arranged for his artist friend Howard Ogden

to do an adoring computer-generated portrait of Clara. Jon presented me with the framed copy of the result, *Bit Map Clara*, and he also gave it to me on a floppy disk. Much to his annoyance—he feels I'm cheapening her image—I use it as a fax cover sheet. My Clara faxes seldom wind up at the bottom of the pile.

A couple of years ago, Jon moved and decided to convert his dining room into an office. (I argued in vain that he should have a kitchen table.) He invited me and Clara to accompany him to the Pacific Design Center to inspect Herman Miller file cabinets that cost more than my bedroom and living room furniture combined. We ate lunch at an outdoor café. Jon ordered a hamburger. Clara, sitting on a stone bench beside him, gently nudged him with her paw. "Would she like a piece?" he wondered. (Did he really have to ask?) When I nodded, Jon summoned the waitress and asked her to bring Clara her own plate, and then he cut the hamburger into neat little pieces.

I must have looked incredulous because he shrugged and said, "Yeah, so?"

Who was I to come between Clara and her swain?

Even though Jon once told me that if he ever got a dog he'd take six months off of work to train it properly, he didn't judge Clara harshly when he joined us for a walk on the Venice boardwalk and she displayed her dark side. First, we passed her mortal enemy, Betsy, a medium-sized, shaggy-haired mutt who always heels beautifully next to her master, Bobby, a suntanned, buffed-up fellow who wears shorts and a tank top no matter what the weather. As usual, Clara spotted her foe from a hundred yards away, even though Bobby tried to avoid a confrontation by making a detour around a building.

Jon watched with amusement as Clara shrieked and lunged for poor Betsy, who immediately forgot her manners and howled at her pint-sized tormentor. I picked up the hell-hound, and she immediately switched from the manic yapping to her trademark stuck-pig car-alarm screech, which sent all the skateboarders, Rollerbladers, tourists, and bums in the vicinity into gales of laughter. "I think Clara is a little presumptuous," Jon said, "but I forgive her."

(Much to my surprise, so did Betsy's master, Bobby. A few years into the feud, on a rare occasion when I happened to be on the boardwalk sans pugs, I stopped him and apologized for my dog's behavior. "Oh, I think she's hilarious," he told me. "Every time she screams it makes my day. She and Betsy are like people who take an immediate disliking to one another.")

Jon and I walked a little further, toward Santa Monica. The unrepentant Clara drove on a Portuguese water dog, a basenji, a bull terrier, and a pair of Irish setters.

"I wonder what that's all about," Jon mused. "She has issues with other dogs. She's a canophobe. Like a homophobe. She knows deep down she is a dog, but she can't stand it, so she attacks the other dog. The bigger the better."

Not long after, I got an answer of sorts. Anna Marie asked me to cover the Second Annual Pug Luck Garden Party in San Diego, a fundraising event to benefit homeless pugs. My husband was less than enthusiastic when I invited him along. "Can I slam my hand in a car door instead?" he asked.

If one reluctant guest wasn't enough, a few days before the party my sister called. Laurie had business in Los Angeles and wanted to fly in early to spend the weekend with me. When I explained we were going to the gala pug party, she decided to come too. "After all, I'm the one who got you interested in pugs," she reminded me.

The temperature was eighty-five degrees and climbing when we arrived at the event, which was being held at the Mission Bay home of one of the rescuers. There was no mistaking the place because the air was reverberating with the sounds of 247 overheated pugs panting and snorting and their owners squealing, "Cute, cute, cute." None of the pug guests, least of all Clara, looked pleased to be confronted with the reality that they were not the center of the universe, but their Humans were cheerfully comparing notes. The pickup line of the day was not "What's your sign?" but rather "Is he fixed?"

"Where's Federico Fellini when we need him?" Laurie gasped.

Imagine—no, it is impossible to imagine—how other-worldly pugs look en masse. (*Men In Black,* the hit film of the past summer, had a memorable scene in which Tommy Lee Jones unmasked a pug as an alien. The revelation was a big surprise to the audience, but not to me.) To make matters even more surreal, many of the pugs were in costume—hula skirts, cowboy hats, even one dressed as Superpug, complete with tights and cape. If a pug appeared in a tutu, I thought I would lose my mind.

As part of the festivities, Sue Goodrich, who bills herself as an animal-communication specialist, was giving psychic readings. A professional dog trainer, groomer, and handler, and formerly a senior keeper at the San Diego Zoo, Goodrich claimed to communicate telepathically with animals. I signed Clara up for a consultation. The earnest, sunbaked swami leaned across the velvet tablecloth and gazed into Clara's Milk Dud eyes. "Tell me," she murmured, "what do you want to know?"

Is she going to meet her twin flame? What is this week's winning Super Lotto number? I fell back on the truth.

"Clara has a dark secret," I began, after crossing the medium's palm with a check. "I got her when she was almost three months old, and as far as I know she has never been treated with anything but adoration. Yet she gets uncontrollably upset if I so much as look at her crossly."

"Let me see what she has to say." Goodrich picked up Clara's paw and shut her eyes, the better to receive enlightenment, which, she explained, Clara was transmitting to her in picture form. Several minutes passed. Finally: "Clara really missed her litter mates, and it was very traumatic for her meeting you."

"Funny," I said, "her breeder says she loathed her litter mates."

Goodrich shook her head. "Clara says you have very vital energy. This is intimidating to her."

"Believe me," I said, "I don't scare her."

"She must be holding on to her feelings. Let me ask her something else."

I threw her a softball. "How does she feel about Sophie?"

The psychic concentrated for an instant, then smiled. "Clara says she loves Sophie. She's really glad to have another friend to play with. She's not jealous at all."

And I am the Queen of Romania. "Ask her why she attacks large dogs."

"She tells me that she doesn't like their energy and feels that they are evil," Goodrich said. "She needs to teach them a lesson. When they see her, they throw their energy at her. They think they're so tough, but Clara has absolutely no fear. She says she scares them."

"She certainly scares me," I said.

Then the psychic dropped a bombshell: "Clara is very into energy and occultism."

Who knew?

"That's why you two have melded so well," the seer said with a trace of irony. "It's like you were sisters. Wait . . . wait.

I see . . . You two have been together before in a previous life. You were a witch and Clara was your familiar, like a cat. You can still use her that way in this body if you so wish. She's a very powerful being."

The powerful being panted furiously.

"The big dogs feel the intensity of her energy," said the psychic. "I'm warning Clara to be very careful. Some mighty being could be a big shepherd or a pit bull. She feels that she can handle it. She's very cunning."

The medium regarded me with grave concern. "Clara is a complex creature, and she knows what you are thinking. You don't have to scold her. She's in your head. All you have to do is picture what you want her to do. Because the bond between you is so close and tight, she gets hurt that you don't understand her. She doesn't feel that she needs to be told things or scolded. Just tell her in a polite voice, 'Please don't do that.' She wants more respect."

Respect? Clara would settle for nothing less than world dominance.

I got up to leave. Goodrich pulled me back down. "One more thing," she said. "Clara would like you to read to her."

"Fiction? Nonfiction?"

"Anything you're interested in learning, Clara would like to know, though she's particularly interested in metaphysics. You've always been her teacher. Speak out loud, picture it at the same time, and express the feeling behind it. You might put a crystal or two by her bed. Clara loves crystals."

I actually did put a crystal in Clara's bed. She sniffed it and then passed it to Sophie, who tried to eat it and almost choked.

In the interest of self-preservation, I felt compelled to escape from the pug party. I rounded up Laurie, who informed me that she no longer felt guilty for making me fly to Chicago in the winter for her wedding, and Duke, who was lying on the ground trying to photograph the Catch the Cheese Ball contest. Sophie and the little witch jumped into the car with unprecedented speed.

"Swear to me you'll never make me go to something like that again," Duke said later.

I gave him my word.

As it turned out, I lied.

Clara the Hero?

I never made a conscious decision to take Clara along on my first book tour; perhaps she made the arrangements and cut me out of the loop. When the publisher sent me a plane ticket to New York, a pet ticket for Clara was enclosed, and it hardly seemed in my best interest to refuse. The pug was a proven crowd pleaser, and I was at the bottom of the celebrity food chain. "It's a shame you aren't a victim of some kind," the publicist for the book had said wistfully. "I could have booked you on all the talk shows." It was the only time in my life I regretted not being a substance abuser.

Like Evita off to Buenos Aires, Clara eagerly hopped into her Sherpa Bag without a backward glance at Sophie, who was staying behind with Duke. He dropped us off at the airport and tenderly bade farewell to the love of his life. She gave his nose a gentle lick before ducking her head into the bag so he could close her zipper. "Write if you get work," Duke told her. He dragged my big suitcases over to the curbside check-in and gave me a quick hug. "Take care of Sugarplum," he called out as he drove away.

Clara contentedly rode through the terminal on my left

shoulder; my PowerBook was slung on my right. I had a few anxious moments when I went through security, as I had to perform a complicated maneuver: Unpack the PowerBook, pass it to a security guard. Unpack Clara, put her bag on the conveyor to be scanned, carry her through the metal detector. Act confident when her bone-shaped silver-plated I.D. tag sets off the metal detector and the pug has to be scanned again with that metal-detecting rod. Hand pug to security guard. Boot up computer to prove it isn't a bomb. Shut computer down, put it back in the case. Pry sluttish pug away from the fawning crowd of passengers and guards who are passing her around like the wonder ball. Stuff her back in the bag. Throw PowerBook and pug over my shoulder and, feeling like a pack mule, trudge half a mile to the gate.

Within a year, I performed this procedure so many times I could do it in my sleep. This first time, though, I made a critical mistake. I left Clara's bag partially unzipped so she could poke her head out. I set the bag on the floor while I waited in line at the gate. The passenger behind me tapped me on the shoulder. "Excuse me," he said, "but is that your dog over there?" Sure enough, Clara had escaped and was introducing herself to a flight attendant who was savoring a dish of vanilla yogurt. When I tried to remove the piggish puppy from the food source, she looked stricken. "Poor thing was hungry," the flight attendant said accusingly.

Frankly, a little hunger is not such a bad thing when you're taking a dog on a five-hour flight. But luck was with Clara: her new best friend was working our plane. The flight attendant allowed the pug to sit on the empty seat beside me and even brought her a disgusting-looking chickenlike product, which Clara accepted gratefully, even though she had already helped herself to half of my fruit plate. We landed at Kennedy Airport at eleven at night. It was freezing; Clara shivered pathetically. I stuffed her into the pink-and-green-striped sweater that makes her look like a bumblebee and pulled on my molting fifty-year-old mink coat. Blessedly, my mother had sent Willy, my stepfather Paul's driver, to pick us up. "Clarita, it's so good to see you," he exclaimed when she jumped into the backseat of the Town Car. And then, as an afterthought, "Hi, Margo."

On our way to Manhattan, I asked a favor that in all his years as a driver he had yet to hear. "Is there any grass between here and the city?" He looked stunned—only later did it occur to me that he probably thought I was asking for drugs—and I hastily explained that Clara would only go on lawn, ivy, or, in a pinch, weeds.

Willy miraculously located a patch of green in Queens. "It's cold out," he warned.

"Don't worry, she'll be quick," I said. I dragged her out of the warm Town Car, said, "Hurry up," and Clara obeyed instantly, much to Willy's surprise. He reported this to my mother.

"I can't believe you say, 'Hurry up,' and she goes to the bathroom," Mother marveled later. "Who told you that dog was brilliant?"

Again we were staying at the Hotel San Carlos, where Clara and I had first met. "Clarita, welcome back," cried Gabriel at the front desk. He admired her sweater and carried her behind the desk into the back room to introduce her to a few new employees. As an afterthought, "Credit card, Margo."

It didn't take long to realize that my book tour was not going to be the ego-boosting experience that I had fantasized about. When you're sitting alone in a room with your word processor you can imagine yourself to be creating a literary sensation, but once it gets published, you realize that what you actually have produced is a product, much like cereal, and I was not Cheerios but rather a quirky brand of granola. Fortunately, I had taken the precaution of buying a baseball cap for Clara embroidered with the name of my book. Mother chauffeured us from bookstore to bookstore, where I signed my books so they couldn't be shipped back to the supplier and Clara drew worshipful crowds. Not the lines around the block that Colin Powell and Howard Stern brought out, but more people than I could have summoned on the strength of my own reputation. Clara made an exception to her only-work-for-food policy: she sat, lay down, shook hands, danced, and for the finale, she parked. Everyone was mesmerized. She even convinced the cynical bookstore managers to move my book from the dingy corner of the humor section to a prominent place in the window.

"I can't get over she doesn't mind wearing the hat," Mother said. "And she is such an agreeable little person. I told her that we had to take a walk because her mom was signing books, and she said, 'Okay, that's fine.' "

Clara took a limousine ride out to Connecticut, where I was booked on a local talk show. She sat in the seat opposite me the entire trip. Later, when I took her for a walk along Park Avenue to see a display of sculptures by the artist Fernando Botero, she was photographed next to a rotund bronze bird by a television news crew. A publicist at Random House even managed to plant the following item about her in William Norwich's column in the *New York Post.*

FROM CLARA'S SCRAPBOOK:

William Norwich, *New York Post,* Friday, March 19, 1993

What else? Just that ever since *The New York Times* declared the pug the society dog of the year, you see them everywhere.

The latest sighting was an eight-month-old pug named Clara who flew recently to New York from Venice, California, with her owner, Random House author Margo Kaufman.

Margo came to town to promote her new book, *1-800-AM-I-NUTS?*, a collection of screwball stories about life in screwball Southern California. The good pug Clara, sporting a neon-pink visor that said "1-800-AM-I-NUTS?" and a pair of lime green sunglasses, was dragged from city bookstore to city bookstore by Ms. Kaufman.

The only hitch was a detour at Tiffany's, the Fifth Avenue jewelers, where Clara got herself caught in the revolving door.

Hardly the breakfast little Clara intended, more about bones than baubles, and surely a sign that a certain royalty check must have been burning a hole in Ms. Kaufman's pocket.

Clara made her radio debut on *The Joan Hamburg Show.* The show's publicist was initially apprehensive about letting her in the studio. But the pug wouldn't dream of soiling the carpet; she was more interested in finding out whether a thoughtful sponsor had sent over a pizza that the host might like to share. When none materialized, Clara took a fast train to Lullabye Land. Her jolly snoring could be heard over the airwaves, but the host was tickled. She told her audience that Clara was the best-behaved puppy she'd ever seen. Clara walked out of the studio unimpressed. Perhaps she sensed that radio was not her forte; TV was her preferred medium. (A few weeks later in Portland, Oregon, she made an electrifying television debut, growling at a close-up of herself on the monitor and chironed with the caption "Clara.") Or perhaps she was saving her strength for the most impressive trick she has ever performed: Escape from New York.

We were scheduled to leave on Saturday, but on Thursday the weather reports were unanimously predicting a weekend of snow. I decided it would be wise to fly back Friday morning, but Mother vetoed my decision. "You can't go," she said. "I've made reservations at the Friars Club for dinner."

"I don't want to get trapped in a blizzard," I said.

"I made reservations," Mother said, and it was futile to argue.

When I awoke at five o'clock on Saturday morning, snow (a substance I hadn't seen in twenty years and hadn't missed) was falling. I took Clara outside, and though she flinched, she gingerly walked over the ice to her favorite patch of ivy at Fiftieth and Second and squatted. Our flight was scheduled to leave at nine, and the storm wasn't supposed to get bad until afternoon. I called American Airlines to confirm a second time. I was put on hold for forty minutes, serenaded with the haunting refrain of "Something Special in the Air." They certainly weren't special on the phone—I never did get through to a human, but eventually I was connected to the automatic flight-information menu, and a computer voice assured me that our flight was leaving on time.

The snow got heavier the closer the cab got to the airport. "Nothing is taking off in this," the cabby said, but at the terminal the curbside skycap was also confident the plane was leaving. I checked my bags. That left me with Clara and the PowerBook, each of which weighed eight pounds but soon felt more like twenty. I did the security juggling act and trekked about a mile to the gate. We even boarded on time.

Just as I was congratulating myself on getting out of New York under the wire, the captain came on and announced a half-hour wait for deicing (a word I usually associate with death). Out the window, I could see swirling snow and the shivering ground crew, looking like they'd just run the Iditerod. An hour passed. The captain announced another deicing delay. Another hour passed. The captain announced that the long runway was covered with snow, a fact I could see for myself. Ten minutes later, he delivered the coup de grace: The airport was closed. I wasn't surprised.

However, I was flabbergasted when I inquired as to what the airline planned to do to assist me and the hundreds of other stranded travelers and the stewardess uttered the consoling words, "You're on your own." In the case of snow—an act of God—the airlines aren't required to be helpful. I asked a customer-service representative at the gate to give me back my ticket. "Nobody else asked for that," she said brusquely. (This has become the stock response to any request for service in the nineties.) I insisted and eventually, after a stampede by other passengers, she relented. "What are we supposed to do?" I inquired.

"Go home," the customer-service representative said. As if that wasn't precisely the service I was depending on the airline to provide. "Call our 800 number for reservations."

If I had called that 800 number, I'd probably still be on hold. Instead, I went to the ticket counter. A tall, distinguished-looking gentleman in a gorgeous cashmere overcoat was changing his ticket for the three o'clock flight the following afternoon. I got in line behind him and was nearly trampled by a herd of my fellow passengers. (I'm under five feet tall, a handicap in a mob scene.) I swiftly calculated the odds of someone helping me versus someone helping an enchanting pug puppy, and I unzipped Clara's bag. Out popped the black head with the bat ears. Sensing my distress, she automatically widened her eyes, cocked her head, and mewed like a dove. Almost instantly, Mr. Cashmere Overcoat took notice and gallantly pushed me to the front of the line. "How old is your pug?" he inquired.

"Eight months," I said.

"I have French bulldogs," he informed me right before he strolled away.

Armed with a return ticket and loaded down with computer and pug, I descended to the baggage claim, the lowest level of hell in this rendition of Dante's Inferno. Realizing that they had in their power a way to make the lives of people who had made the mistake of buying a ticket still more difficult, officials announced that we could not leave our bags at the airport unclaimed. It would take "at least" a couple of hours to get the luggage off the plane. Thousands of stranded passengers were having a mass panic attack commandeering taxis, jousting over luggage carts that rented for $1.50 (I vowed if I made it home alive, I would purchase a collapsible cart), bulldozing through pay-phone lines twenty hysterical passengers deep. Curiously, the New Yorkers coped by hollering at anyone who looked remotely official, while the Californians descended as if driven by some primordial force to the rental-car booths.

Clara looked at me reproachfully. She was not content to be dangling from the shoulder bag. It was my duty to restore her to an acceptable level of comfort. She pawed at my purse, and suddenly I remembered that right before we left, Duke had given me a tiny cellular phone as a Valentine's Day present. "What the buffalo was to the Indian, that's what the telephone is to you," he jested. But I loved the idea that I could call for help in a pinch.

The dial tone sounded like the angels singing. I reached

the Hotel San Carlos and asked them to save me a room. I
didn't have a clue how I was going to get back into Manhattan,
but it had to be easier than spending the night in a crowded
airport guarding two overstuffed bags I couldn't lift, a computer, and a pug who was unlikely to find grass in the terminal. I visualized us lying on our queen-sized bed eating
room-service food and waited for the universe to provide.

Just in case the universe needed help, I released Clara and
showed her off to good advantage in my arms. She made herself look extra small and pathetic and gave an anguished
whoop. Within three minutes, Mr. Cashmere Overcoat sidled
over to her, and within four minutes, Clara was in his arms,
licking his face, and my computer was strapped to his cart.
Between exclamations about how petite was her body and how
perfectly curled was her tail he confided that he had been
headed for Los Angeles with two equally tall assistants, whom
he had immediately dispatched to the rental-car booth. He
gestured to the snaking line to use the phone and grimaced. "I
need to call my hotel."

Immediately, I handed him my phone. He stopped stroking
Clara long enough to phone a smart hotel on the East Side and
tell them that he wanted rooms. Not just any rooms. He wanted
his usual suite with the view of Central Park. "You must be a
photographer," I noted when he hung up. (I've dated more
than my share of photographers and they all maintained a lunatic aesthetic even at the most inopportune moments.)

As a matter of fact, I was talking to Greg Gorman, a name
totally unknown to me at the time but later used by awestruck
friends in the question "Not *the* Greg Gorman, celebrity photographer of celebrities?" (He had just finished shooting the
Arnold.) All I knew at the time was that he was a sucker for a
delectable puppy. He offered to drop Clara—and me—off at

our hotel. His strapping and resourceful assistants, Kevin and Tom, had managed to rent a minivan. Clara accepted without hesitation. Between their luggage and mine it was a tight fit, but they weren't about to leave Clara. Or the phone. (Me, they would have cheerfully abandoned in a heartbeat, so I took the precaution of mentioning I had an extra battery for the phone in my purse.)

Kevin drove, Tom navigated, Greg and Clara slept in the front seat next to the heater, and I held my breath as the van inched slowly through the unplowed snow on the Van Wyck. They had heard rumors that the bridges were closed, so I called Mother to check. The Triboro was still open, she said, but she felt it was a mistake for me to go back to the hotel. "Have them bring you here," she insisted. I pointed out that her apartment was thirty blocks out of the way. "They're more than welcome to stay here," Mother said.

My rescuers dropped us off in front of the Hotel San Carlos. Clara went into the paws-locked position the instant her feet touched the snowbank, so Greg lifted her up and carried her into the lobby, where again she was welcomed like a foreign dignitary. (She refused to set foot outside the hotel, and so I found her some newspaper.) There was a fax waiting from Duke. "If you are reading this, you win the Urban Survival Award," it said. Room service was shut down, but Paul magically managed to make Chinese food from Bruce Ho appear and Clara and I spent the evening snuggling on the bed tuned in to the Storm Watch on television (ironically sponsored by Alaska Cruises). The next day I couldn't get through to American Airlines—I couldn't even get put on hold, just a solid busy signal. The television news reported that Kennedy was scheduled to reopen at four, but I didn't know if our three o'clock flight would go.

I called my husband and asked him to call from Los Angeles. He couldn't get through either. But he was able to get the Kennedy takeoff schedule from an on-line database and discovered that my flight had a departure time—an hour late, but who cared? Clara and I headed back to the airport and arrived in Los Angeles three and a half hours late. Duke threw his arms around Clara and greeted her joyously. He did not believe she was a rescuer akin to the Saint Bernard who dragged two children from a burning house or the Chesapeake Bay retriever who rescued his five-year-old master from a fast-moving creek.

"Boy, was I smart to get you that phone," he said.

Clara Goes to the Office

$\mathscr{D}$ue to a strange quirk of fate or bad karma, or perhaps a pathological corporate skill-set deficiency, I have almost always worked at home. With the exception of a brief interlude when I worked for an advertising agency and had a proper office, I've written in a cluttered spare bedroom with only a pair of pugs snoring under the desk for company. The advantages of this arrangement are mutual, I suppose. I am free to indulge the pugs' every whim, and they in turn provide a distraction, which all writers need.

A couple of years ago, during an extensive home remodel, Duke, Clara, Sophie, and I moved across the street to a pleasant one-bedroom apartment. I spent months supervising the construction and fell behind schedule finishing a book about the project. When it came time to move back to our house, Gamma Rae suggested that I keep the apartment as a work space so I could concentrate without being distracted by boxes that needed to be unpacked, paintings that had to be hung, surly contractors who needed to be called back to repair some mistake in the job. It was an idea that wouldn't have occurred to me in a million years, but I instantly recognized its wisdom.

Every morning the pugs and I walked across the street to the quiet apartment. I became fond of the separation between work and play, and Clara enjoyed the change in scenery. Apart from a colossal flea infestation in the plush carpet that proved to be resistant to all bombs known to man, the arrangement was satisfactory. Alas, once I finished the book, I couldn't justify that apartment's expense. I dreaded being cooped up at home again.

In the middle of our remodel, I'd had a revelation: I didn't like our house. We tried to sell it, but we remain trapped by economic and aesthetic necessity. Our bungalow, fifty yards from the ocean, was purchased when California real estate was cheap. To buy a better house this close to the sea—and my husband has to be near water or his gills dry up—requires us to triple our existing mortgage in exchange for at most a couple hundred more square feet. It makes no sense. Gamma Rae made another suggestion that wouldn't have occurred to me in a million years. "Why don't you rent office space?" she said. That way, I wouldn't be trapped all day, listening to the deadbeats in the Roach Motel, the seedy apartment building next door. (Lest you think I'm exaggerating, recently a new tenant leaned over the rickety fence that separates our property and introduced himself. "Greetings, neighbor," he said. "My name is Danger.")

For several months I canvassed office buildings on nearby Main Street in Santa Monica searching for an inexpensive yet aesthetically pleasing work space close to home that would accept two pugs. It was even more frustrating than looking for a mint-condition two-story bungalow half a block from the beach. The best I could do was a dreary six-hundred-dollar-a-month cubicle with dank carpets and dirty windows that didn't open. I grew so despondent that Gomez, the landlord of my beloved apartment, half-jokingly offered to let me have the one-bedroom for free in exchange for being his mistress. I reluctantly returned to my cluttered home office.

Just when I couldn't stand another day of listening to my neighbor practice "Stairway to Heaven" on his electric guitar—an instrument he's been practicing incessantly for eight years and still hasn't mastered—a miracle occurred. On my way home from the market, I took a shortcut down a Bohemian Venetian boulevard that supposedly has been about to become a happening street for the past twelve years. A sign advertising vacant studio lofts loomed in my windshield. I reflexively punched the number into my cell phone and was connected to a disembodied voice who identified himself as "Lotus, your New Age real estate channeler." He broke the sad news that the loft in question was twelve hundred dollars a month.

"Bummer." I sighed. My budget was a quarter of that.

In spite of my penury, Lotus offered to help. But first he instructed me to close my eyes, inhale to the count of four, and exhale to the count to eight, until I was completely relaxed. It was a little tricky, since I was in a moving car, but this is Los Angeles, where people have three-course meals, put on makeup, and receive faxes in their vehicles. Next, Lotus instructed me to visualize my dream office surrounded by a translucent powder-pink bubble. "Tell me what you see," he said.

"An architecturally interesting space, preferably not on the ground floor, with high ceilings and a decent view," I said. "And it has to be dirt cheap." I didn't mention the pugs. I didn't want to press my luck.

"The universe will provide," said Lotus, and to my astonishment, an hour later he called and said that the universe had come through. "You'll love it," he assured me.

The last Realtor who told me this showed me a half-million-dollar clapboard shack with one bathroom and a view of McDonald's from the master bedroom. But I dutifully wrote down the address, tossed Clara into the car, and drove to an old brick building five minutes away. A steep stairway led to a voluminous loft. I looked around hopefully. Narrow oak peg-and-groove floors. High ceilings. Skylights. So far, so good.

Clara, who relishes stairs, scampered up and then down and then back up again. Her grand entrance was greeted with a delighted guttural squeal.

"Ein schwartzer Mops," cooed a blowsy blonde with a fluttery voice like a wind-up canary. I don't speak German, and being Jewish, I can't help but think of World War II films and worse when I hear it, but I recognized the German for "black pug." Switching to English, the woman breathlessly introduced herself as "Elke, Dave's wife," and explained that she and Dave ran a small graphic-design firm. He was the principal art director; she kept the books. Before she could give me any more details, the *schwartzer Mops* parked on her sandal and fixed her with a Suzy Parker smile.

"Dave's going to die when he sees her," Elke chirped rapturously. "Can I pick her up?"

The *schwartzer Mops* obligingly let all her limbs go limp so she could be easily lifted. She licked Elke's face and purred like a kitten as Elke gave me a tour. "We're downsizing, so we're looking to sublet space," she explained. "We have a photographer here and a couple of freelance artists and a producer."

Kind of like the old *Bob Newhart Show*, with Los Angeles creative people instead of Chicago dentists. It might be fun.

My eyes widened approvingly as I followed her around. Dave, whom I later learned was a master carpenter, appeared to be even more of a visual fetishist than I am, which was sort of scary. Each light fixture, shelving unit, doorknob, chair, and poster in the loft had been carefully chosen for its looks. I passed a vast photographic studio and a communal kitchen. Not bad, I thought. I got more excited when I noticed a giant paper cutter and reams of tagboard. My hobby is building dollhouses, and a giant paper cutter is high on my wish list. By the time we came to the state-of-the-art copier, which Elke assured me I was welcome to use whenever I liked, my head was reeling. Access to free copies is a freelance writer's dream. (Little did I know that I was about to embark on a venture that required incessant photocopying.)

"We also have a fax and a laser printer you can hook up to," Elke said. Two offices were available. The larger one was shaped like a trapezoid and had no windows, just a skylight. The price was right, but sandwiched between two other offices, it felt claustrophobic. "The other is smaller," Elke said apologetically, and led me down a hall to an isolated corner. I gasped with pleasure and surprise. Twenty-foot ceilings. Walls of exposed old brick. Two oversized double-hung windows that looked out on the palm-tree-lined boulevard and beyond that, the sea. A sleek glass desk hung from the ceiling on steel cables. Even an adjoining bathroom. All I needed to do was install a phone line and bring in my PowerBook.

I made a mental note: Call Lotus and see if he can find me a house. (There, the universe failed to provide.)

The only possible deal breaker was snoring in Elke's arms.

"Clara has a sister," I began hesitantly.

"Zwei schwartze Möpse!" Elke exclaimed.

I said, "They don't really like being left alone all day." I thought, "Tough, if worse comes to worst, they'll get used to it." Elke put her Kewpie-doll mouth next to Clara's ear. "Do you miss your mommy?" she whispered.

Clara sent a telepathic response: "You can save this pug or condemn her to a life of isolation and boredom."

"Don't worry," Elke said to me. "We love dogs. Clara is always welcome here."

I naïvely believed that I was renting the office for me. But as usual, Clara reaped the rewards.

On the first morning of our tenancy, the pugs and I developed a routine that persists to this day. After breakfast, I put Clara and Sophie outside. I was trying—and I'm still trying—to convince them to go to the bathroom without a formal audience, but no matter how urgent the call of nature, they will only perform for praise. Clara waited eagerly on the back steps. The balky Sophie disappeared around the side of the house and barked at a fluttering leaf. After my usual frantic search for keys and sunglasses, I staggered out, weighed down by my Power-Book, a bag of books, lunch, and my purse. Lacking a free hand to hold leashes, I ordered the pugs to follow me out to the car, a distance of at most five feet. Clara vaulted into the passenger seat; Sophie wandered off to investigate what new smells had accumulated in the parking lot overnight. She spied a cat and pursued it down the alley. Cursing, I locked Clara, the PowerBook, my purse, and the books in the car and chased after Sophie.

It took three irritating minutes to corral her. I debated whether to leave her home alone as punishment for her disobedience, decided I didn't have the heart, unlocked the car, and unceremoniously dumped her in the backseat. By this time, Clara was hyperventilating dramatically, even though the sunroof was open and the air temperature was only sixty-five degrees.

Five minutes later we arrived at the sanctuary. (Were it not for the PowerBook and the marginal neighborhood between my home and office, it would be a twenty-minute walk.) I hit the automatic door opener and pulled into an enclosed parking lot. Clara jumped out and took the back stairs three at a time. Sophie refused to budge. I finally pulled her out, unloaded my stuff, and climbed up a steep flight of stairs. Sophie rambled over to the far corner of the parking lot and lay in the sun, eyes gleaming defiantly. I wondered if she could be stolen, thought, "Hmm, maybe I'll get lucky," and left her there. Eventually, she heard a chorus of my new office mates fussing over the ingratiating Clara and deigned to join us. (Duke claims the pugs are so jealous that you can punish one simply by rewarding the other.)

On that first day, when Sophie entered, panting, she was the fifth four-legged creature in the place. The office turned out to be a real-life enactment of those tacky paintings of dogs playing poker. Marta, the graphic designer from Poland, brought Spencer, a golden-blond cocker spaniel. Elke and Dave introduced Sailor and Coco, their two springer spaniels. Sailor attempted to mount the diminutive Clara, but she leapt vertically toward his jugular and snapped like a demonic jack-in-the-box. He recoiled and slunk back to Dave's office.

"Good for you, Clara," said Elke. "Teach him a lesson."

Dave was fascinated by the pugs' distinctive design elements. "The way they walk is so unique," he said. "Their front legs go forward, but the back ones shimmy from side to side. Have you ever noticed?"

Of course I had noticed. Duke once picked out a pair of pugs from five hundred yards away on a Santa Barbara beach just by their gait.

For a while we had a tenant with a tremendous Great Dane

named Garrote, but he lunged at Sailor through a glass door, shattered the door, and sent Sailor to the vet for stitches. Ironically, his master was asked to leave, not for mutilating the landlord's spaniel, but for not paying rent.

Naturally, all these dog worshippers had offices stocked with treats, and by the end of our first week I didn't see Clara for huge chunks of the day. She escorted me to my office and waited for me to boot up the computer and start writing, then she vanished to panhandle the other tenants. She knew what time every single person ate lunch, posted herself under the appropriate desk, and turned the power on her Begging Control up to high. At one, Elke and Marta got Chinese take-out. Dave went out to eat, but Clara soon trained him to return with a doggy bag. At three the UPS guy came bearing packages and Milk-Bones. At four the pugs mauled the FedEx lady, who had the nerve to arrive sans treats. She promised to make amends. At four-thirty, Bob, the graphic artist, ate a burrito. I knew things had gotten out of hand when I heard a pizza-delivery man call out, "Clara, I've got your favorite, pepperoni."

For the record, I have never ordered pizza.

Far from being bothered, Elke proclaimed the pugs the official office dogs and began leaving Sailor and Coco at home. "The pugs don't bark all the time like our dogs do," she marveled. "I've never known pugs as pugs. In Germany *Möpse* are very popular. Now I see why."

"They're the best office dogs we've ever had," Dave agreed. "And we've had tons."

It was bad enough that all our office conversation revolved around flea-extermination methods and discount groomers. But soon after I moved in, we were joined by Phyllis, a freelance producer and supermom to Bogie and Bacall, two Labradors. She felt that I was blind to the pugs' needs. Her

Labs seldom came to work; instead Phyllis smugly informed me that they attended a swank doggy day care center in Manhattan Beach. "Every morning Bogie and Bacall get picked up in a big van with half a dozen other dogs," she said. "They all go on park outings and run around and get dirty and work on their socialization skills."

I defensively assured her that Clara and Sophie saw plenty of dogs on the Venice boardwalk.

Phyllis also considered me remiss for not celebrating the pugs' birthdays. "The Labs have a party every year," she said. "I sent out formal invitations, and they get to eat ice cream out of the carton. All the dogs get cupcakes—vanilla of course, because dogs can't eat chocolate because there's a chemical in it that can be toxic. And they wear party hats."

My policy on dog parties remains firm: When the pugs can write thank-you notes, I'll hire a clown to entertain them. Actually, I wouldn't have to hire a clown, as Duke's sister is a clown and his brother is a juggler. It was a shame we didn't have a child because we would have the birthday-party problem solved.

Phyllis was a bad influence. She did a decorating job that Martha Stewart would envy and put me to shame. Loathing clutter, I had brought only my PowerBook, a printer, a couple of ancient IKEA bookshelves that no longer fit in our remodeled house, and some pug bric-a-brac that was too kitschy to keep at home. But she dragged in sofas, dhurrie rugs, a sculpted metal chair, a VCR, TV, coffee table. Every day brought a new design accent. A candy dish filled with designer jelly beans. (Clara liked the buttered-popcorn ones.) A Chinese ginger-jar lamp. Clara took to lounging on Phyllis's white ottoman. "She's such a princess," Phyllis marveled. "How can you let her sleep on the hard wood floor?"

If Clara ever bothered to come into my office, she would have seen there was a thick Pierre Deux cushion on the floor for her comfort. But she felt Phyllis's ottoman showed off her charms to better advantage.

I was flipping through the RC Steele catalog, which sells discounted dog supplies (our office was going to place a group order), when I noticed a camelback loveseat with rolled arms and a cushion that unfolded into a futon (in case the pugs had overnight guests). It cost forty-five dollars and was upholstered in a professional-looking navy blue, with white fleur-de-lis. I jokingly told Phyllis I was thinking of purchasing a power sofa for the pugs.

"You'll have to get two," she said. "So you can set them up in a conversational *L*."

The whole office rallied around the couch quest. Dave, who is so particular about furniture design he once threw out a chair left by a former tenant because, he said, "it was too ugly to look at," came in all excited. A guy on the shoulder of Pacific Coast Highway near the airport was selling scaled-down armchairs. "If you leave right now, you'll probably catch him," Dave said. I was on deadline and not particularly eager to buy pug seating, which I considered another step down the slippery slope toward dementia. But Dave kept after me, and a few days later I convinced Clara's devoted swain, Jon, to drive up there with me. Jon is a skilled haggler, and I figured he could get me a good price. But unfortunately or fortunately, the *ambulante* had taken the day off.

A few days later, Marta knocked on my door. "I hope I'm not bothering you," she said, "but there's a chair vendor on the corner." She insisted on coming with me to make sure that I picked something that met the office's lofty design standards. We walked over and found ninety-dollar rocking chairs upholstered with fabrics bearing likenesses of Mickey Mouse and Cinderella that I was certain Disney didn't license. Clara hopped on Cinderella and teetered like a beginning surfer.

"Dave could take the rockers off," Marta said thoughtfully, "but I don't think they look serious enough."

Phyllis, the design maven, brought in an upscale catalog, In the Company of Dogs, that offered a wider selection. For a moment I succumbed to temptation and debated between a "doggy chic" sofa covered in red floral cotton damask ($65), a plaid Regency model that was a replica of an overstuffed round chair with throw pillows (only $110), and a sleek contemporary sofa upholstered in a black-and-gold harlequin-patterned jacquard with two neck-roll pillows, three throw pillows, and "lavish fringe" (only $145).

"Remember, you've got to get two, for symmetry," Phyllis said, and the others nodded in grave agreement. The gag had gone past the point of no return. I broke down and ordered a pair of the discounted royal blue loveseats that had initially launched this insane crusade. Compared with the competition, they seemed almost reasonable. When they finally arrived, I set them up opposite my desk and Clara and Sophie took to them with disconcerting avidity. All new clients were paraded into my office as part of their introductory tour.

"You know what you need?" Marta said thoughtfully. "A coffee table." I imagined a small glass table with copies of *Pug Talk* laid out in a fan, but I resisted. At least so far.

Great Irony Number One: A few months ago, in the course of researching a story, I had a visitor. He looked around my studio for a place to sit. He noted the pug chairs, which were occupied. "Sorry," I said, "you're the first two-legged visitor I've ever had."

Great Irony Number Two: Right after I sent away for the

chairs, Posh Pups, a boutique specializing in all things un-
necessary for your companion animals—including upholstered chairs—opened up across the street. You will recall
that these old friends used to be located a couple of blocks
from my house on the Venice boardwalk, where for years
owner Gwen Zeller was a fixture, selling thousands of doggy
visors, sunglasses, and even biker hats to tourists. The hats
come in seven sizes—from small enough for Clara to big
enough for a horse.

I took a break one day and asked her how she had been
lured into dog millinery. "I was jogging with my two Afghans
one time, and I happened to notice they were squinting,"
Zeller said blithely. "It just didn't seem fair, so I made the
hats, and sunglasses were the natural progression. A few people think it's undignified for a dog to wear clothing, but dogs
love it. They get a lot of positive feedback."

She suggested that Clara would look darling in her newest
creation, a white sailor cap. I tried it on her and the result was
toxic. "Too cute," cried my office mates when she waltzed in
looking like a pint-sized Gilligan. I took to walking the pugs
over to Posh Pups whenever I needed a break, and Clara and
Sophie were soon the proud owners of a gilt crown, a straw
bonnet, a pair of bunny ears for Easter, and a red cowboy hat.
Worse, Gwen and her assistant, Marie, got the pugs hooked on
revolting chew toys: hooves and pig's ears. A longtime vegetarian, I protested, but when I realized that a pig's ear would
shut Sophie up for hours, I relented, even though my office
floor looked like an outtake from a David Cronenberg movie.

My husband came to my office on a Saturday afternoon to
help me hang a Chinese scroll we had bought in Xi'an. He
froze in horror. It was all new to him. He took in the couches,
the ceramic water dish decorated with paw prints, the PUG

CROSSING street sign (a gift from Marta), the framed lithograph of black and fawn pugs in a basket (a gift from my sister), the masticated ears . . . "Honey," he said, "this is a little terrifying."

Clara, who was lounging on her divan delicately gnawing what appeared to be a human hand, thought he was overreacting, but I looked at my office through his eyes and realized that the focus of my life was askew. I had to take action before I turned into one of those dotty old ladies who leaves her estate to her cat or, in my case, the Pug Dog Sanctuary, a refuge for geriatric pugs located in Gairloch, Wester Ross, Scotland. Duke and I looked at each other with perfect understanding.

If Clara only knew what we were thinking, she would have figured out a way to stop it.

But by the time she realized, it was too late.

Under Clara's Radar

On an overcast Monday morning in January, at the uncivilized hour of 8:00 A.M., Clara's worst nightmare commenced. Yawning, Duke and I sat around the breakfast table and made polite conversation with our guest—Betty, an unflappable middle-aged social worker. Clara perched on my knee, paws on the place mat, and attempted to move the plate of smoked salmon closer to her mouth through telekinesis. Suddenly, Betty looked into the pug's eyes and in the soothing, slightly patronizing voice you'd use to talk a lunatic down from a high building, asked, "Clara, are you prepared to share your mommy's lap?" I visibly startled.

Duke rolled his eyes. "Clara isn't a good sharer," he said.

Betty put down her poppy-seed bagel and put her nose up to the pug's wrinkled brow. "You'll have to make a few adjustments, now, won't you, dearie?"

Clara panted so furiously that her foul breath fogged Betty's tortoiseshell glasses.

I stroked her back and murmured, "Don't worry, Clara. You won't suffer." I thought, "Damn, this is what I get for hanging out in cyberspace."

It was an accident that lends truth to Freud's axiom that there are no accidents. I was lallygagging on America Online (back in the days when it was possible to log on at will without getting a busy signal for a couple of hours). I must have clicked on the wrong icon because like a time traveler I touched down in an unfamiliar culture. "Welcome to the Adoption Forum," flashed brightly colored letters on my screen. I scrolled past reunion registries, adoptive-parenting support groups, and search boards until I saw a menu option that piqued my curiosity—international adoption. Idly, I double-clicked and up popped a roster of choices that I normally associate with a travel agent. Latin America? China? Vietnam? Korea? Philippines? Russia? I hadn't been so awestruck since I heard my first Rodgers and Hart musical. When I finally logged off, bleary-eyed, two hours later, my head was reeling from visions of infants trapped in orphanages around the world who desperately needed a loving home.

Please don't write me letters. I realize that there are many children in the United States in similar predicaments, but domestic adoption struck me as an express ticket to the *Jenny Jones* show. I had seen *Losing Isaiah*. I had followed the Baby Richard case. I had heard overwrought couples at cocktail parties describing how they made scrapbooks and placed ads in the newspapers of small Southern towns, hoping to attract the attention of a pregnant teenager—preferably president of her class or at least head cheerleader—who was willing to give up her child. They flew the aforementioned cheerleader to Los Angeles, took her to Disneyland, bought her star football-player boyfriend a big-screen TV, set her up in the Oakwood Apartments, and paid all her medical expenses, only to have her change her mind at the last minute or, worse, five years down the road, sue them for custody. And I thought, "Not for me."

By contrast, according to my cybersources, international adoption was a straightforward albeit Byzantine process requiring an obsessive-compulsive desire to organize paperwork, the ability to extract information from intractable bureaucracies, a high tolerance for the unknown, and a willingness to journey to a foreign land—in other words, all my best skills. I also liked the fact that we would be saving an abandoned child from a life in an institution, which meant the birth mother wouldn't be coming back and also, given my less-than-stellar health record, assuaged my conscience. It had been four years since my cancer battle and I was doing swell, but just to be on the safe side, I ran the idea past my official reality check, Laurie. She volunteered to be guardian if worse came to worst, and thus empowered, I broached the idea with my husband.

Duke instantly recognized that international adoption was right up our alley, given our mutual passion for travel and foreign cultures. Never one to trouble himself with low-level research, he encouraged me to get more details. Unlike my husband, who spends hours on-line pontificating on the famous San Francisco–based cyber watering hole, The Well (identified by *Wired* magazine as the most influential on-line location but known to me as a hotbed of inbred backbiting, one-upsmanship, and insincere pandering), my forays into cyberspace were primarily to check my E-mail. (I don't like to invest energy in relationships where we don't go to lunch.) But as the seedling took root, I monitored the on-line adoption bulletin boards with the gusto that I reserve for my secret vice, the *Star*.

I discovered that Chinese orphanages are filled with infant girls, abandoned because of their government's one-child policy and a cultural bias toward boys. Korea gives the adoptive parents the most detailed background information—but then again, I was turned off by Mia Farrow's experience with her adopted Korean daughter Soon Yi. Russia sometimes sends medical reports filled with terrifying diseases that my on-line sources assured me were not "always real." Peru and Chile require you to stay for a month.

Ultimately, it came down to a choice between China and Russia. I favored Russia because deep in my conservative heart I suspected it would be simpler to raise a child who resembled us—both our families are of Eastern European descent, and my husband and sister speak Russian. Duke, light-years more liberal than me, was wildly enthusiastic about celebrating the Chinese New Year and studying Mandarin (a few years ago he learned Cantonese for a lark). By all accounts Chinese adoption was less problematic, so I went with my husband's choice. Besides, after twenty years of enslavement to small Oriental dogs, a Chinese daughter seemed like the next logical step. Given my experience fielding stupid pug questions, I was certainly prepared to handle the biggest complaint of parents with adopted Chinese daughters: prying comments from strangers. (I did harbor mild embarrassment at equating a child with the pugs, but Pangloss eased my conscience. "The lower your expectations, the better you'll handle the adoption process," he said. "And it's not like those pugs have a bad life.")

One afternoon I met Duke at a strip mall in Roland Heights. I had scheduled an introductory meeting with Ken Qing, a former government official in the People's Republic who was now facilitating adoptions. He assured us that he had superb connections in the Ministry of Justice and the Ministry of Civil Affairs, then the two agencies in Beijing that governed adoption. Duke was more impressed to discover that Mr.

Qing's office was conveniently located above a noodle shop, and he spent most of the meeting daydreaming about lunch.

Mr. Qing walked us through the steps we would have to take. First, we needed a home study—a written report by a social worker licensed for intercountry adoption. Second, we had to apply to the Immigration and Naturalization Service for permission to bring an orphan into the United States. Third, we had to assemble a bunch of notarized documents. Once our paperwork was in order, Mr. Qing would submit it to the Chinese government. And in time, we would be matched with a baby. Mr. Qing would then escort us and a group of his other clients to China to claim our daughter. From start to finish it should take six months.

"Any questions?" he said briskly.

"How long does it take from the time we submit the dossier to the time we get a picture of our daughter?" I asked.

Mr. Qing shook his head. "I don't believe in picture."

To me, seeing is believing. I couldn't possibly fly to China to pick up a baby sight unseen. I couldn't send away for sheets sight unseen, and sheets I could return. Besides, all my on-line sources got pictures. I took a deep breath. "Other agencies give pictures."

Mr. Qing pulled a disapproving face. "If you were pregnant, you wouldn't get a picture."

"That's true," I thought, "but if I were pregnant, the baby wouldn't be Chinese."

Duke interrupted his dumpling reverie to intervene before I stuck my foot in my mouth. "Do we have to travel in a group?"

Mr. Qing nodded. "Most families love group," he said. "I give banquet every year."

Duke perked up at the banquet part. But I had no intention

of going on a baby-procurement tour with a group of insanely competitive childless couples from Los Angeles.

We thanked Mr. Qing, took an application packet, and went downstairs for lunch. Over a plate of steamed dumplings and fried shrimp chow fun, Duke and I agreed that perhaps Mr. Qing was not the right facilitator for us. "He seems to want to control everything, and we don't do well with people like that," Duke said. He suggested that "we" get started with our home study while "we" investigated other placement agencies.

I posted a query asking for local social workers, and within ten minutes my electronic mailbox was crammed with suggestions. Most directed me to Casa del Niños, a social-service agency only twenty minutes away. I called and talked to the earnest Betty. She explained that a home study consisted of four interviews—one with us together in her office, another with me alone, another with Duke alone, and the grand finale, a visit to our house. The next day, in my snail-mail box was an application so thick and intimidating that it made applying for a mortgage seem like filling in a luggage tag. My husband, whom I believe married me so he would never again have to fill out a form, tuned in to an important Lakers game as I studied the requirements.

Letters from our doctors, bankers, employers, and accountant (because I was self-employed). Five character references. Birth certificates, marriage certificates, divorce judgments, bank statements. Three sets of fingerprint cards—each! A form known only to government bureaucrats and international-adoption veterans, Immigration and Naturalization Service Form I-600A: Permission for Advance Processing to Bring an Orphan into the Country. Another form, this one giving the California Child Welfare Services permission to investigate whether we were known child abusers. A twenty-five-page questionnaire. And, just in case any fact about our lives escaped their scrutiny, we each had to write an autobiography.

I took a deep breath and began filling out the questionnaire. I moved briskly through the name, address, and phone-number part, then I had to stop and ruminate for twenty minutes over whether it was really necessary to mention the ill-fated marriage I entered into when I was twenty-one that barely lasted a month. So successfully had I crated up this interlude in my memory, I couldn't even remember in what state I had gotten a divorce.

Unfortunately, once I opened that Pandora's box, out sprang my deep, dark pug secret—Sammy. It saddens me to reveal that the dearly departed Bess and Stella were not my first pugs. When I was a senior at Northwestern, my mother took me to Baltimore's top pug breeder, Marjorie Shriver, and as a Christmas present bought me a five-month-old fawn male called Sheffield's Sunday Sam. Eager to experience the joys of pug ownership, I drove back to Chicago with the hyperactive little boy sitting next to me in the front seat. (Apart from leaping out the window when I was backing out of the driveway, Sammy, like all pugs, was a model passenger.)

At the time, I was living in Evanston, in a dreary, gold-shag-carpeted apartment under the El tracks, which I shared with my then-fiancé, the Crown Prince of Passive Aggression. He was in a deep funk, unable to decide whether to take over his family's multimillion-dollar janitorial-supply business or go for his master's degree in revolutionary anarchy. My parents were in the throes of their divorce, and the family had been shattered. Sammy was my only source of positive energy, always game for a walk, always thrilled to see me when I returned from class.

Sammy was a little too ardent; in fact, he soured me on

male dogs forever. The handsome fellow humped everything in sight, and anytime he sat down, I was treated to the sight of his coral-pink lipsticklike penis in full erection. Alas, our relationship ended before I could have him fixed. After graduation and my ill-fated wedding, we moved to Washington, D.C., where I enrolled in an MBA program at George Washington University (a spectacularly bad choice for someone with nonexistent math and entrepreneurial skills). Within a week of matriculation, at the precise moment when my statistics professor was trying to explain to me—for the umpteenth time—the mysteries of the Gaussian curve, I realized with long overdue clarity that my life was way off course. I flew to California to sort things out. When I returned a couple of weeks later, I discovered that the Crown Prince had given Sammy away to a family who lived downstairs in our building. It was gut-wrenching to pass their apartment each morning and see my ex-dog humping their eight-year-old daughter's leg. But deep in my heart I realized that the pug was better off. I left the Crown Prince, moved to Los Angeles, and never looked back.

Until I was confronted with the damn home-study application.

If contemplating my misspent youth wasn't depressing enough, I then had to wake my husband from his nap to inquire where he and his first wife were married and in the process learned more than I wanted to know. (Actually, almost anything about your spouse's previous wedding is more than you want to know.) Before I was halfway through the questionnaire, I felt so violated, I had to take a break. A week later, fortified by a couple of glasses of Australian chardonnay, I resumed filling in the blanks. I got to Question Forty-three: "Have you ever been arrested?" Of course, for myself, I checked "No." I walked into Duke's office, where he was busy flaming one of his many on-line enemies. "Honey," I asked, "have you ever been arrested?"

"Oh, sure," he said, without taking his eyes off the computer screen.

I was not entirely surprised. After all, he spent the late sixties in Berkeley and has what I consider to be a negative attitude toward authority. Once we were returning from South America and a customs agent asked Duke if he had gone there on vacation.

"Sort of," Duke said, and they immediately searched his bag.

I moved on to Question Forty-four: "How many times have you been arrested?"

He scratched his head. "Seven or eight?"

"Seven?" I gasped. "Eight?"

Duke shrugged and resumed typing. "What's the big deal?"

One of the difficulties of being the more conventional partner in a marriage is that I frequently feel guilty for being small-minded. I took a deep breath and progressed to Question Forty-five: "What were you arrested for?"

"This and that," Duke said, and he refused to elaborate. Lacking a former KGB agent with an electric-shock machine, I knew better than to push him, though a few days later, over dinner with friends (my usual way of prying information out of my tight-lipped mate), he casually let slip, "Once someone using my name handcuffed a policeman to a tree at Berkeley. But I wasn't arrested for that." I beat down suspicions that he was an unpublicized member of the Symbionese Liberation Army and wrote in "Sixties stuff" on the application. For what we were paying Betty, the imperturbable social worker, I'd let her ferret out the truth.

I labored over a ten-page autobiography that dutifully covered each of the twenty-two topics we were ordered to address. Duke dashed his off the night before our first appointment and summed up his life in under a page. (I made him delete the sentence in the Courtship and Marriage part about how he wasn't particularly impressed by me at our first meeting.) I racked up sizable long-distance bills in order to obtain copies of our birth, marriage, and divorce certificates. Duke signed his name when I placed a typed request in front of him and handed him a pen. I showed up for our initial appointment with Betty five minutes early. Duke breezed in twenty minutes late.

And what was my reward for my diligence? He charmed the pants off the earnest social worker. Her final report would be oddly reminiscent of "Goofus and Gallant," the preachy comic strip in *Highlights,* the old children's magazine. Instead of "Gallant uses his fork. Goofus eats with his feet," she wrote, "He is a thoughtful, highly intelligent, insightful individual who speaks several languages. She says she is a responsible person."

It was a blessing that Duke was so engaging, because the intrusive process made me nuts. Being cursed with the inability to lie to a direct question, I was forced to put a positive spin on the decidedly un–Brady Bunch–like interactions of my family. Unlike Duke's clan, who send out gossipy newsletters and have group pajama parties, mine hasn't shared a warm fuzzy fill-in-the-holiday for twenty years. Betty asked me to explain my role in the family, and all I could do was quip, "I'm the only one who has never threatened or been threatened with legal action by a blood relative," which made quite a splash. I hastily assured her that I was on excellent terms with each family member; it was just that as a unit we were not dysfunctional, but nonfunctional.

Ironically, I got the feeling all Betty really cared about was whether we were child molesters, batterers, drug addicts, or drunks. She converted anything I said into social-worker speak, much in the same way you fill your résumé with action verbs. A casual comment like "I'm very close to my sister" became "So, you're the linchpin of your family?"

"No," I simplified. "I just talk to her on the phone a lot."

"She's just doing her job," said Duke. No doubt he was more sympathetic because his mother was a social worker too, a fact he immediately shared with Betty in his private interview.

"What did she say about your arrest record?" I asked.

"It never came up," Duke said smugly. "We talked about the geriatric programs my mom set up, and I offered to put Betty in touch with some people who might do her some good."

My enthusiasm was at a low ebb when Betty arrived at our house for our home visit. Naturally, she came on a Monday morning, when our home sets records for sloth. I'd been up since 6:00 A.M. cleaning, even though she expressly told me not to bother. I figured this was a trick, and indeed she would later note in our report that our home was "well maintained." The only other positive thing she found to say about me was that I had good taste in furniture and she liked my dollhouses. Of course, she gleefully warned me that I'd have to cover all the nice furniture with plastic when the baby arrived and that my dollhouses were filled with thousands of items that could present a choking hazard.

She had a final question. "You do plan to tell your daughter she's adopted?" Betty asked.

"Believe me," I said, "I think she'll know."

Duke hastily assured Betty that we planned to send our daughter to Chinese school (this was news to me), take her out for dim sum, and teach her all about her rich cultural heritage. He went into a long discourse about a woman he had interviewed on our recent trip to Beijing, a ninety-year-old high-ranking government official named Madame Lei, who once taught Cantonese to Erle Stanley Gardner, the author of the Perry Mason books. Betty brightened.

I walked her to her car. I asked her lightly, "So, did we pass?"

She gave me a funny look. "This isn't about passing or failing," she said. "Why on earth would you ask that?"

"Because you've just interviewed us for six hours," I thought. But I just thanked her for coming and said good-bye. I picked up Clara and gave her a reassuring cuddle.

"I'll try to get your home study finished by the end of February," Betty said.

"Please," I said, "take your time."

Clara in the Pacific Northwest

*I*n late March 1996, Clara (and I) left Los Angeles for a three-city tour of the Pacific Northwest to promote my second book, *This Damn House!* A veteran of one publicity tour, I had no delusions of grandeur and was simply looking forward to a week in deluxe hotels, where I could freely imbibe Diet Cokes from the minibar without my husband reminding me they were overpriced or, worse, clanking through the lobby with a rattling bag of a half dozen replacements. The pug, however, was pumped. A few days before our departure, my publisher arranged for me to speak at a Borders sales-conference dinner in Santa Monica. Also on the agenda was an afternoon trade show.

It was pouring that day, and Clara was holding a vigil on the sofa. Like those of a hibernating bear, her bodily functions shut down in nasty weather, and even when I dragged her outside and stood on the lawn holding an umbrella over her head, she balked at the damp grass and scooted back into the house. "Suit yourself," I said, and got dressed for my public appearance. Clara noticed me pulling on panty hose—a cue she recognized as a sign of impending adventure—and ran through the rain to the car.

The convention was held at the Loews Santa Monica Beach Hotel a mile away. There was no way I was taking a full-bladdered Clara into a mobbed trade show, so I had a word with her in the parking garage. Ever the intellectual, she ruminated for a few moments and finally located a dry impatiens plant situated beneath an underhang in full view of the doorman. In spite of that, he let her in. (Loews has an enlightened pet policy. In fact, when Herb Goldstein, the kindly owner of the Hotel San Carlos, died and the new management barred Clara from their registry, even though she'd been a perfect guest on a half dozen occasions, she switched her allegiance to the Loews New York. But only until I can afford the Pierre.)

The Arcadia Ballroom was mobbed. Being small and claustrophobic, I was somewhat daunted, but the even smaller Clara strode purposefully into the labyrinth of sales booths, all her flags flying. It was like the old E. F. Hutton commercial; publishing representatives stopped in the middle of a sales pitch to gape. Clara played it for all it was worth. Forget about walking demurely at the end of the leash, hoping someone would notice the attractive black pug. She was on a mission. A six-foot salesman had the nerve to ignore her, so she swatted his leg with her paw. When that didn't work, she sat on his Bally loafer. When that didn't work, she emitted an agonized yelp, and he finally figured it out. "Oh," he exclaimed, "what a cute dog." Like a seasoned professional, Clara waited until she was surrounded by devotees before she performed her sit, shake, lie down, dance, and park routine. Such was her animal magnetism, my publisher asked if I could leave her at the booth for the rest of the afternoon. I knew how President

Kennedy felt when he said that he was the man who accompanied Jackie to Paris.

We flew to Seattle on Clara's least favorite carrier, the one that claims to be the last great airline. First, an uninformed gate attendant insisted that Clara's Sherpa Bag didn't meet airline regulations; I had to put the pug in a cardboard box and check her as steerage. Given that my packing motto is "Be prepared," I rummaged through my purse and located an official list of carriers that would accept the bag. The carrier-in-question's name headed the list, and after a consultation with her superior, the gate attendant grudgingly and without apology waved us aboard.

There were no more than eight passengers on the flight, the nearest sitting seven rows behind us, but the snooty male flight attendant had an attack of officiousness when he heard snoring and traced the sound to under the blanket on my lap. "She must return to her bag at once," he said snippily. "I've received complaints about her from the other passengers."

It was a relief to land. We were met by Seattle's preeminent author wrangler, Joy Delf, who had just finished escorting Martha Stewart. Martha got a limousine, but we got Joy's Toyota. Clara, who enchanted Joy on our last trip, was touched that our handler had stocked her car with Naya water and Milk-Bones.

"I remember the first time I picked you up and I didn't know there was going to be a Clara," Joy said. "You had the bag, and all of a sudden it started moving, little protrusions coming out of the mesh. I thought, 'What in the world?' The bag moved but she didn't make a sound."

The sycophant gave Joy an air lick on both cheeks, in the European fashion, and settled in the bucket seat. "She seems to be very much at home," Joy said. "I guess as long as she's with you, she is home."

Certainly, Clara had no trouble settling in at the lush European-style hotel on First Avenue. I installed her water dish on the floor of the marble bathroom; she duly noted its whereabouts, then jogged into the room and stretched out on a salmon-colored chaise lounge. She cheerfully gnawed a pig's ear while I did a drive-time radio show over the phone. Afterward, I called room service and ordered dinner. Clara polished off half my grilled Pacific salmon—not because she was hungry, but because the altruistic critter was looking out for my best interest. "The camera adds ten pounds," Clara warned me.

Early the next morning, Joy drove us to *7-Live*, a popular morning television show. Everybody in the building was drawn to the pug, who thanks to her friends at Posh Pups sported a denim cap with the name of my new book on the brim. "She's a very savvy P.R. tool," Joy said. "Normally when people are walking around the studio, they don't talk. Either in her charming naïve way Clara is a natural, or she is very practiced."

Let me be frank. Clara is a media slut. Joy offered to keep her in the greenroom while I was on air, but Clara followed me onto the set. She sat on the host's lap and got her own chiron, an identifying caption: "Clara, the Pug." Afterward, Joy couldn't remember if they had identified me or my book. I kind of doubt it. During a break between engagements, Clara and I strolled through Pike's Market. A half dozen people stopped Clara and said, "I saw you on TV this morning." One asked if I was an animal trainer.

On our previous trip to Seattle, Joy had expressed trepidation when I insisted on bringing Clara to a live radio show that was done in a Tacoma shopping mall an hour away. We smuggled her in, and I left Joy holding the bag. A few chairs were set up in the rotunda of the mall for the audience, and Joy put the hidden Clara on a vacant seat. As soon as the host introduced me, the bag moved. Joy made frantic pantomime gestures and was unnerved when I mouthed, "Let her out." Clara tiptoed over to my chair. The host exclaimed, "What have we here?" and after fielding a few questions, Clara napped on my lap.

"She has such good media manners," Joy marveled. "I was impressed she could be on mike while live radio was happening and not make inappropriate noises. A few little teeny noises, just to let you know she was there, but she never interrupted the host."

On this tour, I was booked on a different radio show. Joy warned me that the host was visually impaired and relied on a guide dog, a German shepherd, that he kept in the studio. "Clara won't be frightened?"

"We should be so lucky," I said.

To my mortification, Clara lunged at the guide dog, and when I picked her up she treated him to her stuck-pig car-alarm squawk. The German shepherd cowered and was dragged out of the studio by the collar, much to Clara's satisfaction. The pug sat regally on my lap, her eyes glowing with triumph. The host said, "You're listening to the radio station for the blind," and I startled. Unfortunately, my book was not out on audiocassette.

Next, we flew to Portland, this time on the friendly skies. Clara was served pretzels and was allowed to sit in the vacant seat. We were met by my friend Marc, who has known me and my pugs for twenty-five years. He is the only person who actively prefers the dearly departed Bess and Stella to their successors. "I felt more closely bonded to them," he said. "I remember when they were puppies and I came to visit you and slept on the floor. Bess and Stella would attack me, and I'd be smothered with pugs. I'm kind of ticklish and I'd laugh a lot, and that would just increase their ardor."

I must point out that Marc had a financial interest in Bess and Stella. For most of their lives, whenever I flew, I bought airline insurance and made him the beneficiary. I thought he understood that he had to take care of Bess and Stella if anything happened to me, but ten years and dozens of premiums later, I discovered otherwise.

"The policies would come, and I thought, 'Here's fifty or a hundred thousand dollars if Margo's plane does a Lockerbee,' " Marc admitted. "I never put that idea together with pug stewardship. I looked at it as a potential windfall. I would like to think that I'd have done the right thing—taken Bess and Stella in for the month or two it would have taken to find a good traveling circus to sell them to."

At the Heathman Hotel, I left Marc with Clara while I registered. I was sure he would succumb to her charms, but when I returned, my friend complained, "Clara is so manipulative; I can't take her hot and cold. She generally ignores me if you're around, but when you leave, then she's all over me, aggressively and demonstratively affectionate. Isn't this nice, Clara's feeling neglected, but I'm not a tool. I'm not a Price Pfeister faucet." Marc was so underwhelmed he suggested that we leave the pug in my room and go out to dinner.

"I don't think so," I said, even though my room was a spacious suite. Clara makes few demands on the road, but she's adamant about not being abandoned in an unfamiliar hotel room in a strange city. She moans, she whimpers, she throws herself against the door. Once she's accustomed to the hotel, she will tolerate a few hours of solitude if it's absolutely necessary, but never on the first night. "How do you feel about room service?" Marc shook his head. "I suppose we could leave her in your car so if she screams she won't bother anyone," I said without much enthusiasm.

"I wouldn't feel right about leaving her in the car," Marc said, and Clara flashed him a conspiratorial grin. "Why don't we just take her to dinner with us?"

Clara remained still and silent while we waited in line for a table at Pazzo, a noisy Italian restaurant in a celebrity hotel. Marc insisted on a red leather banquette—"I don't think Clara will be comfortable on a chair," he whispered—and I slid the bag in first, up against the partition.

"We may have to order lobsters just so they won't throw us out when they discover her," said Marc.

When it was just the two of us talking, Clara slept, but every time the waiter showed up, the bag twitched and I'd have to shield it with my body. She became more agitated when she smelled Marc's swordfish with capers and olives. I threw a piece of focaccia into the bag to shut her up. In the course of the meal, she put away pasta puttanesca, a good part of the swordfish, and more than her share of garlic bread. Her bag was noticeably heavier when we finally left.

After dinner, Marc insisted on accompanying us while I walked Clara in what looked like a lovely park near the hotel but which he described as "Needle Park, where all the young drug-taking hoodlums hang out."

A vagrant set down his bottle of Ripple and yelled, "Did someone bash her in the head with a shovel?" A junkie knelt down on the ground and had an entire conversation with Clara without acknowledging her human escorts. Another park habitué volunteered that his great-grandmother had a pug and when he died she had him stuffed.

"Maybe I'm jaded," Marc said as he walked us back to the hotel. "But I don't understand why people are in stitches over the pug. People think she's the most amazing thing they've ever seen. It's like no one ever let them out of their home before."

Clara may have looked five pounds chubbier the next morning on *AM Northwest,* but it didn't affect her performance. She galloped onto the set and jumped up on the chair next to the hostess. The live audience cheered. Of course, the hostess felt compelled to put Clara on her lap, and the cameraman zoomed in for a close-up. Clara looked at the monitor just as her face filled the screen and began to growl. The audience cheered louder.

There was a brief altercation after our segment, when another guest, an animal-rights activist, complained that it was inhumane for me to make the dog wear a hat.

"She likes the hat," I said.

"She feels humiliated," he said. "It's dog abuse."

"Believe me," I said, "she's not suffering. She's staying in a suite at the Heathman."

"I'm at the Motel 6," he said sheepishly.

Our final West Coast stop was San Francisco. We went straight from the airport to a drive-time radio show where the host asked Clara to bark on command as part of a pet-store commercial. Always agreeable, she dutifully yipped into the mike. Then we checked into the Clift, a four-star hotel near Union Square. The management sent up a silver tray laden with dog biscuits, feeding dish, and toys. Clara adored sashaying through the opulent lobby, though she wasn't crazy about the menacing rats in Union Square, the closest bit of grass. (Clara's favorite hotel is the Marriott in Rancho Mirage, where she spent a memorable weekend in a room overlooking the golf course. A pug on the fairway looked insanely decorative, like a unicorn in a medieval tapestry. Duke thoughtfully raked the sand trap free of her dime-sized pawprints.)

The San Francisco media wrangler drove us to the public broadcasting station. The guest before me was veterinarian Terri McGinnis, author of *The Well Dog Book*. During a break, she inspected Clara. "I used to own a fawn pug named Boo, who had the annoying habit of growling, running in circles, and chasing her tail," she said.

"Did you cure her?" I asked. Dr. McGinnis nodded. "I gave her so much phenobarbital that she couldn't stand on her feet, let alone get to her tail. Then I instructed my staff to tell her no when she chased her tail and then to give her an alternative behavior, 'Sit,' for which she got a reward. All day long there was this chorus of 'No, Boo, Sit, Boo, Good Boo.' "

Maybe Sophie would benefit from a massive dose of phenobarbital . . . But I refrained from asking for a prescription.

We both agreed the pug was exceptionally demanding. "They're such cute puppies, like little toad beanbags, that most people become immediate victims to pug manipulations," McGinnis said. "I suspect they're bred for that ability. Over time, the people who were interested in them selected the ones who were the best companions."

Clara's ego bubble deflated the next afternoon. We had some free time, and I arranged to meet Alexis, my Internet adoption mentor. I had graduated from the America Online bulletin boards to the A-Parents-China List Server, a cyber-support group composed of more than a thousand families that had adopted or were in the process of adopting children from China. (Banana Republic would kill to get their hands on this list, as it is composed of their target market: aging, solvent former hippies who travel.) After our encounter with the Roland Heights baby farmer who didn't believe in pictures, I'd posted a note asking for agency suggestions. Alexis had responded warmly, and we'd stayed in touch. When she heard I was coming to the Bay Area, she suggested that I meet her daughter, Lia, so I would have a picture of my goal to carry around in my head.

She called me from the lobby. I left Clara in our room and went downstairs. There was no mistaking them. Alexis, a willowy brunette, had Lia, a gorgeous little girl from the Jiangsu province, riding shotgun in a baby sling. Though Alexis is not Chinese, she and Lia looked alike. "The Chinese officials try to match parents with kids who look like them," Alexis said. "Something about the feng shui of the face."

I couldn't help thinking that my red hair and blue eyes were going to be a hell of a test of Chinese geomancy.

Clara greeted me at the door like she hadn't seen me in years, even though we'd been separated for at most six minutes. I picked her up, hugged her, and introduced her to Lia. I didn't anticipate any problems. Clara sees children all the time on the Venice boardwalk. They pat her, pull her ears, uncurl her tail, and she endures these indignities with great patience. But there was something about this child that made her wary.

Clara trotted to Alexis with a pig's ear in her mouth, sat at her heels, and gave her The Stare. Alexis was tickled. She passed me her daughter, so she could focus on the pug.

"Aren't you a pretty baby?" I cooed to the child, and Clara shot me a wounded look.

"You're like a big dog with none of the big-dog problems," Alexis chirped to Clara, and it was Lia's turn to look distressed.

Like a pair of synchronized swimmers, the tot and the pug went through their time-tested "Aren't I cute?" maneuvers. Clara cocked her head. Lia pulled herself up to a standing position and began throwing things off the coffee table. Clara parked without being prompted. Lia cried. I put her on my lap. Clara spitefully jumped on Alexis's lap and licked her face.

"Clara knows a rival when she sees one," Alexis said. "She reminds me a lot of a roommate I once had called Mary Beth. She was a real queen bee. She who must be obeyed. And you didn't question it. It was a force of nature, like gravity."

Lia howled and reached for her mother. "You and Clara are cut out of the same cloth." Alexis laughed. While the two queen bees glowered at each other, Alexis asked me where I was in the adoption process.

"The home study should be ready any day," I said. "Then that goes to the INS and we have to wait for INS clearance. And then we have to find a placement agency."

"It will all work out," Alexis said.

Clara was thrilled to see them go. An hour later my friend Marian called from the lobby. I went down to get her, and when I returned, Clara's Abandoned Pug routine was reminiscent of Lillian Gish's performance in *Orphans of the Storm.*

"What did you do to her?" Marian asked suspiciously. "She's following you around the room like she's scared she'll lose you. That's not like her. Something must be wrong."

Marian frets about the pugs more than I do, which is why she is their appointed guardian. Not long ago, I had to leave town on a rare writing assignment where Clara's presence would be a hindrance. I invited Duke to come along in her stead. As it happened, the night before my departure a dozen of my friends—Marian and Blanche among them—were meeting at my favorite Japanese restaurant to celebrate my birthday. I planned to leave the pugs in the car in the guarded restaurant parking lot and let Blanche take them back to her house, but Marian interfered.

"They'll be afraid in the car," she said, "and they shouldn't spend a night in a cage if they don't have to." Marian proposed that she drive back to our house after the party, pick up Sophie and Clara, take them to her parents' house in North Hollywood, and then drive them out to Blanche's house the following day. It seemed unnecessarily complicated to me, but I acquiesced. To this day, Marian doubles over remembering her parents' reaction to the pugs. "At first my mom was hesitant, but then Clara ran up the stairs and the spell was cast," she informed me. "Mom and Dad stayed up until eleven o'clock petting them. I think they were waiting for the pugs to get enough affection. I finally said, 'You guys, as long as you pet them, Sophie and Clara will just lie there and lap it up, so maybe we all better go to bed.' "

Back in San Francisco, Marian insisted that Clara needed a pick-me-up, so we took her shopping in Union Square. The pug felt the healing rays of the Coach Store, Neiman Marcus, and Gump's. Her confidence returned. She dismissed the interlude with Lia as a hallucination.

Late that evening, I was lying in bed, watching television. Clara was curled up on the pillow next to me, dreaming about the next day, when she was scheduled to appear on the morning news. Suddenly, the door opened and in walked my husband, who had driven up to join us. As soon as she heard his voice, Clara dove off the bed and greeted him, like I wasn't there. "Lemon Drop," he murmured as he enveloped her in a loving embrace. "Is everything just the way you like it?" Clara voiced all her complaints about me but assured him that her life was worth living now that he had arrived. Then Duke whistled and called out in the hall, "Dammit, Sophie, stop woolgathering and get in here."

Clara was so outraged her fur stood on end. "There must be a mistake," she muttered as Sophie meandered into the room. Sophie sniffed Clara from head to tail. Clara clamped her jaw around the scruff of Sophie's neck, and the two sisters rose on their hind legs growling and expressed their mutual disdain.

I watched with a growing sense of unease. Somewhere on the other side of the world, there was a little baby who would have to compete with Clara.

I couldn't say I envied her that fate.

Birth by Paperwork

*C*lara was melancholy when we returned to Los Angeles and she resumed what she considered to be a dog's life. I tried to assure her that her days in the sun weren't over yet; later in the month we were headed to New York to be on *Good Morning America,* and then to Chicago, for *Oprah.* But all the pug knew was that when she woke up in the morning, she was on a cushion under my desk in my study instead of on a down pillow in a four-star hotel. True, she still went to the office with me every day, but what fun was that when the obstreperous Sophie went along too?

More fun than she imagined, as it turned out. Elke and Dave and Marta and Phyllis welcomed her back joyously. Phyllis had a VCR in her office, and by popular demand, I brought in the videotapes of Clara's television appearances. The pug spent the morning in Phyllis's lap, surrounded by my office mates who enthused over her every nuance. Meanwhile, Sophie, who has an honest heart and loves me for myself, slept loyally at my feet while I labored on our top-secret project.

The next step was to obtain permission from the Immigration and Naturalization Service to bring a baby into the United

States. As part of the home-study process, we had submitted Form I-600A: Application for Advanced Processing of Orphan Petition and two sets of fingerprints—each!—on Form FD-258: Applicant Fingerprint Card. My first task upon returning home from my book tour was not to check sales figures but rather to messenger our completed home study to Mr. Muckety Muck, the autocrat in charge of orphan petitions at the Los Angeles branch of the INS. As per Betty the social worker's instructions, I also enclosed our vital documents and police clearances.

To my immense relief, both Duke and I received official-looking letters from the California Department of Justice stating that we had "no criminal history." "I told you there was nothing to worry about," my husband said, and I apologized for suspecting that he had kidnapped Patty Hearst. Supposedly, it took sixty days to receive the next boilerplate, Form I-171H: Notice of Favorable Determination Concerning Application for Advance Processing of Orphan Petition. (Catchy name, got a nice beat, you can dance to it . . .) Without this key form, we could not hire an international placement agency to find us a child.

"*We* might as well put our dossier together while *we* wait," the big-picture guy said helpfully.

The little-picture guy got cracking.

To adopt internationally, you must present a foreign government with a dense stack of documents that reveal every aspect of your life. Given that each step of the foreign adoption process is a test akin to the Wizard of Oz ordering Dorothy to bring him the broomstick of the Witch of the West, it isn't enough to merely obtain the documents. Each has to be notarized, then the local notary's rubber stamp has to be certified by the county, then the county's gold sticker has to be authen-

ticated by the state, and then, in the case of China, the state
seal has to be certified by the particular Chinese consulate
that governs the particular state where the document originated. According to the home page of the Families with Children from China Web site (http://fwcc.org), the basis for this
rigmarole is the concept of chain of evidence. When adoption
documents arrive in Beijing, the only way the government can
ascertain their authenticity is by inspecting the stamps and
seals at each level of the chain. (Attention, foreign bureaucrats: No sane person would do this for a lark.)

It's unfathomable just how time-consuming a task can
be—to this day, the big-picture guy doesn't have a clue—so
here's a concrete example. We needed a notarized letter from
a stock fund based in Valley Forge, Pennsylvania. First, I
called the fund and navigated through an elaborate voice mail
menu before I reached an operator who said I had to call another number. I did. After ten minutes on hold, being assured
by a synthetic voice that "your call is very important to us," I
reached a human being who said that I needed to send in a
written request. I did. Three weeks and four follow-up calls
later, the letter arrived. Next, I placed a few calls, again negotiating several dozen voice mail options, to determine that Valley Forge was in Chester County, the address of the courthouse
and the fee schedule. I sent the now-too-precious-to-entrust-
to-the-U.S.-Post-Office document by Federal Express along
with a prepaid, self-addressed return envelope. When the letter returned home again, like a carrier pigeon, bearing the appropriate rubber stamps, I phoned the Pennsylvania secretary
of state's office in Harrisburg, ascertained their address and
fee schedule, and sent the letter off to them. Four weeks and
twelve follow-up calls later, the letter—now accessorized with
a red ribbon, a gold seal, and a snazzy baby-blue folder—ar-

rived back on my doorstep, only to be stuffed in yet another FedEx envelope and shipped to the Chinese consulate in Manhattan, which validated documents that originated in Pennsylvania. Before the letter ever left for Beijing, it traveled eighteen thousand air miles, interrupted five hours of my writing time, and ate up $150 in fees. And that was only one document. There were more than twenty.

I'd like to report that what kept me going was my intense desire to have a child, but I found it impossible to believe that I could actually give birth by paperwork. In truth, it was Clara who kept nudging me along the road to motherhood. Each day, her sphere of influence expanded until I was forced to do something to reassert my sovereignty. I was sitting in my office, flipping through the Yellow Pages, trying to locate a traveling notary who would drive to my accountant's office in Encino, rubber-stamp her letter, and bring it back to Venice Beach, when I noticed that Clara was in satori, the Zen state of enlightenment.

Investigation revealed that in preparation for a casting session, Elke had cooked a brisket—a substance the pugs had been deprived of all their lives because Duke and I don't eat red meat. I learned that Dave invested in a line of dog vitamins called Vita-Love and, much to Clara's consternation, he was holding an open-casting call. The pugs sat on the floor beneath the brisket, chirping like a microwave oven, until Dave finally locked them up in my office. Salivary glands working overtime, Clara watched through the glass door as poodles, golden retrievers, mongrels, and—the ultimate indignity—her fellow office dogs, Sailor, Coco, and Spencer, disappeared into the photo studio to audition.

"Excuse me, I'm ready for my close-up," Clara said. Sophie battered the glass door with her massive head, and against his better judgment Dave agreed to give the pugs a chance. (He didn't feel they would photograph well because they were black.) To Clara's chagrin, he wanted Sophie and Clara to pose in tandem. Kip, our in-house photographer, set up a bar like a limbo stick, so he could get their paws in the shot. Off camera, Dave dangled a piece of brisket on a string. Sophie knocked down the bar and snatched the brisket. Clara briskly snowplowed Sophie out of the shot with her head and for the next twenty minutes cavorted like her idol, Cindy Crawford. She rotated her head from side to side. Showed a little pink tongue. Opened her mouth like a fish. She even winked.

"Clara's amazing," Kip said, shooting roll after roll. "She knows I'm taking her picture." (She seemed to bring out the best in him too. Kip later took photographs of me and Duke for our adoption dossier, and the results were less than wildly flattering.)

When the pictures were developed, everyone agreed that of all the dogs, Clara was most photogenic. Except Dave, who out of sheer nepotism put Sailor on the cover of the brochure. Clara settled for a vitamin label. Marta airbrushed out a few wrinkles and added a rose-colored tint to her tongue, and Clara wound up looking like an extremely attractive intergalactic whale.

I casually mentioned to Loretta, my agent, that Clara would be appearing on Southern California grocery shelves.

"Is she getting part of the profits?" asked Loretta.

"No," I said.

"Free vitamins for life?"

"I don't think so."

Loretta began to hum, always a bad sign. She took a deep breath. "Don't tell me you let her pose for free?"

"I couldn't help it."

"From now on, I'm representing Clara," Loretta snapped.

I was afraid to tell my agent about Clara's other photo session. *Los Angeles Magazine* had wanted to take my picture to run with an article I wrote. It was sort of a pain, as the photo call was scheduled for Monday, the universal hairdresser's day off. The devil winds were blowing and I was having a terrible hair day, but I hastily pulled myself together. I was congratulating myself on making the best of a situation when the photographer, Scott, arrived. "Where's the pug?" he asked. "The editor said to be sure to get a shot of the adorable pug."

The adorable pug had nothing to do with the story, which was about little girls and dollhouses, but why should that have stopped her from taking charge? Clara cantered over, gave an electrifying demonstration of star quality, and suddenly I sympathized with Sophie. Gently, like he was handling precious cargo, Scott placed Clara on a high stool in front of a dollhouse, lit her, and then, as an afterthought, ordered me to kneel on the far side of the house. "Shield her eyes, I'm going to pop the flash a couple of times," he instructed me.

Reflexively, I obeyed.

You could barely see me in the test Polaroid, but what concerned Scott was that Clara was not at her most becoming angle. He begrudgingly agreed that I could sit next to her. "Move forward and lower your head so you're on the same plane as she is," he ordered. Not my best angle, but who cared. This time, the test Polaroid showed a photograph that my husband later christened Pug and Kaufman, attorneys at law. I tried to look on the bright side. We looked like equals, which in fact we are not.

Scott shot a roll, and I tried not to feel insulted as he called out encouragement, "You look beautiful, Clara. Wow, Clara, that's gorgeous. Margo, wipe Clara's brow." Clara widened her big baby browns and, oblivious to the fact that she was perched rather precariously on a bar stool four feet off the ground, posed like Claudia Schiffer on the Chanel runway.

"Enough of you, Margo," Scott said. "Would you mind if I shot a few rolls of Clara for my portfolio?" Did I have a choice? He relit her, and Clara gave him all she had.

It was a small comfort to remember that a photo of Clara would not be included in our package to Beijing. The Chinese adoption authorities did not approve of pets. "The Chinese think dog is very good friend," my friend Nei explained, "but we eat them." Clara probably would have won them over, but I didn't want to press my luck.

To facilitate my paperwork, I acquired a label printer, a FedEx account, FedEx tracking software, and a scanner. What I should have acquired was my own notary stamp. Blessedly, one afternoon, on my ritual visit to Ocean Park Mailbox to drop off the latest batch of Federal Express requests to far-flung courthouses, I discovered that Christopher, the blond surfer who owned the place, was a notary. Christopher and I went back a few years—a lifetime in Los Angeles—because he packs the dollhouses I compulsively build. (Friends who for years mocked my hobby became wildly supportive once they had daughters.) Christopher verified all our local documents for a heavily discounted rate. By the time we were through, he knew so much about us that if I'm ever black-mailed, I'll know who to blame.

The dossier also gave me a false sense of accomplishment and the best excuse I've ever had not to write. I fell behind on all my deadlines, but all of our out-of-state documents were notarized to the max. To authenticate the California ones, I was forced to take field trips to marginal parts of town such as scenic Norwalk, a half-hour ride on the new Century Freeway, perhaps the bleakest stretch of road I've ever been on. I waited uneasily in the government building, hoping a Ryder truck filled with fertilizer didn't pull up while I was waiting for them to be certified. Then I shipped the papers to the California secretary of state in Sacramento, home of the most expensive authentication fees in the land. They charged twenty-six dollars a document to slap on nine cents' worth of gold stickers. For that price, I expected speed, but the folks in Sacramento took seven weeks and nine follow-up phone calls before our documents made their way home.

Not that it mattered. We were still waiting for INS clearance.

Clara and I flew to New York. To her fury, Brian, my book publicist, announced that she was not welcome on the set of *Good Morning America.* I was reluctant to get in the limousine and leave her behind, but he insisted it was for my own good. He was wrong. I was sitting in the makeup chair, getting ready, and I happened to mention Clara. The makeup artist squealed, "I have a pug too." She asked if Clara was black or fawn. When I said black, she said, "Mine too. Who's your breeder?" Not only did our pugs come from the same breeder, but as near as we could tell, the makeup woman's pug was Clara's brother. I went back to the greenroom and asked Brian to go to the hotel and get Clara, but he refused. (Brian tried to make it up to Clara by getting her invited to a chic literary function. She got to sit on the lap of Victor Navasky, editor of *The Nation,* the country's leading lefty magazine, but she was not mollified. Brian vowed to get back in her good graces.)

Loretta was also furious at Clara's lost opportunity. "Clara has a long-lost brother?" she exclaimed. "Like Snoopy. You've got to get them together, don't you think?"

"I don't think Clara wants a brother," I said.

She didn't want another sister either, and the way things were working out, it didn't look like she was going to get one.

On Day Sixty-five, I called Muckety Muck at the INS. He was on vacation. Day Seventy-two, I called again. He was back from vacation but off for the day. On Day Eighty he was on vacation again. I asked if someone else could help me, but I was told that Muck was the only person in the entire Los Angeles INS office who processed orphan petitions, and he had a big backlog.

"It's not surprising," I said. "He vacations a lot."

"His job is very stressful," an INS receptionist said curtly.

I imagined a post-office-style breakdown involving the lone INS orphan processor and a high tower.

On Day Ninety, I finally reached the elusive Muck. It was ten in the morning. "I only take orphan-related calls from one to three," he said.

"I *just* want to know the status of our application," I said, careful to stress the *just*. My husband uses this *just* construction quite successfully to override my objections. For example, when Duke comes home two hours later than promised, rather than offer an explanation, he goes into the kitchen, opens the refrigerator, and says, "I just have to get a bite to eat to keep myself alive." And then he "just has to take a swim to get his blood going." And then he "just has to check his E-mail to see if there's a fire at the university" that he needs to put out.

Muck put me on hold for a half an hour, during which time he probably called his travel agent to book a flight to Cancun. Upon his return, he announced, "I *just* need another set of your husband's fingerprints. The originals are *just* too blurry for the FBI."

How could this be? Back in February, we submitted two sets of Duke's fingerprints, and they were done at the same place that did mine. I know the finger printer was fastidious because it took a month to get the ink out from under my nails. I also wondered why we weren't informed of the snafu, but I knew better than to question a government official. Instead, I called Duke and informed him that he'd have to get finger-printed again. The next day he went down to the INS (a place I would not set foot in if I could possibly help it), picked up the forms, went across the street and got refingerprinted, and gave the prints to Muck himself.

"He promised he'd expedite FBI processing," Duke reported.

"What was he like?"

"Seemed like a junkie to me."

Such was the efficiency of the Adoptive Parents China List, that at 8:37 one evening, I posted a message inquiring how long the FBI took to expedite fingerprints. At 8:46, I received three E-mail messages with the direct phone number of the fingerprint processor in Washington. Not wishing to harass the FBI, I waited a week, then I summoned up my nerve and called. The FBI fingerprint processor was incredibly obliging. She looked up my husband's name and informed me that his prints were submitted on May 5 and should be ready in a week. This made no sense whatsoever. Duke's blurry prints were sent in February, and his revised version went out in June.

"The FBI has no record of any blurry fingerprints."

I thanked her politely. I figured, "This is what I pay taxes for, government screwups."

I called Muck for clarification. He was on vacation. Surprise.

Clara and I flew to Chicago to be on *Oprah*. A limousine driver picked us up at O'Hare. "I do *Jerry Springer* and *Oprah*," he said. I thought it must be unsettling, driving to the airport, standing at the gate with a little cardboard sign, never knowing who you were picking up. The woman who slept with every member of her family? The devil worshipper turned celebrity hairdresser? "I try not to ask," the driver said.

We shared the limousine with another guest, a dour-looking woman from Boston who had written a documentary on teens with AIDS. She stretched out on the limousine seat and watched disdainfully as I put the shivering Clara in her red sweater with the Scottie-dog appliqué. I asked about her work history. "I did a documentary on children with AIDS," she said, "and then I did one on the parents of kids with AIDS."

"It must be emotionally grueling," I said.

"Yes," she replied. "Next I'll do something different. Maybe eating disorders, maybe depression."

I considered lending her Clara to cheer her up.

Oprah put her guests up at the Omni Berkshire on Michigan Avenue. The desk clerk had me sign a release form indicating that I'd be responsible for any damage caused by my pug. Our suite was done up in the English Library school of decor with mahogany bookcases lined with *Reader's Digest* condensed books from 1972 and appellate briefs from the Illinois state court. When we checked in, I noticed a suspicious stain on the hunter-green carpet and promptly notified the front desk that this was not Clara's doing.

Clara was bitter when a producer from *Oprah* informed me that the pug was not welcome in Harpo Studios. Even though Clara upstaged me during a *Chicago Tribune* interview and was a big hit in all the area bookstores, she was certain that I was trying to sabotage her career. When I returned from the *Oprah* taping, Clara threw up on my new orange blazer, the very one Ms. Winfrey had admired.

A week later, Muckety Muck was back in town but out sick. Probably contracted malaria in Costa Rica, I decided. I called the FBI again. This time the friendly Fingerprint Expediter seemed uncomfortable and referred me to the INS. Frankly, I was so tired of dealing with the INS I wanted to drive to Tijuana and bring illegal aliens back in my trunk, but I called again.

"I can't talk to you," Muck said briskly. "I can only speak to your husband. He has two hits on his FBI report."

These were not words to warm a wife's heart. I called Duke. "Honey," I wailed, "you have an FBI record."

"Can I put you on hold for a minute?" he said, and the line went dead. I was fantasizing about putting truth serum in his morning coffee when he came back on. "Relax," he said, as if I could. "I'm sure it's nothing."

Maybe I'm naïve, but I don't think people get in trouble with the FBI for "nothing."

An hour later Duke informed me that his FBI report showed two arrests for misdemeanors in 1971 and 1972. Charges had been dropped, but no one had bothered to inform the FBI.

"I just have to get documentation from the counties where the incidents took place," my husband said blithely.

"What incidents?" I pressed.

Eventually, he admitted that when he was a brash young journalist in Berkeley he wrote a story "about an unfair and cruel policy in the San Francisco jail." Duke continued, "The story was about a legal challenge that had overturned the policy. I forgot about it, but then I was visiting somebody in jail for another story and saw a large hand-lettered sign that said the illegal policy was still in effect. So I ripped it down, and they threw me in the pokey."

"What did you expect?" I asked.

Duke looked wounded. "They threw me in the felony tank. I wound up in a cell with a slow, hulking guy that had killed a bunch of his relatives in Santa Barbara. Finally they let me go, and they dropped the stupid charge about destruction of county property. The sign wasn't worth anything, and the judge had ruled it was wrong to begin with. I was doing them a favor."

I never got a satisfactory explanation for the second charge. Duke talked about a mysterious case of mistaken identity that occurred while he was hitchhiking through the city of Salinas, California. To tell you the truth, I was afraid to hear the details, so I let it slide.

Muck required an addendum to our home study showing that Betty the social worker was aware of what had happened. Duke wrote up an explanation for Betty, who was unruffled by her golden boy's FBI file. "Happens all the time with older couples," she said. "Would you believe I had one guy who was accused of harboring Patty Hearst?"

Three weeks later we were back on track, or so I thought. Duke obtained letters attesting to his innocence. I messengered the information down to the INS. Muck promised that we'd have our I-171H form in two weeks.

I waited in vain. When I finally reached him, he made a big point of telling me how busy he was. I was unimpressed. Busyness has become the universal excuse for inefficiency. "Yours is the third application in my pile," he said. "You should have the form in three days."

A week later, when we hadn't received it, I made my husband call in the hope that the magic sound of a male voice would produce results. "Our dossier is the fifth document in his pile, and he hopes to get to it by the end of the week," Duke reported.

"Did you remind him that he told me it would be ready weeks ago?" I asked.

"I did," said Duke. "He had no recollection of ever talking to you."

That sent me over the edge. I have a very distinctive voice. I've been on the radio for years, and I've frequently had total strangers identify me on the basis of an overheard syllable. It was outrageous that a child's future was frozen because a government functionary was unable to compare two sheets of paper, given a month to do so. I wrote a long letter to Senator Dianne Feinstein, begging for help. Her office promised to look into it.

When the end of the week came and went without the form appearing in our mailbox, Duke also became enraged. It was one thing for Muck to lie to me but quite another for him to mislead my husband. (Like the difference between right and wrong.) Duke called the INS and then called me with good news. "Muck is gone for good," he said. "His replacement was quite apologetic and swears we'll have the form in a few days."

Whether it was due to the senator's intervention or simply that Muck's replacement was more efficient, I'll never know. But a week later I opened the mailbox and found an unprepossessing form letter from the Immigration and Naturalization Service. Our petition was approved, and a cable had been sent to the United States Embassy in Guangzhou for advanced processing. All that was left to do was to attach a piece of paper to the INS form that said, "We certify that this is a true and accurate copy," and get it notarized, certified, authenticated, and sealed by the consulate.

I made another trip to Norwalk, then shipped the final document off to Sacramento. My new best friend at the secretary of state's office promised that she would authenticate it and send it back overnight. Amazingly enough, she did. I dropped all the documents off at the Chinese consulate downtown, and Duke, who likes nothing better than a high-profile errand in a marginal neighborhood, picked them up three days later. Thus it came to pass that eight months after the start of our great adventure and six months behind schedule, we were finally ready to hire a placement agency to find a daughter.

A human daughter, that is.

PrimeTime Clara

*C*lara was ready for her nude scene. I was a nervous wreck. We were on location at the Princess Resort in San Diego. A crew from the television show *PrimeTime Live* was unloading a van filled with expensive state-of-the-art equipment: big cameras, small cameras, booms, mikes, lights, and monitors. Julia, an earnest young assistant producer from Los Angeles, studied a list of shots sent by her boss in New York. "Let's start with the bath scene," she said, and my stomach churned.

Duke patted me on the back. "Don't worry, honey," he said, "this is how Harlow got started."

Yes, but Harlow wasn't a thirteen-pound black pug.

Clara and I were about to take the nation to a gathering of several hundred pugs at the Del Mar Fairgrounds in San Diego, sponsored by the local chapter of Pug Rescue. (In these troubled times, there are homeless pugs, though I suspect many ran away in the hopes of finding cushier digs.) Careful readers will remember that after the last pug convention, I gave my husband my word that he would never have to attend such an event again. And I meant it, honest, I did.

Alas, fate intervened in the form of an excited call from Brian, my book publicist. With the help of my far-from-pug-crazed editor, David, he had come up with a surefire way to worm his way back into Clara's heart, after the *Good Morning America* fiasco. "*PrimeTime Live* is considering a segment on the increasing popularity of pugs," Brian said. "They want to interview you and Clara." He warned, "It's great exposure for you, so be nice to them." In the twenty years I've owned pugs, I've never received any exposure when standing within a mile of them, but I promised to be polite.

A few days later, Beth, the show's New York–based producer, made contact. She chatted me up for a while to make sure that I had personality (television producers live in fear that you'll freeze on camera). I didn't think her filming me and the pugs at home would make for riveting television, unless maybe I took Clara down to the boardwalk and she drove on a Saint Bernard. But just my luck, the fifth annual San Diego Pug Rescue Party, called Pugo de Mayo that year because it fell on the fifth of May, was three days hence. According to the promotional flyer, one of the costume categories was famous Hispanic personalities. What television producer could resist?

"Clara can go as Carmen," Duke said. "You can put a rose between her teeth."

I'm ashamed to admit that I considered it.

Duke agreed to come along only when I pointed out that it was crucial to Clara's career. We drove down from Los Angeles on Friday night with the star and her understudy, Sophie. We checked into the dog-friendly Princess Resort, surrounded by forty-four acres of lush tropical gardens, with interesting scents from exotic plants to amuse Sophie, whose second-greatest pleasure in life, after compulsive barking, is obsessive sniffing.

The producer wanted to shoot footage of Clara getting ready for the big event, like she was Evita being Christian Dior–ed for her world tour. I was asked to wash the star on camera, in the tub in the cramped hotel bathroom. I pictured myself on my knees, bent over the bathtub, derriere in the air in front of millions of Americans. Or worse, holding the indignant, squirming pug under the bathtub faucet. Not any pug either, but Clara, who is accustomed to aromatherapy treatments and shiatsu pedicures from her personal groomer, Aly, of Alley Cats and Dogs. (Aly treats Clara the way Jose Eber treats Elizabeth Taylor.) It wasn't like I could rely on my dog to sense my concern and be a good sport—Clara wouldn't hesitate to go into her "Poor Little Me" routine if it resulted in more attention. Fortunately, while I was no match for the shameless opportunist, I had a higher bank balance. The night before her national debut, I tipped the concierge and in exchange, a liveried room-service attendant driving a golf cart delivered a garden hose to our semidetached room. My plan was to sit Clara outside on a plastic lawn chair and hose her down.

"Can't we stretch the hose to the bathroom?" asked the jaded cameraman who had shot war, earthquakes, and social upheaval and felt a plastic chair wasn't sufficiently dramatic. "She'd look better in the tub." I made a feeble excuse. It was rude to clog the hotel drain with pug fur, which when damp, Clara sheds at a copious rate.

The cameraman made an aggrieved face. "The tub reads better on film than the chair."

I tried again. "The hose isn't long enough."

"Call room service," said Duke, who can't take a hint. "Get them to send a longer hose."

Julia, the associate producer, checked her watch and shook her head. "Do the chair," she said. "We're due at the fairgrounds in an hour."

The crew set Clara's bath chair up in the parking lot opposite our room, in the shade of a eucalyptus tree. "Action," Julia said, and the coal-black Clara became luminescent, flirting with the camera like Drew Barrymore, ears fluttering, crooked teeth fixed in a *Mona Lisa*–like grin. She widened her eyes pathetically when I hosed her with icy water and she pointedly shivered when I stood her on her hind legs to scrub her gently rounded tummy. But the only real trouble came when Duke noticed that I was drying Clara off with his life-sized Magic Johnson beach towel, the one he mistakenly believes is a collector's item. He filed a protest.

"Shh," said the producer. "You don't want to distract Clara."

I began to question my sanity. There I was, soaking wet, makeup melting off my face from the heat, but the camera kept rolling. Eventually, the crew moved to the vanity area of the bathroom, where the unflattering fluorescent lighting turned my complexion mint green. I know this because I was ordered to blow Clara dry in front of a full-length mirror, where I noticed every smile line and eye wrinkle on my face (I vowed to call a plastic surgeon the instant I returned home). Normally, Clara cringes at the sound of a blow dryer—but mindful of her public, this time she sat placidly, gazing at her own reflection, careful not to turn her back to the camera.

Duke was flabbergasted. "The dog's a pro."

This is what I love about my husband. No matter how many times I tell him something, he doesn't believe it until he sees it for himself. Only the week before, Clara had gone with me to Universal Studios to tape a segment of *Home and Family,* then hosted by Christina Ferrare and Chuck *"Love Connection"* Woolery. While it may not get the ratings Rosie O'Donnell or Oprah get, I like being a guest because the show is filmed in a big house, built especially for the program, that sits on a grassy hill in a remote corner of the studio lot. I always feel like I'm going to the country.

Thanks to a marine layer, it was cloudy and cool at the beach when we left the house. It was a shock to Clara when we arrived in Burbank and it was nearly a hundred degrees. She walked three steps and then demanded I carry her. By the time we got to the greenroom her pink tongue had swollen to the size of a strawberry Popsicle and she was panting so hard I thought she'd break. If she were a car, all the red lights on the dash would have been flashing. The producer turned up the air-conditioning for her and brought her Perrier, which Clara drank from the bottle. Ever the trouper, she did the Hustle while the Captain and Tennille sang "Love Will Keep Us Together" to a captive audience, which was bused in on the Universal Tram. Afterward, Toni Tennille demonstrated another talent on camera: She ironed a shirt. Clara, ever generous to her fellow performers, managed to look interested.

Next Christina and Chuck did a cooking segment. Sherman Hemsley, formerly of *The Jeffersons,* showed off his never-before-publicized sandwich-and-salad-making skills. The pug trotted into the kitchen and plopped down at their feet, fixing them with a keen "Aren't you forgetting something?" stare. Rewarded with a substantial portion of a ham sandwich, she returned to the living room, where I was positioned for my interview. Clara vaulted up onto the plump-cushioned white couch and sat next to me. Then Christina came over and Clara abandoned me in a heartbeat to show herself off to better advantage on the host's lap.

So I was not really surprised that the pug sparkled in San Diego.

Beth, the producer, had asked me if Clara owned any clothes. Long ago, Duke threatened to commit me if I ever dressed the pugs, but I prevailed on Posh Pugs, and Marie, the manager, lent Clara an entire wardrobe.

Julia kept the cameras rolling as I dumped a supermarket bag filled with dog outfits on the hotel bed. Clearly and distinctly into the mike clipped to my National Pug Dog Specialty Show apron, I said, "These are not Clara's clothes. I borrowed them," but of course, that comment wound up on the cutting-room floor. (After the show aired, even my closest friends expressed consternation at my dog's many wardrobe changes. I asked, "Have you ever seen Clara in a pinafore?" but it didn't seem to make an impression.)

Like Iman doing a Versace show, Clara modeled an Uncle Sam stovepipe hat, a red velvet sombrero with spangles, a Stetson, a blue taffeta party dress with a matching straw bonnet, a denim dirndl (what Sam Donaldson would later call "her Daisy Mae outfit"), and my personal favorite—and incidentally the only item that really came from Clara's wardrobe—a gold crown studded with faux jewels. "She does have a red coat that makes her look like Bette Davis in *Now Voyager*," I quipped, referring to a wrap that I had purchased in New York when we got caught in yet another snowstorm.

I felt bad for slighting my older pug, even though she was sound asleep, snoring placidly. Only when I dressed Clara in a black-velvet and gold-lamé frock that Sophie had previously admired did she wake and begin to growl. Clara went for her throat, and the two pugs rose up on their hind legs like bears and batted each other's faces—hoping to run up a sizable veterinary ophthalmologist bill. The crew was invigorated by the sounds of pug combat, but I stuffed Sophie into the lamé gown and put Clara in her Daisy Mae denim number and the two pugs sat side by side on the bed glowering in mutual antipathy. A Kodak moment if there ever was one.

Alas, Sophie wound up on the cutting-room floor.

There was barely enough time for me to change, let alone repair my makeup, before we moved outside to the cruel—if you're over thirty-five—midday sun. I answered questions about pugs, which would later be used as commentary, then the spotlight returned to Clara, who seemed offended that it had ever left her. The cameraman spread out a bolt of red velvet and instructed me to keep the pug still for three minutes. I said, "Stay." Clara, who never stays, remained motionless.

Duke suggested that they photograph Clara sitting next to my book.

"We can do that later," Julia said. "We better get going. We don't want to miss the costume contest."

Two hours after the shooting began, we arrived at the fairgrounds. It was eighty degrees out already, and the temperature was rising. Given the heat, Clara opted to go au natural, adorned only by what Sam Donaldson would later call "a simple, elegant bow," courtesy of Aly, who had had the presence of mind to give me a bunch for the show. (The pugs are very proud of their bows and will keep them on for weeks.) Julia's jaw dropped as dozens of panting pugs rambled in clad as bumblebees, Carmen Miranda, Juan Valdez's burro, Pancho Villa, Fred and Wilma Flintstone, Michael Jackson, and Minnie Mouse. "We could do a whole show on this," she said with a gasp. "It's unbelievable." I thought the fact that my dog was being followed around by a cameraman holding a tiny camera on a long stick—known in the trade as a lipstick camera—in front of Clara's face to get the pug's-eye view was far more implausible.

The jaded cameraman darted around trying to capture sales tables crammed with pug-shaped dishes, refrigerator magnets, mouse pads, needlepoint pillows, you name it. There was a pug in green medical scrubs who arrived in a mini ambulance; pugs splashing in wading pools that had been put on the lawn to prevent overheating (in spite of this, a pug whose owner stupidly left him in the car died of heat prostration); a gaggle of pugs running around in circles. The sublimely calm and organized show chairman, Carol Ferguson, called me and Clara up to the podium and introduced us to the crowd. Thoughtfully, she mentioned my book.

She wound up on the cutting-room floor too.

The camera did record a radiant Clara and me consulting animal psychic Sue Goodrich, the very same seer who had told me that Clara wanted me to read to her. I was confident that Goodrich was good for some off-the-wall advice, but as soon as the soundman clipped a mike on her she turned almost sensible. This time, Goodrich explained that Clara barked at big dogs because "they told her that she was funny-looking." She told me that Sophie, snoozing under her chair, seemed "a little depressed." Her big revelation was that Clara was concerned because my energy wasn't grounded.

Obviously it wasn't, or I wouldn't be there.

After two more sunbaked hours Julia said that we could leave. However, she still needed a shot of Clara wandering off into the sunset after her big day. Julia couldn't find a location she liked at the fairgrounds, so Duke consulted a map and found a junior college a few miles away that was nicely landscaped. First they shot me walking down a long path with

Clara. Then they explained that they wanted Clara to walk away by herself. I was dubious. Clara has a terrific fear of abandonment and follows me closely when she is in a foreign environment (in the house, she doesn't give me the time of day). But I took her off the lead, ordered her to stay, walked twenty yards away, crouched down out of sight, and yelled, "Clara, come!" The ham bounded down the path toward me like Dorothy on the yellow brick road. For the first time, I didn't feel the course in obedience had been a complete waste of money.

"Okay, let's do it again," the cameraman said.

Clara did it again. And again. And again. I felt like the mother of the Olsen Twins. In six hours of shooting, despite intense heat, the little trouper failed only once. Julia wanted to end with a shot of Clara asleep after her big day. We waited around, hoping that she'd fall asleep on the grass. Clara had no intention of closing her eyes on her public. The cameraman argued that it was out of context for her to be sleeping on the grass. I suggested the car and put Clara in the backseat. She stared at the camera. She panted. She mugged. We waited twenty minutes. Duke lay down on the cool grass under a tree and closed his eyes. But Clara kept smiling. I got into the car with her and put her in my lap. Clara was pissed off that I was in the shot but forced herself to look cheerful. Julia gave up. The crew packed up the expensive equipment and sped away, heading toward the nearest FedEx drop, to get the film to New York. Duke got in the car. "It was such an incredible amount of energy we spent on the goddamn thing," my husband griped.

As soon as he turned on the engine, Clara started snoring.

Two days later I received a call from Beth, the New York producer. "I think you should think seriously about getting her on a children's show," she said. ("You should have asked her if she had anything in mind," Loretta, my agent, said to me later, with ill-concealed exasperation.) I asked Beth whether I looked dreadful in the noonday sun.

"Don't worry," she said. "No one will pay any attention to you."

Beth should have won an Emmy for editing the footage. The best moment came when I mentioned Clara looking like Bette Davis in her red coat and Clara morphed into Bette Davis in *Now Voyager*. "I spent an hour on that shot," Beth said. "At first, I thought you were kidding, but the resemblance was uncanny."

I never thought I'd live to see the day that Sam Donaldson commented on my pug, even if his comment was, "Oh, poo!" Somehow it made me believe that anything in life was possible. On the other hand, there was something truly terrifying about the amount of attention my pug attracted after that show aired. Strangers came up to Clara on the boardwalk and conversed with her, ignoring me completely. People even asked for her autograph. (Mother suggested I get a rubber stamp made with her paw print.)

Beth confided that last year she spent months working on an important investigative piece about a sleazy fertility doctor in Orange County. "I've gotten twice as much positive feedback on the pug story than I ever got for that," she said ruefully.

I decided to be charitable.

Clara's days as the center of my universe were numbered.

Hometown Pug

—ᏕᏕᎷᎧ—

$\mathcal{I}$ was riddled with doubt. It was one thing to compulsively amass a seven-inch stack of official papers, and another to ship them to an international placement agency that would in turn ship them to Beijing, where they would be exchanged for a small blurry photo of a baby girl randomly selected from a pool of millions by an unknown government bureaucrat. Dear God of political correctness, forgive me, but that is not the way I like to shop.

The boondoggle at INS gave me too much time to think. When I was first inspired to adopt a Chinese daughter, I easily rationalized the indiscriminate selection process by reminding myself of numerous positive experiences with the I Ching, the ancient Chinese oracle. My right brain was confident the baby destined to be our daughter would appear by chance, in much the same way as when I was out of work a few years ago and threw the I Ching coins for guidance I repeatedly drew the all-too-apt hexagram K'an, the Abysmal, and the message "In the abyss one falls into a pit. Misfortune." Unfortunately, my left brain had eight months to come up with worst-case scenarios, and when it came time to take the leap of faith, I was reluctant to jump. I consulted Pangloss. "You can't get rid of your anxiety right now because fear is the appropriate response," my therapist said. He suggested that I distract myself by doing something tangible—like buying a new car.

Only in Los Angeles would a therapist make this recommendation, but it was not without merit. Just the thought of haggling with a car salesman made adopting a baby seem like fun.

After much soul searching, Duke and I hired Kinderama, a large, established placement agency on the East Coast that finds forever families for homeless children on three continents. We signed up for their newest China program, which placed infants from a flagship orphanage in Shanghai. I liked the idea of knowing where we were going, and Duke was pleased because of Shanghai's traditional symbolic role as a meeting place between China and the West.

The program was run by a radiologist named Meredith, the mother of two darling daughters from Nanjing. Like many people who successfully adopt overseas, she felt a zeal to help others and worked for Kinderama in her spare time. Meredith was bright and efficient with a dry sense of humor, and she completely understood our reluctance to travel in a group. "This isn't the kind of agency that gives everyone a brightly colored T-shirt and tells you all to meet at noon under the big clock," she assured me.

On a sultry August morning in the middle of Los Angeles's traditional summer ant infestation, I went to my office determined to make five copies of the dossier and get it out of my life. It was easier said than done. At least three colonies of ants were feasting on the pugs' pig's ears—to my horror and Sophie's intense fascination, the ear was actually moving across the floor—and I had to call Duke and beg him to stop in Chinatown on his way home and pick up the special anti-ant chalk that is only sold there. (What it contains I don't want to know.) Then I nearly had a nervous breakdown at the copy machine because each of the twenty-plus documents in our dossier contained at least seven pages of authentications and seals, all of which were stapled in such a way that they were impossible to copy without removing the staples. My Internet sources warned that if the powers that be in Beijing detected staple tampering, it could jeopardize our future daughter's fate. I wound up taking the staples out anyway and replacing them with the help of a magnifying glass.

"Do you have a moment?" called Marta, the soft-spoken graphic designer from Poland. I didn't, but when I went into her office I discovered a fawn pug named Pierre, a client of Marta's son's doggy day care center, huddled in the corner shivering. "His mother, a froufrou Valley type, gave him a tranquilizer because he couldn't sleep last night," Marta said.

A pug not sleep? Unthinkable.

"I'm sure she was the one who wanted sleep," Marta agreed. "When she dropped him off he fell down, he was so dopey."

I fell to my knees and tried to revive him with all the fervor of Anthony Edwards on *ER*. I massaged Pierre vigorously. "C'mon, big boy, wake up," I pleaded. Even in his stupor, Pierre recognized a dupe and bravely flopped on his back to allow me to rub his rather massive belly. Only after I produced a rawhide chew stick and Pierre miraculously came to his senses did I stop and consider that perhaps I was overidentified with pugs. I was like a mother who sensed her child was in danger, only my child had bulging eyes, a coat that shed easily, and a tendency to sneeze.

When Pierre was stable, I introduced him to Sophie and Clara, who were lined up in the hall like sledders on a luge. Sophie went berserk with jealousy—howling, throwing herself at the back of my legs, clinging to the hem of my skirt with her teeth. She noticed the interloper was gnawing on her chew stick and confiscated it. Meanwhile, Clara fluttered around Pierre, coquettishly kissing his face.

"They're licking the wrong end of each other," said Marta.

Crisis averted, I returned to my office and checked, double-checked, and triple-checked each document and copy until I thought I would lose my mind. From my window, I spied a Federal Express truck parking and hastily shoved the wedge of papers into a box—noting wryly that it was the same weight as a book manuscript—and ran outside and thrust it into the driver's hands. My prevailing emotion was not excitement or even fear, just abating claustrophobia. I never in my life wanted to see a notary stamp again.

The next day, I received E-mail from the efficient Meredith: Our documents had arrived safely, and a copy was en route to Beijing to be translated. A week later, she E-mailed that the translation and our original documents were at the Chinese Center for Adoption Affairs. "Referrals are coming in about two or three months after dossier submission," she reported. Once we accepted the referral, we had to wait six to eight weeks for formal permission to travel because "the Chinese Center for Adoption Affairs thinks it's important to have a cooling-off period in case the family changes its mind."

As always during periods of stress, I was guided by my mantra, "Run away." Clara and I went to Baltimore, my hometown, to attend my high school reunion. I hadn't seen or even thought of anyone in my Park School graduating class for decades, but an atavistic stirring in my bones prompted me to go. To be honest, it was probably as much ego as sentiment. My publisher had lined up extensive hometown publicity—what better time to get in touch with my roots? (No woman has ever voluntarily gone to a class reunion when her life was at a low ebb.) I invited my husband to come with me. Duke, who had obviously never read a Dear Abby letter from an abandoned husband who refused to accompany his wife to her reunion and lost her to the lug who had taken her to the senior prom, demurred, "I'd rather be french-fried."

Clara was elated to be his stand-in. (This is another thing pugs have over people: They're always willing to do what you want.) She went on alert the minute I began packing and guarded the suitcase like it was her own pup. "Don't worry," I said, "I won't leave without you."

When we arrived at LAX, I unzipped her Sherpa Bag and Clara scooted inside. The porter at the curb asked if she minded being stuck in the bag. "Of course not," I said. Invariably, when she emerges she receives more fanfare than Tom Cruise visiting Rosie O'Donnell. If I got that much attention, I'd crawl into the bag too.

In some ways, it's more relaxing to travel with Clara than with my husband because she doesn't consider it a badge of honor to arrive at the gate at the precise moment the gate attendants are closing the airplane door. Nor does Clara complain if she can't look out the window. I always request an aisle seat in a row where the middle seat is vacant. Not just because I want the extra leg room but because I live in fear that someday I will encounter a situation where the oxygen masks will drop down, and I want Clara to have her own mask. I'm embarrassed to admit that I have given great thought to whether the life jacket that is supposedly under my airline seat will fit the pug and whether or not she'd balk at going down the inflatable slide.

Duke flew with Clara only once, and he who has a genius for complicating situations did just that. A few years before, we flew to Baltimore by way of Cleveland. Our connecting flight was late, and I decided to take Clara outside to visit the grass. I slung her bag over my shoulder. Duke said, "You don't need that. Leave the bag with me."

"They won't let me back into the airport without it."

"Sure, they will."

"No way," said I, who had flown over sixty thousand miles with Clara.

"Trust me," he argued with more conviction than I ever feel about anything. I walked Clara outside, sans bag. On our way back she was confiscated at the security gate. I had to trudge through the airport all the while worried that a passenger would steal her; search for Duke, who had wandered off looking for a cup of coffee; retrieve her bag from the chair outside the men's room where he left it; wrench the pug away from her new best friend, the security guard; and sprint to the gate.

It was unseasonably cool when we landed at Baltimore Washington International Airport—which I still think of as Friendship Airport despite the glitzy façade. As always, I felt queasy about returning home, in part because I am considered a traitor for having moved away. Baltimore is an insular town, a crazy quilt of neighborhoods, sharply defined clusters of similar houses inhabited by similar people, all of whom believe that their neighborhood is the best neighborhood in the best city in the world, who never want to leave Baltimore, who want to turn the world into Baltimoreans (pronounced "Balti-morons" in the local accent, appropriately enough). In the Jewish community of Pikesville, where I was raised, so finely honed is the rumor mill that I once kissed a boyfriend on the street at eleven in the evening and by ten the next morning I received calls inquiring if we were engaged. It violated local customs for me to carry a secret of such enormity as the pending adoption of a foreign-born child, but I was not confident enough to share it. Returning to the scene of my childhood brought my fears of parenthood to the fore.

Fortunately, I was too busy catering to Clara to dwell on my own insecurities. She demanded that I release her as soon as we reached the baggage claim and sat on the Avis counter, quivering with excitement while I got the keys for the rental car. Ever obliging, she spied an acceptable patch of ivy by the parking garage and relieved herself in front of dozens of passengers who wanted to pet her even though she was obviously engaged. She vaulted into the passenger seat of the red Chevy Cavalier and watched with ill-concealed irritation as I searched for the controls. Again, I missed Duke, who unlike Clara and me is instantly comfortable in unfamiliar vehicles. Soon we were motoring down Highway 295, desperately searching for the exit to downtown Baltimore and thwarted by the efforts to save Maryland taxpayers money by limiting highway signs. (Baltimoreans are so oblivious to change that they give directions using landmarks that are no longer there: "Turn left at the fire department where they used to set up model trains at Christmas.")

We checked into the Doubletree Colonnade, a comfortable, pug-friendly establishment across the street from Johns Hopkins University. The management presented me with a release form in which I had to swear to be responsible for any damage caused by my pet. They even asked for a paw print from Clara, which she gave imperiously, certain it would be worth big money someday. Once we were settled in, I decided to check in with Flora, my eighty-nine-year-old grandmother, the belle of North Oaks Retirement Home. I was exhausted, but Grandma insisted that I get back into the car and come over and have a snack. She doesn't usually take no for an answer—in Palm Beach she once convinced my food-snob husband to eat an Early Bird Special at a swap-meet coffee shop. Then I remembered my ace in the bag.

"You brought the damn dog?" she screeched in my ear. "Don't bring her here. They'll throw me out."

This seemed unlikely, since the last time I visited her she led the retirement community in the Macarena. "Oh, that's right," I said. "You don't like animals."

"I don't hate them," she said, "I just don't trust them. You better watch out. Someday she's going to turn on you in the middle of the night."

"I'll take my chances."

"Leave the damn dog in the room and come over."

"I can't," I said, strangely empowered by pug motherhood. "The damn dog doesn't like being left alone."

The next morning we went to Philadelphia to do a television show for the Discovery Channel. I had to get up at seven—four in the morning, California time. Clara snored through the wake-up call, and for once I missed Sophie, who has never outgrown her habit of waking me at 5:00 A.M. Clara remained in a coma until I announced that breakfast was being served. The pug looks at me like I'm a deity whenever I produce her kibble in a strange locale.

Back in Baltimore, after the taping, I fretted about which relative to contact first. I felt like Madeleine Albright on a shuttle-diplomacy mission to the Middle East. My father, brother, grandmother, aunt, and first cousins live within a mile of one another, but it's difficult to visit one without offending another. I decided to choose according to who would be most likely to please Clara. She is partial to my father's wife, Rose, who once cooked her a chicken breast, thoughtfully cut it into tiny squares, and served it on one of her good dishes, but my dad and stepmother were out of town. Instead, I decided to take her to play with Cousin Buster, a big fawn boy pug who lives with my brother, Bobby, his wife, Robbie, and their kids, Adam, Erica, and Samara.

I was leery when they decided to get a pug because Bobby and Robbie aren't what I'd call good Pet Parents. Their last dog was a magnificent-looking Pekingese named Yaki, after Yaqui Lopez, the light heavyweight prizefighter. ("He was a bum," Bobby said, "but he had a big moment and he actually won a huge fight.") Yaki seemed to emulate his namesake, because every time I visited he had just gotten into a fight with a large dog and lost another body part. "Hey," Bobby argued, "he lived to be twelve." (An impressive feat, since they kept the Peke outside in the dead of winter.)

Buster was running full speed around Bobby's front yard. He sniffed Clara eagerly and tried to get her to roll around in a pile of leaves, but she clawed my shins and requested to be picked up. "Buster really is the nicest person," Bobby said. "He's always glad to see me. And he's loyal."

Loyal?

Bobby shrugged. "You're right. He's a whore. He'd sell me out for a Slim Jim. But a whore is fine as long as you know what it is. He eats, he sleeps, he lies on the floor. He has no ulterior motives."

My brother seemed so fond of Buster that I felt ashamed for worrying. Then Bobby casually let slip that Buster was an unbelievable swimmer. Feeling like Betty the social worker, I asked a few probing questions, which elicited a description of what my brother called the Pond Incident. "I was taking Samara around the neighborhood to sell coupon books for her school," Bobby said defensively. "The pug was behind me, but I didn't know it. Our neighbor had this thing in his yard. You couldn't tell it was a pond—it had algae, it looked like grass. When we got home, the pug wasn't anywhere to be seen. We weren't overwhelmed. We figured he was cruising the neighborhood."

Call me overprotective. But none of my pugs have ever been allowed to wander free. Once, Clara jumped a wall and wound up at the crack house down the street. I posted signs offering rewards, and she returned, smelling a bit smoky but otherwise unharmed.

Bobby continued unabashed. "After a while, when Buster didn't come back, Robbie and Samara went to look for him. You'll never guess where he was."

I got it in one. "The pond."

"He had to be treading for forty minutes, easy. It's a good thing he's so strong, or he'd be belly-up in the pond. He was covered in algae."

I considered placing an anonymous call to Pug Rescue or another organization not averse to confronting pug abusers.

"Relax," Bobby said. "Robbie gave him a bath and he's fine."

"Robbie gave him a bath?" As a rule, Robbie doesn't like dogs because they don't smell like human beings.

"Yeah," Bobby said. "She cared more than anyone."

A pug really does have miraculous powers of persuasion.

Clara felt Buster was a bit too sporting for her taste, and she was relieved to bid him adieu. I smuggled her in to see Grandma. She had just won a bundle playing mahjong, and I had to drag her away from the game room. "I've got a surprise for you," I said when we got to her apartment. I unzipped the bag, and Clara's head popped out.

Grandma gasped. "It's the damn dog."

Clara climbed onto a leather sofa that looked comfy and curled up in a little ball. Grandma watched her suspiciously. "She's cute," she said begrudgingly. "Just don't turn your back on her." Despite the warning, I could tell Grandma was tickled because she introduced Clara to all her friends. When we finally left, Clara in bag, Grandma sidled up to the guard. "You'll never guess what's in there," she said. "My great-granddaughter, from California."

As a surprise, my childhood friend Melinda arranged for me to visit the house where I grew up. I had not been there for twenty-five years, and I expected to be haunted by memories. Instead, as I walked nervously down the parquet-floored hall up thirteen stairs to my old room, I had a revelation. When my parents were my age, I was a senior in high school. Here I was wondering if I could handle an infant, and they had had to cope with a teenager. I was overwhelmed with understanding and a newfound courage.

The next day we went to Washington, to have lunch with my friend Bob Garfield, who is a commentator for National Public Radio. I had met him when he came to Los Angeles and was casting about for people with weird jobs to poke fun at. He had just struck out with the cheese sculptor when a mutual friend mentioned that I was Hollywood correspondent for *Pug Talk*. When the segment aired, I received calls from people I hadn't heard from in years and Anna Marie reported a sharp rise in subscription requests.

Clara and I met Bob in his office at the National Press Club. I planned to leave Clara with an adoring secretary, but there was no one around so I fell back on Plan B; lock her in

Bob's office. Clara rejected Plan B. I suggested that we bring her along in her bag. "She'll be quiet?" Bob asked.

"Of course," I lied.

We stopped by the Gallery, where Bob Dole was making a speech. Clara, a Democrat, heckled him with agonized yelps, so Bob Garfield hustled us up to the dining room. I carefully hung the shoulder bag on the back of my chair and sat down. Clara's eyes glowed like coals through the mesh, but she accepted the arrangement as satisfactory. Unfortunately, lunch was served buffet-style, and when I got up to get some food, I became aware of poltergeist activity from the supposedly inert bag. I dumped some salad onto my plate and returned to my seat just as Clara began her dying-smoke-alarm-battery chirp. The dining room was filled with reporters, and not one expressed any curiosity.

Clara was far better behaved at the class reunion; then again, her reception was more to her liking. By the time we arrived, she had been featured on local TV and radio (she made such a good impression at the A.M. station that she received an impromptu invitation to appear on the F.M. affiliate.) People who tormented me in high school lined up to meet the furry star. She didn't cling; she worked the room, mingling with the other guests. A former classmate balanced a plate of cold cuts on his lap, while Clara sat motionless beneath him, fixing him with a stare.

"She likes me," he said.

"She wants your dinner," I replied.

"Oh, I'm sorry," he said, and handed her a slice of roast beef.

Clara had a minor lapse when she took advantage of a conversational lull and climbed onto the buffet table to sample the Brie, but no one begrudged her the snack. Julie, the alumni director, later reported that Clara was voted the best-behaved guest at the gathering and invited us to return for Homecoming Weekend.

I declined. By then we would be in Shanghai, picking up our new daughter.

The first thing I did when I returned to Los Angeles was check my E-mail. The China Adoption List was awash with rumors and dire reports. China had just reorganized its adoption process, and the reaction in cyberspace was a collective panic attack. It used to be that foreign adoption was jointly controlled by the ministries of Justice and Civil Affairs. But in May 1996, to end the intramural squabbling, Beijing gave the Ministry of Civil Affairs total control. More than a thousand dossiers were held up for months at the Ministry of Justice before they were transferred to Civil Affairs. When they arrived, they clogged the adoption pipeline—already strained by the thousands of applications and staff shortages.

Meredith called the next day. "I have bad news," she said. "Beijing pulled the plug on the Shanghai program." The new officials canceled all designated orphanage programs and limited each American adoption agency to one facilitator. Kinderama had three, including Meredith. She was out, and Ding, another expatriate who claimed to have excellent connections, was in. "Here are your choices," Meredith said. "We can try to withdraw your dossier from the ministry and give it back to you so you can work with another agency. We can try and refund your program fee. Or you can stay with us and Ding can handle your dossier. Of course, I've got to tell you that Ding's program costs fifteen hundred dollars more. I realize it seems like bait and switch . . ."

She took the words right out of my mouth.

I was ready to throw in the towel, but Duke as always remained pragmatic. "Can we talk to Ding?" he asked.

"Ding doesn't like to talk to the families," Meredith said. She would act as liaison between Ding and the families. Ding would secure the referrals and travel dates, and his associate would act as a translator/guide for the families when they went to China.

Call us unreasonable. We refused to pay someone who wouldn't talk to us.

Meredith offered to see if Ding would make an exception, and a couple of days later, a conference call was arranged. I was speaking on the phone in my office, and Duke was on the extension in the living room, and when the conversation ended we walked into the kitchen and shook our heads and in one breath we both said, "Shady."

"I thought he was part of the secret police who was trying to parlay secret-police connections into money," Duke said.

That would have been the end of it. That should have been the end of it. Except we had ten months invested and had a hard time letting go. Ding's references were glowing, and it seemed in our best interest to try and work things out. I explained to Meredith that I required more control over the selection process, which Ding had described as follows: "There are two piles. One has the dossiers and the other has the pictures. The ministries take one from the top of each pile."

One from Column A and one from Column B was a scenario that didn't work for me. Especially since *The New York Times* had just printed a horrifying story about the lack of iodine in Chinese villages. I asked if Ding could get us a referral from Shanghai, Nanjing, or Xi'an. I received an encouraging E-mail.

Ding could get us a referral from Xi'an, a city we'd visited before and wanted to see again.

Duke began daydreaming about the steamed dumplings he'd eaten in that town. "We can name our daughter Xi'an," he said happily.

"Over my dead body," I replied.

A Change in Plan

$\mathcal{I}$ am a creature of deadlines. I'm used to working intensely on a book or an article for a finite period of time and then I turn it in and move on.

It was early December; the rains had come, and the roof was leaking, along with my resolve. On the Internet, couples who had sent dossiers to China in the spring were still waiting for referrals. The only excitement was that a male poster renowned for his amusing anecdotes left his wife and ran away with a female poster renowned for her laments about men. Meredith didn't expect the logjam to clear until after the Chinese New Year, several months away. For all she knew, we could be waiting another six months.

I was emotionally equipped to handle a time frame along the lines of a pug pregnancy—sixty-three days—but not an elephant one, where the gestation period is twenty-two months. The strain began to wear me down. Relatives would call and ask, "What's new?" and instead of telling the bizarre truth—"Our would-be Chinese daughter is caught in a bureaucratic snafu"—I'd mutter, "Same old, same old." I spent so much energy keeping our secret that I reached a point

where I could hardly speak at all. I had never been as unhappy being childless—after all, I had Clara and Sophie—as
I was being in limbo. Finally, I told Duke that if the situation
wasn't resolved by year's end, I was pulling the plug.

"I don't think it's that stressful," my husband said.

"That's because you're not doing anything," I replied.

Faced with a looming deadline, I felt the wheels begin to
turn. Perhaps our baby wasn't in China; perhaps we were looking in the wrong place. I'd always been attracted to Russia. If
truth be told, what I secretly wanted was a child with red hair,
red hair being the cornerstone of my identity. (This is something only another redhead can truly understand, but I offer as
evidence an excited phone call I recently received from
Mother. "I just saw the most fabulous royal poodles," she said
in the exact tone of voice she would have used if she had won
the lottery. "You would have fainted. The dogs both had red
curly hair. They looked exactly like us.")

Kinderama had a program in Russia and a reputation for
getting good placements there. I suggested to my husband that
it couldn't hurt to get some information.

"I'd rather go to Georgia," Duke said. "They drink less. It's
a wine-growing culture."

I rolled my eyes. He is prone to making these proclama-
tions—recently, when I was sending a baby gift to a cousin
who lived in Paris, he sagely informed me, "The French adore
velvet." I checked the AOL adoption board, found out there
was an A-Parents Russia List, and subscribed. I posted an in-
quiry about Georgia, and to my consternation all the respon-
dents mentioned the winegrowers.

Meredith didn't know about the wine or the Russian or
Georgian programs—her heart belonged to China's children—so she referred me to Nancy Ann, the agency director.

It took five tries to get her on the phone, but when I did the news was heartening. "If you want to go to Russia," she said, "then I can get you a referral almost immediately." I dutifully asked about Georgia. "It's not any faster than China," she said, "though you're certainly welcome to leave your dossier in China, apply to Georgia, and see which referral comes through first. But you can't travel to Tbilisi to pick up the child. The baby has to be escorted to Moscow because Georgia is in the middle of a civil war."

If I had to pick two words in the English language that would automatically deter me from pursuing a given goal, they would be *civil war*.

"Civil war's okay from one point of view," Duke said cheerfully. "It explains the supply of orphans." (Six months later, we would read in *The New York Times* that all international Georgian adoptions had been halted because of the fierce opposition of President Shevardnadze's wife.)

There is a magical place that you can only get to when you are willing to walk away. In this paradisiacal spot you can negotiate effectively for what you truly want because you no longer give a damn. It's like when you've been dating the same guy for three years and he still hasn't asked you to marry him. If deep in your heart you are prepared to dump him, then the odds are in your favor that a diamond solitaire will materialize. But you can't feign indifference; the universe only responds when you're serious.

I called Nancy Ann back. It only took three tries to get her on the phone, and I quickly got to the point. I didn't want to wait for China or Georgia. Duke was nervous about adopting from Russia. He worried about fetal alcohol syndrome, wind patterns from Chernobyl, you name it.

The director thought for a moment. "How do the two of you feel about flying?"

We've never seen an airline ticket we didn't like.

"Have I got the program for you," she exclaimed. It was based in Nigdyetsk, in the easternmost part of Russia—oh, let's be frank, Siberia. The in-country coordinator was a Russian-born former podiatrist named Olga who was married to an American accountant. Olga went over to Nigdyetsk several times a year and hand-picked children from the orphanages in the region. She had just returned to the United States with videos of the children.

Videos. Now, there was a concept I liked.

I asked how long it would take until we could travel. "A couple of months," Nancy Ann said. Having a strict warm-weather vacation policy, I wasn't wild about visiting Siberia in the dead of winter, but I figured that since so far the adoption had embodied everything I hate most in life, this would be the perfect grand finale.

I suspected correctly that Duke, who can't resist an off-the-beaten-track destination, would be intrigued. He later told me it was near Birobiljan, the Jewish colony that Stalin had set up in the thirties. "We could probably buy a round-the-world ticket from Los Angeles to Nigdyetsk to Moscow to Los Angeles," he said. Then he added wistfully, "It's near the Chinese border. I bet there's a good Chinese restaurant by now."

I asked the director how long we would have to wait for a referral if we opted for this program.

"If you were paper-ready, next week," she said. By paper-ready she meant if we had a dossier ready to ship to Russia, which of course we did not. Our original notarized documents were in Beijing, and we couldn't get them back. Not that they would have done us a lot of good. Russia required similar but altogether different paperwork.

I refused to notarize another document until I saw our baby. Kinderama had four copies of our China dossier, so they were aware we met their qualifications. Unhinged by sheer frustration, I even revealed my shallow nature: I requested a cute child, under a year old, preferably with red hair. I didn't care what sex.

Nancy Ann promised to get back to me. Two weeks passed without word, and I lost hope. But not entirely, because instead of Christmas shopping, I hung out in cyberspace. First, I read ninety messages from the China group and then another fifty from the Russia list. The latter was infinitely more disconcerting. The adoptive Chinese parents had lively threads about celebrating the Year of the Snake and how to deflect rude comments from strangers. The Russian board agonized over how to decline when your host family plies you with vodka, and what to do if you went to Russia to pick up your little one and were suddenly told wee Svetlana has five brothers and sisters who would also like parents. Then there were the horror stories about disturbed children who could not successfully bond. I had visions of adopting Alyosha the pet slayer or Masha the fire starter.

I actually made Duke promise that if the baby hurt the pugs, we could send the baby back. "We love Clara and she's part of our life," he said, and I felt better. Though only the day before, he had dispassionately noted Clara's resemblance to some ill-fated lab mice.

On December 19, a Thursday afternoon, at 1:55 Pacific time, 4:55 on the East Coast, I received a voice mail message from Nancy Ann. "I have an assignment of a child for you," she said. "Call me right back."

My hands burned, my throat closed, my heart raced, I cursed myself for not having call waiting, an invention I detest. Naturally, when I called her back five minutes later, she was gone for the day. (This was as inevitable as the plumbing spouting a leak on a national holiday.) Naturally, she'd left no clue as to whether our referral was a boy or a girl. I loathe suspense. I looked at Clara and thought, "Boy, if you only knew."

Clearly she was aware something was up, because the next morning when I let Clara and Sophie out of their room and opened the front door, my younger pug gave me a horrible scare. Clara arched her back and without warning began swaying back and forth. Her feet were splayed out in front, and she couldn't walk. I thought I was going to have a heart attack.

"Maybe it's the pug equivalent of limbs falling asleep," Duke said.

Duke held the convulsing Clara while I went into the kitchen to call the vet. Dr. Shekel was gone for the holidays. He left the name of an emergency clinic. They put me on hold. Meanwhile, Sophie hurled herself at the back of my knees and demanded attention and kibble.

Outside, Clara saw the white light at the end of the tunnel, and all her deceased relatives beckoning. Then she heard the sounds of kibble falling into Sophie's bowl. She recovered instantly.

I called Blanche for advice. "Don't immediately think that the seizure was pug encephalitis," she said, as if that would have occurred to me. "Maybe her blood sugar was low or her trachea collapsed. It could be anything. See if it happens again." (It didn't, thank God.)

I waited until Clara was stable—that is to say, after she devoured my morning bagel—before I called Kinderama. Nancy

Ann was in a meeting. I was frantic. It was three days before Christmas. Duke and I were leaving town the next day to spend Christmas in Desert Hot Springs. Half of the agency staff was also leaving town for the holidays. An hour later I called back. Nancy Ann was at lunch, but she left word that I should speak to Tiffany. I do not have a high opinion of any Tiffany other than the Fifth Avenue jeweler.

Tiffany had just been hired to act as a liaison between the families in the Nigdyetsk program and Olga, the in-country coordinator. Tiffany wasn't sure which baby was ours, so she put me on hold while she checked. I listened to canned classical music for five minutes. I haven't felt so queasy since I called my oncologist to check on the results of a biopsy. Finally, Tiffany came back on the line and I got the news we'd waited a year to hear.

"It's a boy," she said. "Born on August 15, 1996."

"Is he cute?" (Forgive me, I'm shallow.)

"I haven't seen his video," Tiffany said and put me on hold again. More canned Mozart, then she returned and announced that her colleagues thought he was adorable.

"Is he healthy?" Russian medical reports are often filled with bogus and nonbogus diseases. Already I had downloaded a list of doctors around the country who specialized in analyzing international adoption videos and medical reports.

"The medical report is skimpy," Tiffany said. "I'll fax it to you."

"Please," I begged, "read it to me first."

"I'll fax it," Tiffany said. "It will just take a minute."

Two hours later, when my fax machine was still silent, I called Tiffany. She was at lunch. I waited another hour and tried again.

"You won't believe this," Tiffany said. "But I lost the medical report. I've been looking all over. I had it when I spoke to you, but I don't know where I put it."

"It happens," I said charitably. "Does anyone have a copy?"

"Olga does," she said, referring to the Nigdyetsk coordinator. "But she's gone for the holidays. I left her a message."

In the meantime, Tiffany promised to send me a copy of the baby's video, which she had now seen for herself. "He's darling," she assured me. "Meredith saw it too, and she is certain you'll be pleased."

I gave Tiffany my Federal Express account number and instructed her three times to be sure to request Saturday-morning delivery because we were leaving town on Saturday afternoon.

"Oh, I don't need your FedEx number," Tiffany said. "We use Airborne."

"Please," I begged, "use FedEx." I knew the driver. He knew where to leave packages. I wasn't in the mood to take any chances.

"Don't worry," she said. "We send things all the time. I'm making a note to myself to mark the package for Saturday delivery."

That night I called Meredith to get her impression of our future son. "I never saw him," she said. "Who told you I saw him?"

"Tiffany."

"Who's Tiffany?" Meredith said, and I audibly groaned. To assure me, she added, "They're a little disorganized in the Russia program."

This proved to be the understatement of all time.

Gamma Rae called. She'd had a premonition that something was up and was pleased when I confirmed her hunch. She immediately consulted her *Ephemeris,* the astrologer's bible, and reported that Baby's star signs were favorable. "He's a Leo, and my view is that being a Leo is one of the most fabulous things that can happen to a human being."

Being a Leo, I appreciated that.

"I'm pleased to tell you that the following autocrats and dictators were born on the same day," Gamma Rae continued. "Napoleon Bonaparte, Menachem Begin, Shimon Peres, Julia Child, Princess Anne, Edna Ferber—"

The conversation was making me nervous. "That's enough," I snapped.

It bounced right off her. "Lillian Carter, Sir Walter Scott, Frederick William I, the Prussian kaiser . . . but here is the truly amazing thing. The fifth house of the horoscope refers to children. In your chart, you have Pluto, the planet of transformation. The baby's sun is at the same degree forming an exact conjunction."

Call me a skeptic, but I couldn't adopt a child on the basis of the angle of the sun.

"See if you can find out what time he was born so I can calculate his rising sign and the degree of his moon," Gamma Rae said before she hung up.

Nine o'clock Saturday morning found me pacing by the front door, waiting for my new baby to be delivered by the nineties version of the stork. My friend Marian came over and kept me company while Duke took the pugs for a walk. In the course of our friendship, Marian and I have waited for boyfriends to propose, employers to tender offers, the stock market to go up and down (she's a financial analyst), pathologists to give us the results of scary tests. Never were we so charged with anxiety as we were that morning as we sat on my porch, downing Diet Cokes, looking up and down the street for a courier who never arrived.

At one o'clock I called Airborne and asked—in a not particularly friendly way—what happened to my package.

"It's scheduled for Monday delivery," the operator said.

But we wouldn't be returning from Desert Hot Springs until Wednesday. "Didn't they mark Saturday delivery?" I asked.

To ask such a question is to answer it. Airborne offered to try and divert the package to Desert Hot Springs, but Duke and I decided it was safer to have a neighbor retrieve the baby, I mean the envelope, and leave it in our house. It meant waiting five more days, but we'd already waited a year.

We drove to Desert Hot Springs, a trip we've made a dozen times before. It's hard to explain why when there are dozens of destinations within weekending range of Los Angeles, time after time Duke and I return to this remarkably unremarkable town on the wrong side of the Coachella Valley outside Palm Springs. Certainly it's not for the glamorous night life (the only movie theater has been closed for years) or the luxurious accommodations, none of which we've managed to locate in ten years. The main drag, Palm Drive—so uncongested you can make a U-turn without looking—is dotted with phantom businesses with quaint names like the Alibi or the Suzy Q patronized by seemingly freeze-dried clientele.

For us the attractions are the restfully empty desert landscape (snowcapped Mount San Jacinto in the distance, lots of sagebrush, cactus, and the occasional bullet-riddled rusting car hulk), peace and quiet and hot water. The San Andreas fault cuts through the valley and gives rise to warm mineral springs, reputedly beneficial for arthritis and unquestionably a stress reliever. Not that there is stress in Desert Hot Springs. It's like an alternative universe where time stands still. A video shop opens. A frozen-yogurt stand closes. It's comforting to know what to expect.

We take the waters at the Stardust, one of a handful of unpretentious fifties-style motels in the area named for Vegas casinos. To check in is to feel secure that bad news can't reach me because the room has no phone, my husband will be attentive because there's no data jack to connect him to his on-line enemies, and we will sleep soundly, unbothered by neighbors or traffic. We've grown fond of the Stardust's eccentric owners, Linda and Martin, and more important, they're fond of the pugs, who are honored guests.

"Be careful walking the pugs," Martin warned when we checked in. "A coyote took a poodle off a leash."

The strain of the angst-filled year eased as we soaked in the hot tub, along with half a dozen people that Duke immediately pegged as computer-industry digiterados because of their weight and pallid complexions. Sophie chased a road-runner around the pool and tried to catch flies. Clara lounged in a patch of sunlight and worked the crowd like Edith Piaf. The computer people stopped speculating about what the URL for the Vatican would be (I suggested http://www.god, which provoked a mind-numbing debate about whether God would be a dot com or a dot org or a dot something else) and turned their attentions to the pug. When I went back to the room to shower, I called Clara. She was loath to make her exit, but I insisted. She looked back at her audience as if to say, "Sorry, but it's time for me to go." There was a huge collective gasp, and she trotted offstage.

Duke and I took a drive through Joshua Tree National Park and spied a lone coyote in the road. He looked at us with what was obviously begging behavior. "He wants a Big Mac," Duke said.

"More likely, pug sushi."

That night, when Duke was walking the pugs, he spied another coyote ambling down Ocotillo Street. It was dark, and he was nearly invisible except for his luminescent eyes. "The coyote really wants to meet Clara," Duke reported. "She feels he wants to get to know her for herself."

Such is the enchantment of Desert Hot Springs that I managed to put the baby waiting at home in a Jiffy mailer out of my mind. On our return trip Christmas Day, when Duke suggested that we stop for dim sum at our favorite Chinese restaurant, I didn't complain. We discussed names, and in one breath we both agreed on Nicholas. Only after the third helping of har gow did I flip into panic mode and insist we get the check and go.

"What's the rush?" Duke asked.

His powers of denial are greater than mine. (Once when we were in Turkey, sitting outside having dinner, I felt myself being eaten by mosquitoes and asked Duke, "Do you think it's buggy here?" "No," he said, at the precise moment he slapped an insect away.)

At home, Duke suggested we take a walk, "just to get our blood going," before we opened the mailer that would forever change our lives. I dragged him to the sofa. Clara and Sophie settled on our laps. I ripped open the envelope and pushed the tape into the VCR.

We both fell in love at first sight.

The future Nicholas was two months old when he made his audition tape. His hair looked reddish, his eyes were brown and alert. Sophie barked as soon as he started to cry, and Clara put her paws on my shoulders and licked my face slavishly.

For the first time in her memory, I ignored her. Duke and I turned to each other and smiled. "So," I asked, "should we give him the job as Baby?"

"If his medical report checks out, I don't see why not."

We showed Baby's audition tape (and the skimpy medical statistics, which arrived the next day) to three doctors. All agreed that he was adorable (which of course was crucial) and that he appeared to be in good health.

"Let's go get him," Duke said.

It goes without saying that it was much easier said than done.

My Sanity Is Questioned
(and Not Because of Clara)

$\mathcal{I}$f the thought of Baby lying in a crib, waiting for his parents to come and rescue him, wasn't sufficient motivation to get cracking on the paperwork, Tiffany, or as she styled herself, Tiff, offered another incentive. Olga, the agency's point person in Siberia, was returning there in late January (high tourist season, no doubt), and if our dossier was ready she could carry it with her to speed things up. It was fortunate that the future Nicholas was such a charmer because the document list was daunting, even for a world-class paper pusher such as myself. Lest anyone think that it is easy to adopt a baby overseas, here is what we had to supply:

- INS Notice of Favorable Determination
- Formal Letter of Intent to Adopt (boilerplate provided by Kinderama)
- Affidavit specifying the child we were adopting
- Affidavits asking the court to consider our suit in our absence
- Powers of attorney naming Olga to act on our behalf
- Home study

- A copy of the license of the home-study agency (remember this one, even though it sounds like a snore)
- A separate letter from the home-study agency introducing us and recommending us for adoption
- Another separate letter from the home-study agency stating that Betty, the social worker, would submit written reports at six months, one year, two years, and three years after our adoption
- Police and child-abuse clearance
- Birth certificates
- Marriage certificates
- Divorce decrees
- Medical reports on an English/Russian form
- Evidence of employment
- Three letters of reference
- Photographs of our home

If this wasn't enough, Kinderama required that we compile and notarize two complete dossiers—one to send to Russia and one to take with us in case something went wrong. (I didn't even want to think about what that something could be.) Like China, Russia required all the documents to be notarized and certified, but this time around each paper needed an apostille issued by the state where the document originated. An apostille, as medieval as its name, is a curiously cheesy-looking cover sheet that can be used in any country that has signed the 1961 Hague Convention Abolishing the Requirement of Legalization for Foreign Public Documents (Convention de La Haye du 5 Octobre 1961). I spent a diverting moment imagining a convention of international bureaucrats gathered to debate the color of the international rubber stamp. But I looked on the bright side. Because Russia had signed the agreement, I wouldn't have to send our documents to Russian consulates for further verification.

My friend Marc claims that things are either easy or impossible. Whether my grunt-work skill set had improved with practice or it was just meant to be, I'll never know, but I powered through the document-collection phase in record time. It helped that when compiling the Chinese dossier I had ordered extra copies of our vital documents, and we were fortunate that the most time-consuming items, the home study and the troublesome INS clearance, simply needed to be amended to reflect our new destination.

I called Betty and asked how long it would take to get a home study for Russia.

"Does Duke speak Russian too?" the social worker asked.

"He does," I said. He studied it in college, and after watching Baby's audition tape, Duke purchased a box of one thousand Russian/English flash cards, which he reviewed while he was watching late-night sumo wrestling.

"Then it's just a matter of pulling your old home study up on the computer and replacing *China* with *Russia*," Betty said. I faxed her the list of supporting letters we needed, and she had all the documents notarized and ready the following day. I took Clara with me when I went to pick them up. "Are you excited you're getting a little brother?" Betty asked her. Clara remembered a pressing engagement and nearly yanked my arm out of its socket tugging me toward the door.

Even the Immigration and Naturalization Service was cooperative. It didn't hurt that the new person in charge remembered Senator Dianne Feinstein's intervention on our behalf. Overnight, we received Form I-824: Request for Action of an Existing Petition. I filled it out and messengered it back, along with a check and a copy of our revised home study. In three days, I had our revised INS approval in hand.

Suddenly, I was feeling in control, always a mistake in an international adoption. Pumping with adrenaline, I dispatched a traveling notary to our doctors, to our accountant, to Duke's employer. By the first week in January our Russian dossier was assembled. I dragged Duke away from his Russian flash cards and force-marched him to Christopher, the surfer notary. Duke signed his name, then disappeared to look at CDs at the record shop next door. Meanwhile, I watched carefully as Christopher notarized twenty documents for a heavily discounted fee. He debated whether it was necessary to attach the California all-purpose notary form. I lobbied for it, but he didn't have enough on hand. "You'll be fine without it," Christopher said.

Duke and I were so grateful we gave him a bottle of quite good champagne.

Being a woman on a mission, when it became apparent that I was exhibiting distinct signs of flu, I ignored them. I called the notary division of the secretary of state's office, in Sacramento, to inquire how long it would take to get our documents apostilled. After an hour on hold, listening to a synthesized voice tell me that they realized my time was valuable (then hire more operators!), I reached a human being, who revealed that mail-order apostilles took four weeks. But if I brought them into the office, they would do them on the spot. A bonus: Doing so, I would not have to make the one-hour drive to a remote county office for certification. I immediately bought a round-trip ticket and figured I'd fly up and back for the day. Clara wanted to come along, but as much as I would have enjoyed her company, I passed.

Tiff called right before I left for the airport. The document list had expanded. "We need something stating the market value of your house," she said. She suggested a notarized real estate appraisal. I had one in my files from when we refinanced, but that was three years old, and the Nigdyetsk government wanted something up to date. It would cost several hundred dollars to have the house reappraised, and it would take a couple of weeks. Meanwhile, Baby was lying in his crib, cooling his heels. "A notarized letter from the company that issues your homeowner's insurance would work," said Tiff.

I called the insurance company. I spent forty minutes on hold, again being assured my call was important. Not that important, because before someone could pick up the phone, I was disconnected. I called again. An hour later, I finally heard a human voice. "Nobody else has asked for a notarized letter," it said. I asked for a supervisor and waited another twenty minutes. But in exchange for my efforts, a notarized letter was ready the following day. I faxed it to Kinderama.

Five minutes later, Tiff called. "Olga says an insurance letter isn't good enough," she said. I wanted to tap her gently with the bumper of my automobile. But I stayed calm. Duke suggested a certified copy of our property-tax bill. I faxed it to Tiff. "That will be okay," she said. I dashed over to Christopher's shop and had it notarized.

No sooner had I returned home than Tiffany called again. "I checked with Olga, and the property-tax bill won't work," she said. This time I visualized her squirming under the wheels of my car, but again I remained obliging.

"Olga now feels the best thing is a notarized letter from your home-study agency stating the market value of your house," Tiff said. It was preposterous, getting a real estate valuation from a social worker, but I faxed a copy of what we needed to Betty. Meanwhile, Tiff told me to send a certified check for the bulk of the foreign fee. (The balance had to be hand-carried to Russia in new hundred-dollar bills.)

Why they needed a certified check when the agency had certified copies of all our bank accounts was beyond me. We weren't leaving for a month. There was plenty of time for a personal check to clear. But again, I didn't want to argue. A child's life was at stake. "Will you please send me a receipt?" I asked. I had yet to receive a receipt for the agency fee we'd paid three months ago. In that case, I paid by personal check, so at least I had a record for our accountant.

"We don't do receipts," Tiff said.

Maybe I was being paranoid. But I couldn't send a hefty certified check to a person with a track record for losing documents when she wouldn't give me a receipt. Tiff referred me to her supervisor. The supervisor said, "Nobody else wants a receipt."

"Forgive me," I said. "My accountant is fussy."

"We can't send you a receipt when we receive the check because we won't know if it's any good."

"But it's certified," I argued. "That means it's good."

"We can't be sure, so we can't give receipts," the supervisor said.

"You must get a lot of bounced checks," I said.

"Why would you think that?" the supervisor asked.

I felt like Alice talking to the Queen of Hearts.

As predicted, Betty was not crazy about vouching for the market value of our home, real estate appraisal not being a prerequisite to a master's in social work. "Nobody has ever asked me to do this," she grumbled, but bless her heart, she did it anyway.

I made reservations to fly to Sacramento the following day. Again Tiff stopped me in my tracks. Wouldn't you know it, she had sent me the old version of the boilerplate Letter of Intent to Adopt. The only difference between the old one and the new one was that the address was flush right instead of centered and a sentence had been changed from "We, the adopting parents . . ." to "The adopting mother and father . . ."

"You can't get the child without the right letter," Tiffany said.

I typed up a new version, dragged Duke over to Christopher's, where I supervised the notary and my husband wandered next door and bought three more compact discs. When I got home, I discovered a fax from Tiffany—the latest version of another boilerplate letter, Home Study Agency's Agreement to Do Post Placement Reports. This one contained an entire sentence that wasn't in the original. I faxed the letter we had to Tiffany.

"You'll have to redo it," she said.

Betty was not exhilarated to receive yet another request from me, but she drew up a new letter and had it notarized. "This is the last one," she warned. By now, the stack of adoption documents was up to my knees and my flu had advanced from discreet symptoms to the full-blown thing. I warned Tiffany that I would not make two trips to the Sacramento statehouse. "You're all set," she said.

Woozy from Contac, I flew to Sacramento clutching a briefcase with forty-two notarized documents inside. I was afraid to let the briefcase out of my sight. The folks in the notary division promised I'd be out in a couple of hours so I could make my return flight. I tried not to scowl at all the rolls of gold stickers lying about, for which I would have to write a four-figure check. I curled up in a chair, took out a book, and waited. An hour passed. Suddenly, I heard my name being called. Dirk, the assistant head notary, said, "There's a problem with some of these documents." He explained that Christopher, our surfer notary, forgot to write the phrase "as sworn by" on all of the twenty-two documents he validated.

"So write it in," I said.

"We can't apostille a document with inappropriate notarial wording," Dirk said gravely. (In some countries this could be easily dealt with by handing over a wad of the appropriate denomination. But not in the offices of the state of California.)

"I'm going to kill Christopher," I said. "I'll be tried in Los Angeles. Nobody gets convicted in Los Angeles."

Dirk hastily offered an alternative. He instructed me to take the improperly notarized documents to a Sacramento notary and ask them to attach another affidavit, known in notary public parlance as a jurat. I was wary, since Duke's notarized signature was on the offending documents too, but Dirk assured me that all I was doing was adding another layer of rubber stamping to the documents so they could be apostilled. I asked if I could get my four-figure fee back if it was unacceptable.

"Oh, I don't think we can do that," Dirk said. I didn't even want to think about how much a strange notary would charge to validate twenty-two documents.

Here's what mystifies me about bureaucracies. Coughing and sneezing, I wandered around downtown Sacramento until I located a credit union with a sympathetic notary. I handed over twenty-two exquisitely typed documents on heavy bond paper, signed by Duke and me and notarized with an artistic flourish by the errant Christopher. The credit union notary removed a stack of flimsy paper out of the copy machine, instructed me to write an explanatory sentence to describe each document—not a specific, impressively legalistic sentence, just a casual statement like, "This is a power of attorney." He made me raise my right hand and swear an oath: "Do you affirm that the statements in this document are true?"

"Yes, yes," I said, and resumed scribbling.

The credit union notary slapped a purple rubber stamp with the magic notary words underneath my signature. We did this twenty-two times with the speed of an efficient assembly line. I was frantically trying to write sentences that would be acceptable to the Russian government, desperate to get back to the notary public's office in time to get the documents finished in time to make my plane. My handwriting, which is usually a credit to Miss Greenspun, my second-grade teacher, began to resemble Duke's writing, which looks a lot like an electrocardiogram and requires about as much experience to read. The end result was a set of the most unofficial-looking documents imaginable, ones that would raise my eyebrows if I was scrutinizing a foreign dossier. But incredibly, the secretary of state gave it the gold stamp of approval and no one from here to Siberia had a problem. Even more miraculous, the credit union notary public only charged me ten dollars for twenty-two jurats. "Think of it as a baby gift," he said, and I almost cried.

Two hours later, I was on the United shuttle, homeward bound with our finished dossier and a copy of the *Notary Public Handbook,* which the secretary of state's office pointedly told me to give to Christopher. I stopped at home to get the pugs. Clara was incensed that I had left her at home and had left me a steaming present in my bathroom. I cleaned it up and walked the pugs over to Christopher's. Brandishing the copy of the handbook, I told him that all our documents had been notarized incorrectly. He responded as only a man would. He said, "The secretary of state's office is wrong." I avoided reminding him that the secretary of state's signature appears on his license.

"I seriously doubt that," I said. Christopher must have reconsidered because he let me make free copies of our dossier on his machine. Then he packed it all in a giant carton and sent it off to Tiffany.

An hour after my FedEx tracking software confirmed the dossier had arrived, she called. I expected good news, positive feedback even for putting the dossier together in under three weeks. "There's a problem with your home-study agency license," she said.

Our home-study agency has a stellar reputation. It was unlikely. "What's wrong?" I asked.

"There's no expiration date."

"You didn't ask for an expiration date," I said. "You asked for the license."

"We need an expiration date," Tiff said, "or you can't have the child."

I hung up and called Betty. When she heard it was me, she said, "What now?" I explained the problem.

"There is no expiration date on California licenses," Betty said. "They're good until we screw up."

I hung up and called Tiffany back. She said, "We need an expiration date."

"But there is none."

"Then you can't get the baby," she said.

I felt like I was being held hostage. Forgive me, Baby, I snapped. "Keep him." I sighed. I was tired of being threatened with the removal of Baby, who for all I knew could be the video equivalent of the photo of the cute girl with the sixties flip that used to come in wallets. "How do I even know he exists?"

Tiffany said, "You've seen the video."

"I've seen *The Lion King* too," I said, "but that doesn't mean I believe that animals are dancing in the forest." Then I burst into tears. I was sick, I was tired, I had just learned my father had had a heart attack in Spain. The stress was wearing me down. Tiff seemed to understand.

Betty faxed Tiffany a notarized letter explaining agency-licensing policy.

Tiffany said, "I think that's okay, but I have to check." She promised to get back to me by the end of the day.

I went to the office to escape. Pierre, the day care pug, was visiting, and I greeted him joyously, as did Clara. Sophie was lounging on her blue armchair ripping the pig's ear to shreds. Pierre came in and nuzzled her. Sophie let forth a fierce guttural roar, and her suitor fled. Clara ran after him crying, "Please come back, darling. I'll never be mean to you. Pierre, come back."

A minute later, Marta cried out for help. "The pug is not bright," she said. She pointed out the window where the lovesick Pierre was standing on the ledge, looking down twenty feet at the traffic. Clara begged him to reconsider. "Sophie isn't worth it," she said. "If it were me, I could understand . . ."

A memory popped into my mind. When Duke and I were dating, I brought Bess and Stella to stay overnight at his fifth-floor apartment, the Sty in the Sky. I took a shower and Bess wandered out on the ledge. Duke told me he turned pale and prayed he could talk her back in. I like to think I would have married him even if he had been unsuccessful.

We offered Pierre a bagel, and he decided to live.

I came home feeling almost cheerful. Then the phone rang and a voice identified himself as "Kinderama's legal counsel," hereafter "Esquire." He was calling because he had heard we didn't want to go through with the adoption.

"Huh?" I said. "Who told you that?"

"Tiffany."

I couldn't believe she had taken me seriously. Of course, we wanted Baby. For the second time that day, I apologized for getting upset.

Then, to my stupefaction, Esquire accused me of harassing poor Tiffany, of calling her many times each day.

"What choice do I have?" I asked. "Tiffany calls and tells me she needs a document. I have to call the home-study agency and see if I can get it. Then I have to call Tiffany back and tell her what documentation the home-study agency can supply. Tiffany never knows if it's acceptable and has to check. So then I have to talk to her again."

"If you can't handle paperwork, how do you expect to handle a child?" Esquire asked.

I couldn't believe I was having this conversation. I pointed out that since I had previously prepared a Chinese dossier for their agency without any difficulty, then maybe the problem did not entirely lie with me.

Esquire tried another angle. "None of the other families are demanding a receipt."

This has to be a first, I thought. A lawyer complaining because you want legal documentation. I said, "Imagine you had a client who was buying a house in Russia solely on the basis of a video sent by a Russian real estate agent whom she doesn't know. The agent loses key documents and sends your client outdated escrow papers. Then the real estate agent asks your client to pay for the house with a certified check and refuses to give her a receipt. What would you advise your client to do?"

Esquire considered this. He said, "I know what your problem is. You're expecting normal business practices, but they don't apply here."

I avoided going through this door and instead tried to focus on the problems at hand. "The IRS has just passed a tax credit for adopting families," I said patiently. "My accountant will need a receipt."

Esquire promised that if I was audited, he would make sure I had adequate documentation. (I wouldn't hold my breath.) He warned me not to call Tiffany; he would let me know if Betty's letter explaining the nonexistent home-study agency expiration date was satisfactory. I thought the matter was settled.

The next morning Betty called. "What the hell is going on?" she asked in a very un–social worker voice. I learned that Esquire had called her boss and reported me for harassing poor Tiffany. Esquire also demanded to know why Betty had certified such a high-anxiety type to parent a child.

"This has never happened to me in twenty years of social work," Betty sputtered indignantly. "We never hear from legal counsel unless a parent has gone to jail."

I was touched to hear that Betty had defended me valiantly. She was able to attest to the endless paperwork snafus, since I had called her a dozen times to redo documents. Betty suggested to Esquire that Tiffany call her directly if she needed anything. "There's no way you can answer the questions she has," Betty said, and I felt a little better. She promised to let me know as soon as she heard if the letter explaining their expiration date was okay.

Duke and I drove to San Francisco for the weekend. I left

Sophie and Clara with Blanche. She wasn't home, but her daughter let me go outside to see the new puppies. I watched them posing on stumps, running around the tennis court, barreling through the dog door—*thwack, thwack, thwack.* I thought: "Why am I complicating my life? I should just buy another pug." To hell with the skimpy Russian medical records, the complete absence of information about Baby's background. With a new pug I'd get a four-page genealogical chart. I know Clara's mother was Cubby Bear, her dad, Moon-shadow Elwood Blues. Sophie's mother was Phoebe, her father Champion Flarepath Rupert of Rowann. At no point did Phoebe's lawyer or Cubby's lawyer call and suggest that I was mentally unstable. And both breeders took my check.

On the way back from San Francisco, Duke suggested that we take a half-hour detour to pick the girls up early. "I miss them," Duke said. "They're so self-absorbed."

Sophie and Clara were sharing a big cage. Sophie was so pleased to see us she jumped into the car voluntarily and threw up. Clara was wildly affectionate for half an hour, then once she was certain she was not going back, she gave me the cold shoulder.

The next morning, Betty checked in. Her letter had been rejected. Kinderama insisted on a notarized letter from a state official, and the California Department of Social Services wouldn't comply. I couldn't believe poor Baby was trapped in a Siberian orphanage because of an expiration date that didn't exist. "I've put in a call to the Community Care Licensing Bureau," Betty said, "but I don't have a lot of hope." She recommended another adoption agency in Northern California with a good Russian program. I passed. It was Baby or . . .

"How would you feel about a fawn puppy?" I asked Duke. He remembered how funny it was when the fawn Stella lay between the black Sophie and Clara. He used to call it the Pug Flag.

"I'd prefer a border collie," he said.

January came and went. Esquire never got back to me, and he didn't return my calls. I didn't know if our dossier was in Russia. I was more depressed than I have ever been in my life, including the bout with cancer.

Then, out of the blue, Betty called triumphantly. A woman in the state Licensing Department took pity on us and sent a notarized letter explaining California's policy on expiration dates. My friend in Sacramento apostilled it and FedExed it straight to Tiffany.

Two days later Tiff faxed applications for our Russian visas along with a cheery note with smiley faces. I ignored Esquire and called her. Tiffany acted like nothing untoward had happened. She even had good news. The bulk of our dossier went with Olga to Nigdyetsk. It was translated, and our documents were in official hands. The final piece of paper would be hand-carried by another adopting family. If all went well, we could rescue Baby in late February.

"Baby Gap, here I come," I said.

"Don't buy anything yet," Tiff cautioned, "until you have an official court date. A Russian family could still adopt him." (In fact, this had just happened to a woman I knew on-line, who was in the same program.) In the meantime, Tiffany needed a certified check.

I sent a personal one. Tiffany charitably ignored my uncooperative attitude and even sent me a receipt.

Ready, Set . . .

$\mathcal{F}$or a year, Duke and I had kept our families out of the loop because neither handles uncertainty well and international adoption is nothing but vicissitudinous. Our original plan was to break the news when we had an official travel date, but my father-in-law, Earl, forced the issue. Scheduled for cataract surgery in late February, he wanted Duke to come up to Santa Barbara and drive him around. Would we be in Siberia at the end of February? Even by Groundhog Day, we didn't have a clue.

"I've got to tell him the truth," Duke said, "or I'm going to expire from guilt." My life would not be worth living if Mother didn't hear the news first. So I went to my phone and Duke went to his, and we let the cat out of the bag.

Mother was ecstatic, so ecstatic that at first I felt wretched for keeping her in the dark for so long. "I'm thrilled for you, darling," she said. Then she thought for a moment. "But what about Clara?"

"Clara will love having a brother."

Mother chortled. "I definitely think Clara would be happier if you sent her to live with me in Manhattan." Mother's miniature poodle was seventeen—and as she put it, "He's alive, but not for long." On her last visit to Los Angeles, she asked me to drive her out to the remote desert suburb of Antelope Valley to look at a possible replacement, a petit basset griffon vendeen (known as a PBGV). "Mary Tyler Moore has one," Mother said. That wasn't sufficient incentive for me to embark on what would be at least a three-hour expedition in rush-hour traffic, humming "You're Going to Make It After All," so I called around and located a PBGV puppy in Venice whose owner was willing to let us come visit. Mother and I walked through the gate and were greeted by a bizarre, vaguely insectlike hound with a swishy fishtail gait. "Most disgusting dog I've ever seen," Mother said, then turned on her heels and left. As far as I knew, she was still shopping.

"Forget it," I said. "I'm not giving you Clara."

"We'll talk about it later," she said ominously. Then she asked what we planned to name our son.

"Nicholas," I said.

"You should call him Harry, after my father."

"It's Nicholas," I said.

"I can't wait to meet my grandson Harry," Mother said, and hung up.

An hour later, she called back. "So when is Harry coming?"

"He's not coming. We're going. As soon as we get a court date," I said. "And his name is Nicholas." I explained that we couldn't name him Harry, even if we wanted to, because Duke's father's middle name was Harry. It violates an ancient Jewish tradition to name a baby after someone who is alive.

"Whatever," Mother said and hung up. She called back ten minutes later. "When did you say you were leaving to pick up Harry?" She believes if she asks me the same question enough times, eventually she'll get the answer she wants.

Duke's parents, who adore grandchildren, were overjoyed by the news, though they worried what the pugs would make of it. They generously offered to pay our expenses while we were in Russia, even though they too weren't crazy about our choice of name. They preferred Baby's Russian name, Igor. Though it was good enough for Stravinsky, we feared it would guarantee him a childhood filled with taunting *Young Frankenstein* imitations in American school yards.

"When are you going to pick up Igor?" Earl asked daily. He was holding up a special edition of the family newsletter until we had a firm court date.

"I don't know," I said.

"When are you going to get Harry?" asked Mother.

"I don't know." I sighed. It was turning into my mantra.

(Duke said that if he heard one more question about Harry, he was naming the child Orenthal James. Questions about Harry ceased with gratifying speed.)

Once our parents knew, word spread rapidly. "Wouldn't you rather go to Germany and get a BMW?" asked Jon, looking after Clara's interests. "You could name it Bismarck."

"The little princess is not going to like the competition," Laurie warned. She sent a book of Russian fairy tales and suggested I read them to Clara to prepare her for the shock.

My brother, Bobby, asked if we were aware that our lives and the pugs' lives would change forever. The thought had occurred to us. He asked if we wanted to talk to a friend of his who had adopted a Russian baby and had had nothing but trouble ever since. "No, thank you," I said. (I think he was just trying to get even with me for questioning his ability to parent his pug, Buster.)

"You better look out. The damn dog is going to be jealous," cautioned Grandma, who wanted to know if the baby was Jewish and circumcised. "He will be," I assured her. I had already had a conference with a *mohel* who had his own Web site. (No, the address was not http://www.snip.com, but close enough.) "The pug is Jewish too," I teased. "I took her to the Mikvah."

Valentine's Day came and went. I walked a tightrope, trying to act as if things would work out without taking any action that involved a serious outlay of cash, in case our plans were derailed. Our friends Diane and Eliot gave us a crash course in infant care using their son, Adam, born one week later than Nicholas, as the model. They demonstrated the mechanics of bathing, feeding, diaper-changing, and bottle mixing with grave seriousness, like they were running through the sequence for launching a nuclear weapon. But I was secretly amused. Baby care was exactly like pug care, without the flea comb. Eliot lent me a baby catalog called The Right Stuff. I swear that if you programmed a computer to replace the word *baby* with the word *pet* in its ad copy, the result would be almost identical to In the Company of Dogs's copy. The merchandise was similarly divided: waste-disposal systems (Diaper Genie versus Doggie Dooley), bath aids, safety gates, and toys that make annoying noises "for maximum stimulation."

I firmed up our travel plans. Duke, who loves globes, knew the simplest way to get to Siberia was to purchase a round-the-world ticket and fly over the Pacific, pick up the baby in Nigdyetsk, continue on to Moscow, where we had to get our son's visa from the American Embassy, then fly over the Atlantic home. Geographically speaking, he was correct, but there were other factors involved. Kinderama wanted us to spend a few days in Moscow before we picked up the baby— getting over jet lag and setting up appointments. Also, the only carrier that made the global loop was Aeroflot, an airline that was still going through post-Soviet modernization. Every travel agent I spoke to—and I spoke to at least six—told me it would be more comfortable, safer, and cheaper to fly from Los Angeles to Moscow on a known carrier.

My husband blanched at the idea of flying across Russia twice. "It's a long damn way," he said. "It's nine thousand miles round trip."

"We'll save a lot of money," I argued. I had enough frequent-flyer miles on Delta for either two free coach tickets or two business-class upgrades. If ever there was an occasion to upgrade, this seemed like it. But Duke, yearning for circumnavigation, hung on to his loop like a dog to a sock. He went on the Web and located a travel agent who could issue a round-the-world ticket. I called her. She said, "You know, it's half the price if you fly through Moscow."

I suspected that my husband had projected all his adoption anxiety onto our itinerary. Fortuitously, my childhood friend Melinda, who had lived across the street from me in Baltimore for most of the time we were growing up, proposed a surefire way to override his objections. Melinda offered to donate however many miles we needed to fly business class to Moscow for free. "I've got millions of miles, and I'm never going to use them," she said, "and I'm a strong believer that children should not sit in coach." Her act of kindness moved us to tears. Ever practical, Melinda urged me to call Delta and make reservations. "You can always cancel them," she said sagely.

By Presidents Day, I managed to stay calm only because Mother generously took it upon herself to manifest the strain of uncertainty for us both. I could tell it was driving her nuts because I didn't hear from her for a week. When I checked in, she explained that she was trying not to put any pressure on me (a first), but my worst suspicions were confirmed when she casually let slip, "I'm looking around New York for a baby, and as soon as I find one, I'm going to send it to you."

I was flummoxed. "You can't send me a baby." Though maybe she could. Once on my birthday Mother FedExed a large, whole smoked fish from Barney Greengrass.

"Don't tell me what I can do," Mother said. "There will be a knock on the door, and boy, will you be surprised."

Indeed I would be, I thought with horror. "Mother," I said quietly, "where are you going to get a baby?"

"I know lots of people," she said.

I imagined John and Carolyn Bessette-Kennedy being trailed by my mother in her Town Car.

At Duke's suggestion, I sent her a copy of Baby's audition tape. Mother instantly called off her search, but having seen her future grandson, she became frantic to outfit him in Ralph Lauren infantware. "When are you going to get him?" she pressed. "It's not healthy for him to be stuck in an orphanage without any stimulation." It didn't help matters that around this time *Newsday* ran a terrifying three-part feature about all the hazards of adopting from Russia: attachment disorder, fetal alcohol syndrome, hepatitis, you name it. (Thank God we were too early for the story about the couple who allegedly beat their new children on the plane ride back from Moscow.)

I broke down and called Tiffany. She was out to lunch, but Petrova, her associate, took my call. Petrova had just talked to Olga. Baby was doing just fine. No, we didn't have a court date yet, but Olga wanted us in Nigdyetsk in two weeks.

Two weeks? We had no nursery, no baby clothes, no baby gear, no warm clothes.

"Don't worry about the court date," Petrova said. "Just get ready to go."

It was as if I were pregnant and my water broke. I threw

Clara into the car and dashed to the baby-boom-echo shrine, Baby Gap, where I finally bought the teensy denim overalls that I'd been coveting for months. I called Melinda and gave her the travel dates. She promised to transfer the miles to our frequent-flyer accountants. She had trouble doing so, so she simply sent us two round-trip business-class tickets to Moscow, for which we will be eternally grateful.

Duke, who under the best of circumstances is off the radar screen during vacation preparations, accelerated his moviegoing and Web-surfing schedule. Like a duck, he swam around the bottom of the Pond Denial, surfacing only to quack boisterously about something completely inconsequential. "Our old stereo speakers are crackling, popping, and buzzing and must be replaced immediately," he announced one night at dinner. (Like I was in the mood to invest in a sub woofer.) If I gave him a specific assignment, for instance, "Get a heavy jacket," he airily responded, "Maybe I'll rent one," and left me to sort out the details.

It seemed improbable that a three-week parka-rental fee was cheaper than buying one, especially when you considered that the renter would be handling a tiny baby who in his audition tape showed a gift for spitting up. I called Marian, an avid skier, to check. She didn't have a clue, so she asked her husband, Mark, the best-dressed skier on any slope. "I've never heard of a place that rents parkas," he said.

However, our forthcoming adoption inspired the most heartwarming acts of kindness. Marian called back the next day, somewhat incredulous. Her husband, without any prodding, had gone through his extensive ski wardrobe and sent Duke a state-of-the-art jacket with a zip-in liner. Never particularly gracious, my husband remained skeptical until he opened the package and saw that the parka was black with no designer labels that would brand him as an American. Then he looked at me and smiled. "It's astonishing how these things just manifest themselves," he said. I caught a flash of his orange webbed feet as he dove back down to the bottom of the pond. "Do you want to go to a woman's basketball game downtown?" he asked.

I couldn't. I was busy remodeling.

Our house is less than twelve hundred square feet. Technically, we have three bedrooms, but we sleep in one and the other two are his and hers studies, with floor-to-ceiling bookshelves—an earthquake hazard, since we have no place to relocate all the books. We decided to put Baby in the tiny laundry room off our bedroom. The stacked washer and dryer were set in a recessed corner and couldn't be moved, but we figured the child would generate more than his share of dirty clothes.

For years, the laundry room had doubled as my dollhouse workshop, and it looked like the "Before" picture in an ad for a baby-proofing service. I spent two days clearing out potential hazards: paints, glues, nails, screws, packets of seeds, scraps of old linoleum, a Dustbuster, electric drill, cleaning products, X-Acto knives. Everything toxic I moved to an outside shed. When the room was finally empty, Duke, the high-profile guy, sealed a door leading to the porch so Baby couldn't escape. (I didn't see how an infant could unlock a deadbolt seven feet off the ground, but Betty had insisted it was a necessary precaution.) By the end of the weekend we beheld the miraculous: an Empty Room.

That was when Clara sensed disaster and dragged her faux leopard-skin bed from my office into our bedroom. Her worst suspicions were instantly confirmed when I lacked the will to resist.

I'd always been strict about my pugs' sleeping arrangements. Even when I lived alone and hadn't slept with a warm body for six months, I refused to allow Bess and Stella to share my bed. Even the most pampered pugs occasionally harbor fleas, snore, and shed. In fact, in the course of any given evening one pug releases enough hair to create a whole new pug, and they have a repertoire of sleep-disturbing behavior including pathetic whimpering, liquid sucking sounds, and the relentless shuffling and clawing of nails across the wood floors, which Duke once called "irritating almost beyond comprehension." Bess and Stella were content to curl up in a wicker basket in the corner of my study.

There they snoozed until the psychic end of their lives, which I define as the day Sophie arrived. At the time, my study was carpeted—not the optimum decorator choice for a puppy as diffident about housebreaking as Sophie—and for lack of a better option I moved Bess and Stella into the bedroom and Sophie into the adjacent bathroom. As mentioned, Sophie escaped each morning to waken me at dawn. "You just have to hit the snooze button when she does that," said Duke. I later learned he shook Sophie briefly for a snooze-alarm effect.

For a time, Clara shared the bathroom with Sophie. The pragmatic pug realized that waking me wasn't in her best interest and instead waited until we fell asleep, then snuck under the puppy gate, jumped on the bed, and crawled under the covers between us. Invariably, in the middle of the night, Sophie noticed her sister was missing and howled to join the party. Within a month I was tired, confused, and uncharacteristically depressed. I consulted Pangloss. After a few probing questions, he diagnosed sleep deprivation and asked me what was keeping me up. I explained about the pugs.

"Why don't you move them into another room?"

"Really?" I stammered. "You mean I can?"

"Sure," said Pangloss. "You are the dominant species."

Having been granted permission, I went to Dog Stars, the snooty pet store on Main Street, and reluctantly purchased two Sky Kennels so large that side by side they were about the size of our bathroom. The owner of the store was torn between her desire to sell the big-ticket items and her smug conviction that if I really loved Sophie and Clara, I would buy them their own double bed with duvet. "Sweetie never wakes me up," she informed me. Sweetie, a teacup poodle, also wore a bikini to the beach in the summer, so I didn't think she was a good role model.

My husband was horrified when he saw the new arrangement. "They're not lab animals, they're pets," he said.

"Crates provide a sense of security."

"Clara doesn't have a self-esteem issue."

"Trust me," I said. "They'll love it."

Sophie did like her cage, but Clara resisted incarceration every night for a year. I threw in the towel and offered the pugs a compromise. If they agreed to sleep in my study—we'd pulled up the carpets and refinished the wood floors so it was safe—I'd buy them each a faux leopard-skin bed and junk the crates. It wasn't Clara's first choice, but she accepted it. She'd lie on Duke's lap at night watching the eleven o'clock news. Afterward, he said, "Clara, go to bed," and she hopped off the sofa and ran into her bedroom.

If someday it should happen that my sanity is questioned, no doubt the prosecutor will bring up the fact that I spent more time agonizing over my dog's sleeping arrangements than I ever did preparing my baby's nursery. Mother, far more enthusiastic than I, sent catalogs with pictures of snazzy Italian cribs, with names like Gianni and Maria. She dispatched me on fact-finding missions to fancy baby-furniture stores to inspect changing tables that cost more than our dining room table. Usually, I can make a design decision in a minute flat, but purchasing a crib, with all its implications, sent me into a tailspin. I postponed the nursery-furniture acquisition and focused on a task less emotionally charged.

Clara's insecurity mounted the next day, when we visited her least favorite store on the planet, Ingrid's Fur Boutique, in Beverly Hills. Ingrid, an Angela Lansbury look-alike whose features seem to have been locked in place with sutures or epoxy hair spray, is the only daughter in a long line of furriers. Her brothers in Minnesota send her their traded-in minks, nutrias, and sables, and she passes them on to Southern Californians at discounted prices. Her tiny coat-crammed shop looks like a hunting lodge.

The pug trotted inside with her usual insouciance, looked around, then froze in the paws-locked position that she only assumes when she's in the vicinity of an escalator. "What a glossy coat," Ingrid said with a sigh, professional appraisal in her voice. Clara trembled. I set the pug on the chair. She sniffed the mink cushion and scrambled for the exit. "Stay," I ordered, and she sat, shaking.

I had gone to Ingrid to see if she could salvage my mink coat. I have no guilt about owning this fur. My mother gave me the coat five years ago, right before I got Clara, when I went to the hospital for a mastectomy and breast reconstruction. Mother thought the full-length mink would cheer me up, which in a funny way it did. After I recovered, I went to New York with Clara and the mink. A longtime vegetarian, I felt squeamish about wearing it, but the weather turned nasty. The only other wrap I owned was a black satin baseball jacket em-

blazoned with the insignia of the Baltimore Orioles, my hometown team. I wore that first. After the third Yankee fan snickered, "How dare you wear that jacket in this town?" I figured,
"As long as I'm going to be hassled, I might as well be warm."

The mink, which originally belonged to an elderly relative
now dead, was very warm, but alas, it was fifty years old and
molting, and each time I wore it I'd hear an ominous ripping
sound and had to call the hotel concierge to send up brown
thread. I was hoping it could be repaired for the trip to Siberia.

Ingrid made a face, not an easy thing to do with immobile
facial features. "Honey, the coat's dead," she said flatly. "Do
us both a favor. Buy a new one."

Clara's eyes widened in horror as Ingrid draped me in
swing coats, princess coats, blanket coats, jackets, each with
its previous owner's name embroidered in the lining. None
took my breath away, probably because I was already hyperventilating from fear of impending motherhood, but Ingrid
kept pressing. Finally, the mailman came to the door. Clara
seized the opportunity and fled. "I'll think it over," I called out
as I tore after her.

Back at home, I downloaded a packing list from the Families with Children from Russia and the Ukraine Web site
(http://www.frua.org/index.html). It stopped my heart: pow-
dered formula (three cans a week), disposable bottles, drop-in
plastic bags that fit in the disposable bottles, an assortment of
nipples (who knew what kind the baby was used to?), baby
wipes, bibs, body suits known as onesies, hooded towels, un-
dershirts, sleepers, outfits, snowsuit, hats (this would prove
crucial), powder, baby shampoo, baby soap, manicuring scis-
sors, toys, diapers (the Web site advised that I figure on using
fifteen a day), and medical supplies.

There I got lucky. I made an appointment with a pediatrician, Dr. Vicki, whom I chose only because she happened to be on our insurance plan and her office was close to our house. (By contrast, Dr. Sheckl, our vet, was selected solely for proximity.) Choosing a pediatrician turned out to be the only easy part of adopting. When I asked about medical supplies, she stood up and said, "Follow me." Dr. Vicki walked into a storeroom, opened a cupboard, and like she was rewarding a trick-or-treater, filled a bag with samples of baby acetaminophen, antibiotics, topical-rash ointments, Neosporin, lice-killing shampoo, Vaseline, medicine droppers, decongestants, oral-rehydration liquid, and fungal creams.

Sadly, I was shut out of the only part of the shopping experience that I was looking forward to—buying baby clothes. It's hopeless to search for garments appropriate for a Siberian winter in Los Angeles, so I called Mother for help. "How big is the baby?" she asked.

"I'm not sure," I said. The measurements I had were six weeks old. Tiffany told me to buy everything in the twelve-months size, just to be on the safe side.

"I hate when people say practical things like that," Mother said. "You have to know exactly how big he is. Otherwise, his clothes won't be flattering." I took the old measurements, extrapolated using a growth chart, and told her to do her best.

Mother's best gave our UPS carrier a workout. Every day he appeared lugging cartons filled with Ralph Lauren shirts, track suits, jeans, sweaters, Italian sleepers, French sweaters, woolly hats, blankets, a down snowsuit warm enough for landing on the moon, and strict instructions from Mother as to which socks went with which outfit. I became concerned when I noticed all the clothes she sent were in three- to six-month sizes. My friend Melinda, doting aunt to two nieces, hit the sales racks and sent a cache of larger clothes and nifty inventions like Baby's First Laptop, disposable-bottle burpers, and a Boo Boo bunny.

Just when I thought I had a handle on things, Tiffany faxed a gift list. But wait. I've forgot to mention the gifts, probably because I blocked them from my mind. It was not enough that we had to transport clothes, diapers, supplies, and a staggering supply of brand-new hundred-dollar bills that I had to specially order from the bank. We were also required to bring presents—what the Russians call *pedarky*—for local officials.

Tiffany faxed me three pages of guidelines that memorably began: "These are gifts, not bribes. Gifts are part of the Russian way of doing business. With gifts, you are recognizing the status of the people you are dealing with, and showing your appreciation for the assistance they are giving you."

This is not to suggest that we were expected to bring a small token of our gratitude. There were strict rules. "Please bring a variety of gifts, not a dozen of the same item. Do not bring anything you would not like to receive yourself." And wrapping suggestions: "The best way to present the gifts is with gift bags and tissue paper, as wrapping paper may get wrinkled en route."

My eyes widened as I read the specific requirements: For upper-level officials, six gifts between thirty and fifty dollars in value. Fourteen gifts between fifteen and twenty-five dollars for lower-level officials. Gifts for the orphanage—the only present that was my pleasure to buy—a hundred dollars' worth of over-the-counter medicines, toothbrushes, developmental toys, or clothing. Two gifts between twenty-five and thirty dollars for our Moscow host and his wife, plus a twenty-dollar little something for his three-year-old son.

I was surprised they didn't register at Bloomingdale's.

"They like American designers," Tiffany added helpfully.

"Damn," I said. "I'll have to return the Chanel suit."

Some women have labor pains; I had mal-de-mall, a brain fever brought on by overexposure to the canned music and artificial lighting found in large shopping complexes. In less than a week, I bought more than I have in a lifetime of Christmases and Chanukahs. Silk scarves from the Metropolitan Museum of Art, Lancôme tote bags, Williams Sonoma tablecloths, Starbucks coffee, Calvin Klein ties. I had a revelation at Geary's, a landmark Beverly Hills gift shop. Upscale stores have a better selection of impressive-looking inexpensive gifts than downscale stores, also more impressive boxes and bags. In eight minutes, the Geary's sales consultant unloaded all the flashy items that they had overstocked for Hollywood producers' Christmas-shopping lists. I dragged home sterling silver jiggers, letter openers, business-card cases. All my girlfriends lent their shopping expertise. Debbie went with me to Beverly Hills, and in an hour we snapped up soaps from Barneys, patent-leather makeup cases emblazoned with the Saks Fifth Avenue logo, Neiman Marcus shortbread, Godiva chocolates, Tiffany key chains, and dozens of shopping bags. On a busy Saturday, Suzy braved the parking lot at the Target (though she persisted in pronouncing it like it was a French word, "Tarzhay") and helped me select masses of spring clothes for Baby's fellow orphans.

It had to be spring in Siberia for at least a week, I reasoned.

Five days before our departure, Baby was outfitted like a prince and Duke had a parka, but it looked like I was going to freeze. Duke suggested I wait and buy a fur coat in Russia, and I was so crazed I considered it. But fortunately, while returning home from yet another shopping trip to Beverly Hills, Clara and I passed a furrier who doubled as an art dealer (only in Los Angeles). Clara cowered behind a hideous iron sculpture of the Tree of Life, while David, the furrier/art dealer, gave me a choice. He could glue my mink coat together, no guarantees regarding durability, or he could sell me a fabulous new one. Looking at a mountain of expenses, I chose A. (Besides, it seemed sentimentally appropriate that a coat Mother gave me should accompany me on my mission to motherhood.)

Three days before our departure, Clara helped me conquer my baby-furniture phobia. She was the same length as the baby, and the Nursery Expediter, tired of my dithering, decided to use the pug as a model to close the sale. She popped Clara into portable cribs, cribs that turn into junior beds (what is a junior bed, anyway?), cribs with built-in bookshelves, cribs hand-carved by blind monks in the Andes. None set my heart aflutter, but Clara looked so comfy, I burst out laughing. It's impossible to laugh and panic at the same time, so I summoned up my courage and chose a copy of a simple Italian crib that was on sale, probably because it didn't have a cutesy name. I even picked a changing table after Clara obligingly lay on it on her back so I could make sure it was the right height.

"Do you want white or pine?" asked the Nursery Expediter. I froze. I was decisioned out.

I called Mother from the store. "White is too institutional," Mother said, after she ascertained that the crib did not have flat slats, which she felt would make her grandson feel like he was in jail. "See if it comes in a pickled whitewash." Pickled whitewash was back-ordered for two months, so I went with pine.

Susan, the dollhouse maven, took over from there. Used to sprucing up itsy-bitsy spaces, she cheerfully measured Baby's room, figured out the best way to arrange the furniture, and declared that what the room really needed was a quilt to hang on the wall. Clearly, I was in no condition to go quilt shopping, so the next morning, Susan appeared with a beautiful and rare hundred-year-old denim log-cabin quilt, which she gave me as a gift. She promised to hang it and decorate the nursery while we were gone. "Don't forget, you need bedding," she said when her errand of mercy was through. I placed a desperate call to my sister. Laurie made an emergency trip to Bellini and sent the most extravagant crib set on earth.

Two days before our departure, our Russian visas arrived. "You do plan to stay in the agency's Moscow apartment?" asked Tiffany. It was $170 a night, including meals and transportation. (Olga's assistant, Boris, would pick us up at the airport and chauffeur us around.) We would arrive in Moscow on a Thursday. Tiffany didn't know when we would leave for Nigdyetsk. Maybe Saturday, maybe Sunday. Once we were in Russia, it was all up to Olga.

I had made inquiries about the agency apartment. The reports were not raves. "How many other families will be in the apartment?" I asked.

"I don't know. I have to check," Tiffany said for maybe the three-thousandth time in our relationship. She put me on hold. I lost a hand of computer solitaire. Eventually she came back on the line and announced, "Two other families, maybe three."

It sounded claustrophobic. "Where is the apartment?" I asked. "Is it on the metro line?"

"I don't know," she said. I lost two games of solitaire and won one, while she checked. "An hour outside the city," she reported. "Off the metro. Do you want me to fax Boris and have him hold a room?"

"I don't know," I said. "I'll have to check."

The last thing I wanted was to be trapped in a Russian

apartment in the middle of nowhere with a bunch of anxiety-ridden fellow adopting parents. I called Duke and he agreed. Moreover, faced with a high-profile glamour problem worthy of his attention, he emerged from the bottom of the Pond Denial and sprang into action. Within hours, don't ask me how, he got himself accredited with the Russian Academy of Sciences, who arranged for us to get a special rate at the Hotel Budapest, a charming old establishment less than a kilometer from the Kremlin. The Academy even offered to pick us up at the airport. Needless to say, Duke got more positive feedback for making these arrangements than I got for orchestrating the entire adoption.

Ironically, until I told Tiffany that Duke had made other plans, Kinderama had pegged me as the more difficult partner in our marriage. In fact, they had never even spoken to Duke, or else they would have realized that he was far more subversive and spoke enough Russian to be dangerous.

. . . Go

I choked back tears as I bade good-bye to Sophie and Clara. Blanche tried to cheer me up. "Just think what a surprise they'll get when they come home," she said. "Most pugs just love babies. There were six pugs and Jennifer. The only thing they were afraid of was that Exersaucer thing that rolled around. They got their feet run over and crashed into. But don't worry. It will be fine."

"You're sure?"

Blanche chuckled wickedly. "Of course, one time my sister had a pug named Cinnamon. She was terribly spoiled."

More spoiled than Clara? As if!

"Cinnamon went everywhere with them, they did the whole number. She was the child until the child was born," Blanche continued, clearly relishing the memory. "Cinnamon would go into the nursery and poop on the rug, like the baby did it. She figured that way, the baby would be punished. The pug knew if there was poop on the rug, someone would get it. She came out with this attitude, 'I didn't do it.' It didn't work."

"So I should expect a housebreaking lapse."

"You may find little piles," Blanche conceded. "It may take a little period of adjustment, of course. But as soon as they figure out they can get attention from the baby, you won't matter anymore."

I gasped. "I'll be replaced as the object of their affections?"

"You may very well be," Blanche said. "So you see, you shouldn't worry about the pugs. You should worry about your own position."

Like there was room in my psyche for yet another reason to fret.

The crib and changing table arrived twenty-four hours before our departure. I was too busy packing to take much notice, but Lupe, our longtime housekeeper, went into paroxysms of delight and promoted herself to Nana on the spot. (I accepted instantly, lucky for my sanity.) It was Lupe who sanitized the nursery with Lysol, Lupe who bought dozens of gift bags from the *mercado del centro,* and Lupe who insisted on coming in while we were gone to help Susan, the dollhouse maven, decorate the nursery. I got saddled with the tedious last-minute details: locating our money belts, buying film, convincing Tiffany to fax a letter stating we were carrying humanitarian supplies, which I planned to use to convince Delta to waive the inevitable overweight-baggage charge. (Normally, we travel with two small bags and a carry-on, but this trip required two enormous duffel bags, two big suitcases, a tote bag, a camcorder, a computer, and a briefcase.)

"Nobody else wanted a letter," Tiff said.

It was a relief when the taxi came to take us to the airport. Delta was going to charge a couple hundred dollars for our overweight bags but relented when I produced my letter. Duke, who had paid almost no attention to my pretrip preparations, looked impressed. I collapsed in my business-class seat and didn't stir during the entire flight to Frankfurt. The stewardess waited on us hand and foot, and I was relieved to have someone look after me for a change. "It's the first time you've looked happy in weeks," Duke said, smiling.

As soon as we touched down on Russian soil, my husband turned from an attractive but immobile piece of furniture into Action Man. While I was overwhelmed by exhaustion, jet lag, culture shock, terror, and an inability to read Cyrillic, Duke swaggered through Immigration. At Customs, we had to fill out forms stating how much cash we were bringing in and list valuables like jewelry and computers. I'd heard reports from other adoptive parents that they were required to give bribes to Customs agents, but upon hearing Action Man's Russian, they waved us through. Valentina, a representative from the Ministry of Science, was waiting, sign in hand. We managed to cram all our luggage into her tiny Lada, and her driver drove us to the welcoming gates of the Hotel Budapest.

"Do you have a gift for her?" asked Duke, who heretofore had scoffed at my obsessive present-buying.

We gave Valentina a deluxe bubble-bath assortment; her driver a leather steering-wheel cover; and her boss a silk tie. Valentina was so pleased that she offered to drive us to the American Embassy the next morning. Tiffany had assured me that Boris, the agency's Moscow representative, would be honored to drive us around in exchange for his gifts and a sizable cash stipend, so we passed.

Thanks to the Russian Academy of Science connection, we were treated like dignitaries. Our room was spacious and comfortable, with fifteen-foot ceilings, CNN, a deep bathtub with plenty of hot water, and a view of a beautiful prerevolutionary building with ornate stone carvings. Once we were settled, I called Boris and his wife, Natalya, and announced our safe arrival. I was expecting a warm welcome, but Boris, who spoke at most twenty words of English, said, "You no stay here. You not my problem," which made me sort of wary.

If you're thinking of investing in Russian bonds, think twice. The lack of natural capitalist tendencies in Moscow was jolting. After we unpacked, Duke and I strolled around the city. He spied a hot dog stand. There were hot dogs. There were customers lined up for the hot dogs, but the proprietor arbitrarily decided it was time to close, and so he did.

The next morning, Friday, I made Action Man call Boris to find out what was going on. In his native tongue, Boris was oilier. He said, *"Nye valnuyetyes,"* which means, "Don't alarm yourself."

Duke asked, "When are we going to Nigdyetsk?"

Boris said, "Don't worry."

Duke asked, "When would we see him?"

Again, Boris said, "Don't worry."

Duke said, "What about our plane tickets to Nigdyetsk?" (We planned to buy the tickets through Boris because he could get us a heavily discounted fare.)

Boris said, "Don't worry."

Maybe a Zen master would stay calm. But I have not reached that high a level of consciousness.

Duke and I went to the embassy ourselves. The hotel *schveitzer,* the doorman, got us a "cab," a rusted-out white Lada with two incredibly heavyset Archie Bunker clones in the front seat. (In Moscow there are few proper cabs; you just flag down a passing car and negotiate.) I had just finished reading in the guidebook not to get in a "cab" with more than one passenger, but Duke assured me the men looked jovial.

The American Embassy resembled the personnel office of

a medium-sized company in Chicago. In fact, Russia reminded me of Chicago, only the weather was worse. When I called the embassy from Los Angeles to make sure our immigration paperwork was in order, I asked if there was anything the staff would like from the United States. "Fashion magazines" was the reply, so I brought dozens. Duke, getting into the gift-giving spirit, suggested we bring a bag of Starbucks coffee.

The embassy was mobbed with American couples trying to get visas for their newly adopted Russian children. Virtually all the couples were shepherded by agency personnel, and twice when I asked someone what line to stand in to make a visa appointment, I was told, "Your agency is supposed to handle this." Fortunately, when the head of Orphan Processing beheld the bag of mocha java, he came to my aid. "Your agency is supposed to handle this," he said, pro forma, and I shrugged helplessly.

He outlined the three-step process. First, we needed to make an appointment to get the baby's visa. This was a little tricky, since we still had no idea when we were leaving for Nigdyetsk or when we were flying back to Moscow. We had reservations to return to Los Angeles on Wednesday, March 19. We'd be in a pickle if we missed that flight because Delta had no seats available until late April. I made a visa appointment for Monday, March 17, figuring if we ran into any problems we'd have a day to sort things out. We weren't assigned a specific interview time: all visa applicants have to be at the embassy by 8:30 A.M. The head of Orphan Processing gave me a number to call if we ran into any problems.

Of course, there was another cleverly named piece of paper to fill out: Form I-600, Petition to Classify Orphan as an Immediate Relative. We had already been preapproved as suitable parents, but before we could get a visa for our son we had to provide extensive documentation that Baby was technically considered an orphan under United States immigration laws. I was warned not to leave Nigdyetsk without the orphan's original birth certificate, an amended birth certificate with our names on it, a final adoption decree, Baby's Russian passport, proof that the orphan had been unconditionally abandoned, proof that Baby had been on the Russian Data Bank for three months (giving Russian citizens a chance to claim him), and English translations of all foreign documents including a certification by the translator that he or she was qualified and that the translation was accurate.

"Where will I get these?" I asked.

"Your agency will give them to you if they're any good," he said. I must have looked skeptical because he also handed me an Agency Evaluation Sheet.

Finally, before we could bring all these papers to the embassy, we had to take Baby to an approved clinic for a medical evaluation. The embassy orphan processor suggested the Filotov Clinic, a large Russian medical complex a mile away. It was freezing outside, but I was wearing thermal silk underwear, a cotton turtleneck, a wool sweater, a jacket, fleece boots, and a full-length mink, so I didn't fuss when Duke suggested that we walk down the boulevard. (After seeing a Russian taxi, I understand the problems on the space station Mir.)

Miraculously, Duke found the sprawling Filotov Clinic. There were no signs, but Action Man noticed a well-dressed Russian woman holding the hand of a well-dressed child, asked her, and she said, "Follow me." He mentioned we were adopting, and we were directed through a maze of inside rooms until we wound up in a modern office with a modern phone. In a typically bizarre Russian arrangement, nothing was quite where it was supposed to be; Duke was told that even though we were at the clinic, we couldn't make an appointment in person; we had to call Anna, an unknown doctor's secretary. "Your agency should handle this," a receptionist said, but she let Duke use the phone. He made an appointment to come in at 7:00 A.M. on the same day as our visa interview. Anna, the appointment taker, had worked with Boris and Natalya before.

It was nice to know they existed.

We called Boris again to see when we were leaving for Nigdyetsk. He wasn't in, but Natalya said, "Maybe Sunday." Ever the indefatigable sightseers, we decided to enjoy ourselves. We visited the Kremlin (I was more astonished by the absence of tour buses than by Saint Basil's Cathedral) and took the metro (each station has a different design theme but, incredibly, hardly any advertising). At the Pushkin Museum I admired a Moroccan-themed Matisse triptych, which was casually displayed on the wall, and the collection of exceptional Van Goghs, priceless Blue Period Picassos, and Rousseaus. A museum attendant, an elderly woman, lamented the lack of funds. Her colleagues were in worse shape. One sadly reported, "They're going to close my hall."

Saturday came and went with no word from Boris. I removed a watch from his gift bag and was thinking of deleting the tablecloth earmarked for his wife. Duke and I ate Japanese noodles in the outdoor market, the Arbat (not the market where at the turn of the century pugs could be purchased for ten cents each), and bargained for stacking dolls in the shape of NBA teams—the Lakers had Shaquille, Campbell, Kersey, Jones, and Van Exel. In an underground crosswalk, we heard seven musicians play an excellent version of Vivaldi's *Four*

Seasons. Sunday, too, all was quiet on the Boris front. It was International Women's Day, and all through Moscow vendors were selling flowers for men to give their mothers, sisters, daughters, and wives. We went to the Old Moscow Circus. It was sold out, but a scalper, the only capitalist we met in the city other than the Laker-doll salesmen, asked three times the cover price. Duke pointed out that the show was about to start, and we got in for only twice the price. We saw bears gleefully riding bicycles and scooters and twirling Hula-Hoops. The bears clearly did not like the Hula-Hoop trick and were eyeing the trainer closely, waiting for the opportunity that they knew would come.

Just when I was beginning to wonder if we were adopting a child or on vacation, Boris called with news. We were leaving for Nigdyetsk on Tuesday night. But we didn't have tickets.

"Nye valnuyetyes," he said, predictably. He would pick us up at the hotel on Tuesday afternoon, buy our plane tickets, then take us to the airport. He didn't want to make two trips into Moscow, and we had to check out of the Hotel Budapest, so he suggested we spend a few hours at the apartment our agency rented to lodge adopting families. He asked if we would be staying there when we returned to Moscow.

Originally, we figured it would be helpful to be in an apartment with the baby. But that was before we learned that Duke spoke much more Russian than Boris spoke English and that our room at the Hotel Budapest had a refrigerator for storing formula. We decided to return to the hotel. We left three bags there and made reservations for three days hence. Neither of us was certain we had made the right choice.

Tuesday afternoon, Boris finally appeared. Duke gave him cash for our plane tickets and a hundred dollars for his time, along with a gift bag containing a set of place mats and napkins, a leather steering-wheel cover, and a Lakers T-shirt for his son. He didn't open the bag or thank us. We waited in his blue Skoda while he purchased one-way tickets to Nigdyetsk, on Aeroflot, business class. "You no want stay in apartment?" he said plaintively. Duke and I felt guilty, honest we did. At least for the first ten minutes of the drive out of Moscow. An hour later, Boris finally parked in front of a housing project at the edge of Moscow. We saw pine trees and birches and rolling hills and heard planes taking off.

Inside, five adults and a child were crammed in a dilapidated two-bedroom apartment with one bathroom. Two robust-looking sisters from Tennessee who were staying in another apartment came by to use the shower because they didn't have any hot water. Over lunch, we met a couple from New England who had just returned from Nigdyetsk with their new three-year-old daughter. The husband was a judge, the wife a lawyer. "I'm so glad to meet you," the lawyer said.

"Why?" I asked.

"I was sure that I was the biggest pain in the ass Tiffany ever had to deal with, but she said no, you were."

I was flattered.

Four people flew with us to Nigdyetsk: the married couple, Ginny and Joey from Tennessee, and the hardy sisters, Midge and Karen. Midge had already gone to Nigdyetsk the previous November planning to adopt a daughter, but when she got there the child was in poor health. She chose another child and returned to the United States while Olga sorted out the formalities. Before I would make two trips to Siberia in winter, I'd commit myself, but the outdoorsy and intrepid Midge behaved as if she were returning to a lush resort in St. Barts. Her easygoing sister, Karen, a vision in L. L. Bean active wear, was not adopting, but she had come along to give Midge moral support.

Ginny, a perky blonde with a thick Southern drawl, had never been out of the country before. She confided that she had brought along an illuminated makeup mirror and a chart of what she planned to wear every day. Her good-natured husband, Joey, a sales closer at a Ford dealership, sensibly glommed on to my husband the minute he realized that Duke spoke Russian. All the Tennessee contingent had used an agency other than Kinderama. Olga, I learned, coordinated adoptions for both agencies.

"Ah just love my agency to death," Ginny drawled on the way to the airport. "Ah don't see why y'all had any trouble." She reconsidered when Boris unceremoniously dumped us all off in front of Sheremyetovo One, the domestic terminal, and sped away, calling out a final "Don't worry." Joey froze with panic but gamely followed us over to the Aeroflot counter. Duke handed our tickets to the clerk, who scowled and said, "Does anyone here speak Russian?"

Duke said he did a little, and she said, "Your bags overweight."

"How much do we have to pay?" Duke asked.

The ticket taker said, "I don't know." Duke asked what we were supposed to do. She gave him a chit and told him to take it to the cashier's office.

Duke asked how much we had to pay, and the ticket taker said, "I don't know. You have to ask the cashier." Duke wanted to help Joey, so he dispatched me to deal with the cashier. I knew about twelve words of Russian, but I pulled out my trusty pocket calculator, which has served as my translator in countries from Peru to China. Boris had indicated that our overweight baggage would cost a fortune, but it turned out to be only fifty dollars.

Then we all had to find the gate, which wasn't easy because there weren't any boards displaying departure gates, you just had to ask people. Joey was now trailing Duke like a bodyguard, and Ginny was my new best friend. Duke eventually found the plane. I'd heard all sorts of negative things about Aeroflot. Not being a skittish flyer, I thought, "It can't be *that* bad." Business class was like coach on ValuJet. I was wedged in a narrow three-across row between Duke and a burly chain-smoker who was less than fastidious about personal hygiene. Actually, with the exception of Ginny and Joey, who were behind us in business class (Midge and Karen flew coach), the entire cabin was crammed with burly chain-smokers who were less than fastidious about personal hygiene. (I suppose when you live in a country that is in an economic free fall, Right Guard is not a high priority.)

"They're all going on vacation," Duke teased. "Don't you see the scuba gear?"

For eight hours we flew through the Russian night, but I was too overwrought to sleep. I had no idea what time it was; my body clock hadn't adjusted to the eleven hours gained when we flew from Los Angeles to Moscow, and we were about to lose seven hours. Ginny and I debated over which one of us despised the cold more. When I gave her one of my pocket hand warmers (I had brought along three dozen), I made a friend for life.

Joey and Duke pulled out the camcorders as we landed, local time 10:00 A.M. All you could see for miles was snow, mountains, big frozen rivers, more snow, more mountains, more big frozen rivers. I couldn't imagine flying so long and still being over land, but the landscape didn't change. (If my son refuses to go to the store for me when he's sixteen, I'm bringing out the video.) The pilot announced that the air temperature outside was minus twenty degrees centigrade. Ginny and I shivered before we even left the plane.

"What's that in Fahrenheit?" she asked.

"Trust me," I said, "you don't want to know."

There was no jetway at the Nigdyetsk Airport, so we walked across a frozen tarmac to the arrival lounge, which was filled with soldiers. Olga wasn't waiting to greet us, but after ten minutes or so her associate showed up and announced that Olga would be there soon. While we waited for our bags, Duke wandered outside. When he rejoined us, his pants were ripped from his hip to his ankle.

It seems he ran into some Gypsies. They offered to tell his fortune, and Duke, never one to resist a bizarre experience, didn't back away. Their methodology was one not seen on the Psychic Friends Network. They pulled a hair from his head and then tried to put it back in what they assumed was his bulging wallet pocket. (All Duke had in the pocket was his bulging Russian/English dictionary.) "Not a good idea," he thought, and resisted. A group of people looked on without making a move to help. "They watched like they were keeping score, wondering if the Gypsies were going to get lucky today," Duke reported. "Afterward, they came over and asked me if they'd gotten anything."

Our luggage arrived intact, and after another twenty minutes so did Olga, soignée in Chanel and black shearling. She herded us into cars and drove us to the hovel, I mean the agency apartment where we were staying. Another housing project, though better located than the one in Moscow, right in the heart of downtown. She'd crammed six adults into a minimally heated three-room flat with a squalid bathroom, no maid service, a galley kitchen, and a steel door that Olga insisted we keep locked at all times.

"I feel like I'm in *The Diary of Anne Frank*," Duke complained. He confided that on the way to the hovel, Olga had cautioned the driver. "Be careful what you say," she warned. "He speaks Russian."

Our room was at most eight by nine feet, with a double bed, a crib, and a small armoire that held a third of our luggage. The walls were covered with peeling flocked wallpaper; the uneven floors were faux wood contact paper. I wouldn't bother to mention the shoddy decor, except we were being charged $150 a night.

Ginny and Joey grabbed the larger front room and lived to regret it. They had the best view and the only space heater, but the door was glass and Ginny griped about having no privacy. "This is my idea of what hell would be like," she wailed. Poor Ginny had a lot more to complain about ten minutes later when we assembled next door for lunch in Olga's infinitely more attractive and spacious apartment. Olga had bad news for our traveling companions. The judge scheduled to hear their adoptions was presiding over a criminal trial and refused to see any adopting families until it was over. "How long do you think that will be?" Ginny asked.

"Two weeks, maybe three," Olga said, "if I can't straighten things out."

Midge began talking about all the fun things they could do while they were stuck in Nigdyetsk. Ginny and Joey looked stricken. Duke and I exchanged looks. I knew exactly what he was thinking. China is across the icy river. What better place to kill time?

But as it happened, we had no time to kill. "When can we get our baby?" I asked Olga, after the others had left the room sobbing.

"Thirty minutes," she said.

Half an hour to motherhood, and what did I do? I hurried back to the hovel, ransacked the luggage, and stuffed all my carefully selected gifts into festive presentation bags. My overriding concern was not "Is the baby healthy?" but rather "Would the orphanage workers prefer a Saks Fifth Avenue cosmetic bag or a box of Barneys soap?" While I was wavering, Ginny, bless her charitable heart, squeezed into our room and neatly packed my diaper bag. Meanwhile, in a fugue state, Duke sterilized nipples and mixed formula.

I knocked on Olga's steel door and asked how many presents I needed to bring. I was sort of looking forward to playing Lady Bountiful. "Don't bring anything," Olga said. "I'll distribute the gifts later."

"I can't possibly fit a baby, my husband, our luggage, and forty gift-wrapped packages in our room."

"Leave the gifts in the corner of my living room," Olga said airily. (There, Ginny later informed me, they remained for weeks.)

I grabbed the diaper bag, pulled on my fur, and followed Olga to the car. Duke sat in the front seat in anxious silence videotaping the snowy street. I was dead calm. All I was praying for was clarity. Emotionally, I was prepared to accept or decline the baby, depending on what we found. I was not prepared for ambiguity. Eventually, we came to a nondescript brick building, Baby Hospital Number 9. "This is it," said Olga.

She led us into the office of Anastasia, the orphanage director, a raven-haired middle-aged woman. As we shook hands, I couldn't help thinking, "Is she the Tiffany-bookmark type or the crystal-clock type?" On the floor was a brightly colored rug decorated with little cars and a highway, the very same rug that I had admired at the office of Dr. Vicki, our pediatrician in Santa Monica. Olga and Anastasia chatted in Russian for a few minutes while Duke and I exchanged worried looks. "Don't worry," Olga said. "We're just gossiping about another official."

At last the women rose from their chairs and led us down a corridor where lots of female attendants were hanging around. We were relieved to see that while the baby hospital was obviously run on a shoestring budget, it was not Dickensian. Duke and I entered a small room with a changing table and six narrow pink metal cribs. The baby in the first crib on the right lifted his flaxen head and turned to see what was going on. "That's yours," Olga said, pointing. "Take him."

"Oh," I gasped. "He's adorable."

As I bent over to pick him up, Baby, whom the Russian attendants called Gorya, a diminutive for Igor, looked me straight in the eye and grinned. Thank God, I thought, he's responsive. "Hello," I cooed, "are you my little baby? Are you my Nicholas?"

The baby looked like he had been expecting us. "See?" he said to the other infants. "Here are my parents. I told you they were coming to take me to California."

Duke captured the moment on videotape. Nicholas looked straight at the camcorder and smiled again. "Another Clara," I noted wryly.

Olga herded us back to Anastasia's office, where I counted our new son's fingers and toes. He laughed merrily and kicked his feet in the air. He was tiny, only eleven pounds, and his skin was so pale it was translucent. For a while, we referred to him as the Baby Lestat.

Anastasia said something in Russian. Olga translated. "Give them back their clothes." Nicholas was decked out in a yellow undershirt with cotton pants and no diaper. I stripped off his duds, diapered him, and bedecked him in Baby Gap cotton long johns and a fancy French fleece sleeper with a penguin appliqué, a gift from my sister. It was sized for six months, but his feet only went down as far as the knees. Baby accepted the sleeper but filed a protest when I slipped him into the heavy snowsuit. Anastasia asked if I'd brought a hat. I didn't know it yet, but it is an unwritten law in Russia that babies must wear hats at all times, and all the citizens moonlight as Hat Police. I brandished a polar-fleece bonnet that my mother had bought. It fit perfectly. (In fact, the only clothes that fit were the three-month-size togs that Mother had sent.)

We expected to go to court (in fact, we had both packed suits, and Duke had prepared a little speech in Russian) or sign papers, but to our surprise Olga had managed to take care of the formalities by proxy with our power of attorneys. The orphanage director had one final question: Will you bring him back to see us when he's older?

"*Da,*" Duke said.

"In the summer," I added in English, and everyone laughed. And then Olga herded us to the car. Total time elapsed: twenty minutes, not counting the year of paperwork. I was reminded of taking possession of Clara in her black bag.

Nicholas sat in my lap pulling my hair. Blessedly, he didn't get carsick, though he was displaying a gift for spitting up that would later endear me to our dry cleaners. Olga's driver stopped at a photo studio for the child's Russian passport and American visa pictures. He posed willingly for the passport picture, then Olga insisted we stuff him back into the blue snowsuit for his visa picture, which had to be a three-quarter view, in color, with a clear shot of his right ear. Nick's aversion to the snowsuit was tempered only by his fondness for the camera, and five minutes later, Olga herded us back into the car and returned us to the hovel.

We had been gone for under an hour, long enough to turn us into parents for the rest of our lives.

Assuming, of course, that we managed to get our new son out of his native land.

In Praise of Pug Parenting

$\mathcal{A}$s proof of our new status, Joey and Ginny nobly surrendered the apartment's only space heater, though like a modern-day Scarlett O'Hara, Ginny declared, "If I ever get back to the United States, I swear I'm never going to be cold again." Our roommates crowded around to welcome the new baby. Nicholas beamed beatifically and allowed himself to be passed around and admired, much like Clara. Then he decided he was hungry and wailed. I stuck a bottle of Similac in his mouth, and he wolfed it down with great gusto and spit it up later with equal enthusiasm. (That first week, Nicholas went through more wardrobe changes than Princess Diana. God bless Mother—again.) Compared with the kefir, a fermented cow's milk beverage that he had been getting at the orphanage, the Similac was like rocket fuel, and the lad settled in my lap with a contented sigh.

"If only my problems could be solved so easily," Duke marveled.

My husband and I were shell-shocked, but we coped valiantly, mostly because we had no choice. We worked in tandem like surgeons in a MASH unit. Duke prepared bottles, I changed diapers; he went out into the Siberian cold and foraged for fruit and Diet Cokes that I would be too busy to eat or drink. Nicholas swiftly realized that his fortunes had improved, and he adjusted with gratifying speed. The first evening he cried for ten minutes. We put him in bed between us, and he snuggled in and slept through the night. It was somewhat of a shock the next morning to wake and behold not Clara's wrinkled mug, but Nicholas's big brown eyes regarding us with grave fascination. "Oh dear," he thought. "I don't think I'm in California yet."

Meanwhile, in the hovel, an insurrection was brewing. Despite Olga's best efforts, the balky judge refused to be bribed and our four flatmates were trapped in Nigdyetsk for the next three weeks. Ginny was in meltdown mode. She was freezing, she hadn't packed enough outfits to see her through the prolonged stay, she wanted to go back to Tennessee. They were only permitted to visit their baby in the orphanage for an hour each day. The rest of the time they were stuck in the decrepit, underheated, overpriced apartment. Midge kept trying to organize activities, like "Let's clean up the apartment." "When H freezes over," said Ginny. She didn't see why we should clean an apartment when we were being charged a combined five hundred dollars a night to stay there, and frankly, neither did I.

After twenty-four hours in the dreary apartment I felt like I had crawled into a cave, given birth, and was hibernating. I lost all track of time. Sometime late on Day Two, Duke went out on a Diet Coke run. When he came back, his eyes were glowing. "I've found a nice hotel two blocks away," he announced. "Heat. Refrigerator. CNN. Pack up and let's get out of here."

I would have loved to, honest I would. But as Nick was

napping and it was almost dark (it got dark in Nigdyetsk around noon), it seemed prudent to wait until morning. That night I asked Olga when we would return to Moscow. "The baby's passport should be ready tomorrow afternoon," she said. "You can fly back Saturday."

"Why not tomorrow?"

Olga made a face. "The passport won't be ready until after the only plane leaves," she said, with ill-concealed impatience.

"When will we get the baby's documents?" I asked.

"Don't worry," she said dismissively.

Friday morning I left the baby with Midge and Karen and went with Duke, Joey, and Ginny to see my husband's discovery, the Hotel Emerald. It was the first time I'd been outdoors in forty-eight hours, and I was so grateful to be in natural light that I didn't feel the cold. (Every one of the minks that died to make my coat should be canonized.) Duke was proud of his find, and rightly so: the hotel was clean, comfortable, secure, and fifty dollars cheaper than the hovel. Ginny was overjoyed it was amply heated, Joey was ecstatic to see Bernard Shaw on television. Duke began discussing the logistics of moving our bags.

"Forget it," I said. "It's not worth it."

Duke was shocked. It was the only time in the entire history of our relationship that I have turned down superior accommodations. "We'll be more comfortable," he argued, and he was right. But we only had to spend one more night in the hovel, and then we would be back in Moscow, in safe harbor, at the Hotel Budapest. We were still waiting for our return tickets to Moscow, Nick's Russian passport, and all of the documents we needed to get his American visa. And it wasn't like Olga was the organized sort who said, "I'll give you the documents at four o'clock." Preferring to keep her families on a tight rein, when she wanted something, she knocked on the heavy metal door, called out a name, and dragged her captives off to see their child, or sign a document, or buy a plane ticket.

Duke agreed it made sense to stay, but Ginny and Joey made arrangements to check in to the hotel at once. (And if we had had to stay for three weeks, we would have joined them in a flash.) Olga was furious and refused to give them directions to the orphanage or let them pay for meals at the hovel. "I cannot be responsible for you," she warned as they left triumphantly. Duke went with them and got them settled.

"You and Duke, I wouldn't worry about," Olga said to me later. "But those two know nothing."

Our decision to remain was validated almost instantly, when Olga knocked on the door after lunch and summoned Duke to go to the Aeroflot office and buy our plane tickets back to Moscow. My normally frugal husband found out we could fly first-class for an extra seventy-five dollars and decided to surprise me. A few hours later, Olga banged on the door again. She needed one of us to go to the local KGB office and sign for the baby's passport. Duke volunteered to babysit so I could get some fresh, albeit frigid, air. Curiously, Nicholas's Russian passport—in an old USSR jacket, not a new Russian Republic one—had English translations, and yet all the names were in French. Go figure.

After midnight, Olga knocked again. She had our documents. I got out my checklist from the embassy. "You don't need that," Olga said. I brought it anyway, and I was glad I did because I noticed we were missing the original birth certificate. "Don't worry," Olga said.

It was easy for her to say. Olga was leaving early in the morning to inspect an orphanage several hours away and wouldn't see us again. She promised that her assistant, Katya, would bring the final document over at ten-thirty. I asked for Katya's phone number in case we had a problem. "Don't worry," Olga said.

"Write it down," I snapped, and she reluctantly did. Olga also gave me an envelope to give to Boris. He was going to pick us up at the airport. It seemed out of character for Boris to provide such service, but then I learned that he had misplaced another couple's dossier at the American Embassy. We were hand-carrying a replacement dossier.

By eight o'clock Saturday morning, I was packed and anxious to go. At nine, Ginny and Joey returned from their Great Siberian Hotel Adventure, tails between their legs. It seemed that Olga had called their parents in Nashville and told them about how a tourist had been murdered in Nigdyetsk last year. Ginny asked if she could have our room, and I dragged all our bags out into the narrow hallway.

Ten-thirty came and went without word from Katya, who was bringing the final document. By eleven-thirty, I was frantic. Duke called and found out she was on her way. At twelve-fifteen, Katya finally appeared, document in hand. While I stuffed it into my briefcase, Duke dragged our bags down the stairs. Vitale, Olga's backup driver (I suspect she employed half of Nigdyetsk), was outside waiting. I bundled Nicholas into his snowsuit and bade our flatmates good-bye.

Ginny shook her blond head reproachfully. "You're deserting me." She sighed as she hugged me. "But I forgive you."

Vitale was a stark contrast to the good-for-nothing Boris. He waited with us at the airport, carefully delivering us to the gate, and refused to accept a ruble. I was dreading the eight-hour flight with the baby, and it certainly began ominously. Nicholas cried with panicky unhappiness because he was hot in his snowsuit. We had to take a bus from the terminal to the plane, and all the fellow passengers began yelling at me because the baby wasn't wearing a hat. The snowsuit had a hood, but that didn't mollify the Hat Police. I was so flustered I couldn't find the baby's hat or our plane tickets, but they let us board anyway. First class was a tremendous improvement. "Best seventy-five dollars I ever spent," Duke said. As soon as we were aloft, the stewardess fastened a bassinet to the bulkhead, and the baby slept most of the way to Moscow, covered by the bright-red-and-royal-blue polar-fleece blanket Mother had sent. He looked like Kalel, the infant Superman, sent to Earth in a capsule when Krypton exploded.

Boris drove us back to the Budapest. We gave him more cash and a box of chocolates for his trouble and asked if he would drive us to the clinic and the embassy on Monday. Ever the hustler, Boris declined. "You not my problem." It was snowing, Nicholas had a runny nose, and Duke and I felt like we were both coming down with an exotic infection from the Siberian taiga, the endless evergreen forest. But it was a relief to be back in civilization. I took a hot bath. We called our families.

"What pattern do you want the Pack n Play?" Mother asked. I didn't have a clue. Mother explained that this collapsible playpen came in different designs. She had to know my color scheme right away because her friends were dying to send gifts.

"Anything but pastels," I said.

"Do you want an umbrella stroller or a baby jogger, or a car seat that turns into a stroller?" Mother pressed.

"Can this wait?" I begged. In a week, we had flown from Los Angeles to Moscow to Siberia and back to Moscow—over twenty time zones of air travel—and we still had to get our son's visa at the American Embassy and make the long flight home.

"I want him to have everything he needs," Mother said.

Monday morning we got up at five-thirty, the start of a day that would be like Kafka's rendition of Dante's Inferno. By six-thirty Nicholas was fed, dressed, and complaining vociferously about his snowsuit. We went down to the lobby, outside of which a quasi-cab was supposed to be waiting but was in fact nowhere to be seen. Muttering, Duke tried to flag down a vehicle. Meanwhile, Nick, or as we now called him, "the Carrier Monkey," was struggling to remove the snowsuit. My resourceful husband located a car and we drove to the Filotov Clinic for the baby's medical exam.

Unfortunately, we were dropped off at an unfamiliar-looking entrance and we couldn't find the clinic. Duke, in overdrive, ran around trying to find the doctor. I waited in the quasi-cab with the hysterical child. Duke returned, even more hysterical, dismissed the car, and told me to wait in an empty building. Twenty minutes later, Duke returned furious. He had found the clinic, but the doctor was angry because we were late and was refusing to examine the child. No examination, no visa.

"You talk to him," Duke said. "I may kill him."

Clutching my new Laby, I followed Duke through a courtyard slippery with ice and snow. My husband walked full speed, and I struggled to keep up. In my haste, I slid on a sheet of ice and fell flat on my back. Miraculously, Nicholas landed on my belly, cushioned by my mink coat and his despised snowsuit. A half dozen medical professionals were standing in the doorway and watched me slip, but no one made a move to help.

Badly shaken, body aching, I limped to the primitive

clinic where the doctor, who had also seen me fall, didn't ask how I was and instead began lecturing us. We were wrong to come late, wrong to come without an agency representative, wrong, wrong, wrong. In my experience, only one defense will succeed with a man in this mode, and I promptly burst into tears. It didn't take much acting; I was in pain.

"You're right," I said sobbing, "we are at fault."

The doctor looked disturbed. Not disturbed enough to stop his lecture, oh, no, we heard all about how he had called Boris and was told that he was not responsible for us. I cried harder. I explained that on the day we came to the clinic to make the appointment we had just landed from California and were too jet-lagged to note our exact location.

"California," the doctor said with sudden interest. "I studied at USC and then Boston University."

I stopped whimpering long enough to mention that Duke works at USC and his Uncle Henry is a world-famous Harvard specialist.

The doctor decided that maybe he could squeeze the baby in if his next appointment was late. Luck was with us. Twenty seconds after the next appointment was scheduled, when nobody appeared, the doctor relented and showed us into an examining room.

The joke was that the entire examination took five minutes. Long enough for the doctor to announce that the baby had bronchitis—as, it turned out, did we. He wrote a prescription for infant antibiotics and told us we could have it filled at a pharmacy on the other side of town. (My husband would later take back every snide comment he has ever made about "Margo's Traveling Pharmacy" when I informed him that I had brought along antibiotics for the baby—and for us—and saved him a trip.) As for the rest of the exam, Nicholas played with the doctor's stethoscope and the doctor pronounced him a happy boy, cute but small. "I'm not so big myself," I said, and the doctor smiled and said, "You're petite." I hustled Duke out of the clinic before he could leave the doctor with his feet sticking out of the trash can.

We left clutching a sealed envelope containing the medical report. Duke flagged down a quasi-cab, and we sped to the embassy. Nicholas threw up a couple of times, but I couldn't blame him. I was pretty queasy myself. We passed through the embassy gates at eight-fifteen, fifteen minutes early. Inside was unimaginable chaos. At least thirty American couples were waiting with their new children and their hovering, solicitous agency representatives. I parked Nicholas with Duke, who had no idea of what was required and piteously asked, "Papers, we do have papers?" I got in line behind a firefighter from Paterson, New Jersey, with a new sixteen-month-old daughter from St. Petersburg. The firefighter was tall, an advantage in a mob scene, and he made sure I wasn't jostled by the crowd. When my turn came, I handed the head of Orphan Processing all our paperwork plus copies plus another pound of Starbucks coffee, this time Colombia Supremo.

The way it worked was that an embassy official reviewed your paperwork and then you were called to a window for an interview. I returned to Duke and Nicholas, who, relieved of his snowsuit, was cheerfully playing with a rattle made up of plastic footballs, basketballs, and baseballs. Half an hour passed. The head of Orphan Processing called my name and told me that I had to go to the cashier and pay two hundred dollars for my son's visa. I pushed through the adopting hordes to American Citizen Services. A Coke machine offering Diet

Coke beckoned like a mirage in the desert. Alas, the only dollar bill I had was limp, and the machine rejected it. No one in American Citizen Services would trade it for a fresh one.

Back in the mob scene, I turned in my receipt, and another half hour passed. The former orphans looked dashing in their new Baby Gap, OshKosh B'Gosh, and Gymboree clothes. Nick's were covered with spit-up formula. Finally, we were called to Window Nine. A kind immigration officer went through all our documents, one by one, making sure we knew exactly what they said. She seemed surprised that we did. I was asked to raise my right hand and swear that everything I had stated on the INS form was true. (Among the more notable questions: Is the applicant coming to the United States to practice polygamy or overthrow the government?) I swore and we were free to go, though one of us had to return at five o'clock to pick up the visa.

On the way back to the hotel we stopped at the Delta office and bought Nicholas an infant ticket. Back in the hotel, I gave him antibiotics, and the three of us curled up in bed and watched the falling snow. Duke went to pick up the visa at five. The metro stop nearest our hotel was closed, and as a result Duke got lost walking back and nearly froze. But he returned waving a sealed envelope containing the paperwork and a visa with Nick's picture affixed to the outside. We were instructed to present the sealed envelope to immigration officials when we landed at Kennedy Airport, our port of entry to the United States. Our ordeal was almost over.

Up to this point, I was too busy to contemplate how I felt about having a child. But once we had our visa, my thoughts turned to the pugs and, strangely enough, to my dollhouse collection. Ten years ago, when I left my ex-husband, he insisted that I leave him all our full-sized furniture. Rather than fight a man for loveseats and Farberware, I simply took my doll-houses—all of which were furnished down to the wee copper pots and pans hanging from a silver-dollar-sized rack on the ceiling—and departed. As I struggled to create a new life for myself, I realized with self-consciousness that the dolls were living better than me. I felt silly for pouring so much energy into a hobby. Yet, as it turned out, in the years when I first began to write, I was able to support myself by selling the doll-houses that I built. And thus I realized that no effort based on love is wasted.

In the months leading up to our adoption, I had begun to question my commitment to the pugs. A woman devoted to a child is considered a paragon, but one whose energies are fo-cused on her four-legged creatures is considered, well, dotty. Yet, as I sat with my new son in Moscow, watching the snow fall from our hotel window, I realized that the reason that I was not freaking out was because of Clara and Sophie. I had spent twenty years caring for small creatures, nurturing them, at-tending to their every need. And in exchange, they prepared me well.

Granted, I treated Nicholas like a pug. The first time he rolled over, I heard myself say, "Good puppy!" He squirmed frantically when I tried to squirt the antibiotics in his mouth with a dropper, and I thought, "Now, what would I do with Clara and Sophie?" I remembered that I administered their antiflea and antiworm pills in a wad of cheese and promptly mixed the baby's medicine in his bottle. After years of pooper-scooping, I wasn't squeamish about changing diapers. And when Nick assumed the paws-locked position in the bathtub, I calmly climbed in with him. (Okay, I did wonder for an instant if Aly, Clara's groomer, would like another client.) As for his rapacious appetite, I didn't bat an eye. After the gluttonous pugs, it seemed normal.

On the other hand, to be honest, I missed Clara, who could be left alone while we went out to dinner and didn't wake me up in the middle of the night. If I were flying from Moscow to Los Angeles with Clara, I would not be dreading the trip. I would be confident she would enchant all the passengers on the plane. Then again, Clara's adorable goblin face couldn't gladden my heart like Nick's angelic smile.

It was snowing—again!—when we arrived at the airport. The baby was having his now familiar snowsuit tantrum. The driver dumped our bags on the curb, and I realized we couldn't possibly carry them all. A porter offered to help us for fifteen dollars. Duke said, "Dream on," and bargained him down to ten. I looked so miserable that the porter agreed. It turned out that Moscow Airport isn't like every other airport in the world. You can't check your baggage right away. First, you have to go through Customs and write down everything that you are taking out, and then that list is compared with the list you made when you came in. The heroic porter pushed us through the Customs line and then over to Immigration, where a woman who looked like the villain in a Bond film scrutinized Nick's visa for five minutes while my heart stood still. Finally, she waved us through to the Delta counter. "Do you have a jet-way?" I asked, and when the clerk nodded, I removed the dreaded snowsuit. "You won't need this in Los Angeles," I said, and Nick grinned and thought, California, here I come.

Duke gave the porter twenty dollars and apologized. "I was stupid," he confessed. We tried to spend our rubles at a duty-free store, but the line was too long. Not as long as the line to pass through the only metal detector in the airport, but long enough for me to decide that I didn't need another bottle of Shalimar that much. All I wanted, with every fiber of my being, was to get on the plane, which I regarded as American soil. On the jetway, an official inspected the baby's visa again. At long last, we were allowed to board, and I collapsed into my business-class seat. We took off, and the stewardess brought a bassinet and clamped it to the wall. Nicholas played and slept without protest until we landed in New York. Clara could not have been more engaging.

"Anything to declare?" asked the Customs official. We proudly held up our new son and were directed to Immigration. I held my breath until the officer took Nicholas's visa, disappeared for five minutes, and then stamped his Russian passport. "Welcome to the United States," he said, and the baby smiled. (Two months later Nicholas became a United States citizen. No, he didn't have to take a test, which was fortunate, because he kept forgetting that Martin Van Buren was the only bachelor president.)

Mother was waiting at the gate with bags from F.A.O. Schwarz. I have never been so glad to see her in my life. She hugged and kissed her new grandson and pronounced him gorgeous and exceptionally bright.

"You laughed when I said it about Clara," Mother reminded me. "But remember, I was right."

Epilogue

We landed in Los Angeles at nine-thirty at night. I was over-joyed to be back in California. The palm trees swayed in the balmy breeze, the early spring poppies bloomed in the flower beds around the airport parking garage. Marjorie and her hus-band, David, picked us up, installed Nicholas in his first car seat, and drove us back to Venice Beach. To my surprise, Susan, the dollhouse maven, had transformed our laundry room into a cozy nursery that Martha Stewart would approve of. It reminded me of a cabin on the U.S.S. *Baby.* Duke video-taped the baby as he curiously fingered the ribbons on his fancy quilted blue-and-white crib bumper. Ever the trouper, he waited until the camera stopped rolling before he fell asleep.

Scarcely twelve hours later, we were at the vet, I mean the pediatrician's office, making sure our son was in good health. (Not that I didn't trust the arrogant doctor in Moscow. But to quote the old Russian proverb—or was it Ronald Reagan who said it?—"Trust, but verify.") My husband and I exchanged nervous glances as Dr. Vicki examined the lad from his tiny towhead to his pudgy square feet. "He's okay," she said finally. "You can relax." At that moment my anxiety shifted from my two-legged animal to my four-legged ones, twenty-five miles away in Blanche's guest wing.

I waited until Dr. Vicki asked if we had any specific concerns to express my biggest one: "How soon can I bring the pugs home?" I hadn't seen Clara and Sophie for two and a half weeks, but Mother warned me that it was unfair to make Nick compete with Clara on her home turf for at least a month.

"As soon as possible," said Dr. Vicki. "He has to get used to them. They're part of his family."

I gave myself the rest of the day to get organized. (Duke, reverting to duck mode now that the high-profile adventure was over, went straight from Dr. Vicki's office to his own on the bottom of the Pond Denial.) Fortunately, anticipating the dive, Nana Lupe showed up to welcome home her new charge. She and Nicholas took to each other like Romeo and Juliet. Me, she dispatched to bed for a long-needed nap.

I had not let our son out of my sight since we'd sprung him from the hospital only a week before. But not wishing to deprive Sophie and Clara of their mother-and-pug reunion, the next day I left him with the saintly Lupe, whose affinity for games like fetch-the-rattle proved to be infinitely greater than mine. With mounting trepidation, I sped out to Woodland Hills to inform Clara she had been demoted from diva to dog. I felt worse about disrupting the pugs' status quo than I did about leaving my son with a sitter.

I couldn't find a pug artifact in Russia to give Blanche, so I had bought her a butter dish instead. I figured it would come in handy for her annual I Hate My Heart Thanksgiving dinner. Blanche seemed pleased and led me to the guest quarters. I inquired as to how the pugs had enjoyed their stay. "Sophie really made me laugh," she said. "You know that thing she does in the morning where she jumps up and grabs your shirt with her teeth?"

How could I forget her patented Crippling Maneuver? I was terrified she would try that with the baby.

Blanche chuckled. "I was wearing a long shirt, and she grabbed it. I ignored her and kept walking. I felt this weight, and I looked down and there was Sophie swinging from my shirt. She's a funny dog."

I suppose she is, if you enjoy defiance. "She didn't run in the other direction when you called her?"

"She behaved beautifully," Blanche said. "She just gives you trouble because she knows you favor Clara."

Mea culpa. Mea maxima culpa.

Both the favored pug and the intractable one were elated to see me, and I was overjoyed to see them. (Six months later, I was still more accustomed to my role as pug mother than my new role as Mama.) Sophie sprang from her cage into my arms and sneezed in my face. Clara submissively wet for thirty seconds. I stroked Sophie with my left hand and Clara with my right, and almost instantly Clara sprang for Sophie's throat and the two rose on their hind legs and began their hellish growling. "Maybe Mother was right," I thought nervously.

"They don't do that here," Blanche said. "They're fighting over you like you're an object. You can't allow it."

Like I had control over the pugs.

The pair raced down the driveway. Clara vaulted into the car, and Sophie flew through the air after her. To delay the inevitable, I took the slow, twisty scenic route home, through Topanga Canyon, and the ecstatic pugs refused to remain in their customary position in the passenger's seat—they kept bounding over the armrest into my lap. I felt a sick-making combination of love and dread. An hour later, I pulled into the driveway and braced for the moment of truth.

The pugs tore through the house like a thundering herd. Clara greeted her water dish like a long-lost friend. Meanwhile, Sophie dashed into the living room, where the saintly Lupe was sitting on the floor on a quilt showing Nicholas how to stack brightly colored plastic blocks. Sophie sniffed him with interest. "Oh, no," she thought. "Another pug. Another Clara, only this one's white." Nick looked at her with fascination, like she was the coolest mobile in the world. I was just relieved he didn't sneeze. A recurring adoption nightmare was that the infant would be allergic to pug dander.

I was embracing my son when Clara walked in and caught us flagrante delicto. She froze in her tracks, and her Bette Davis eyes filled with ill-concealed horror. I recalled the first of Kübler-Ross's Five Stages of Grief: Shock, followed by Denial. Adapting the posture she takes toward cats—pretending they're invisible—Clara coolly walked over the baby and settled regally in my lap. She licked my face. "This is not happening to *moi*," she thought.

I'd been warned never to leave the pugs alone with the child. This was easier said than done. Sophie, never one to pass up a soft resting place, took up permanent residence on the rubber mats that I bought so Nicholas wouldn't fall and hurt himself on the hardwood floors. She was more interested in chewing her pig's ear than devouring the child, so I eased my vigil. Clara wouldn't let me out of her sight, so she was not a threat.

A couple of weeks passed. Nicholas began creeping on his belly. Clara advanced to the second stage—Denial replaced by Anger, Rage, Envy, and Resentment. The first time I took my son down to the boardwalk with the pugs, Clara charged at a corgi and nearly overturned the stroller. Sophie just thought, "Damn, this dog has a lot of toys," and gave up gnawing her revolting pig's ear and started chewing Baby Legos, known to the cognoscenti as Duplo. But the suddenly insecure Clara sat forlornly on his play mat, thumping the brightly colored plastic toy piano with her paw. "Anything he can do, I can do better," she informed me. She was too cagey to express her displeasure with a housebreaking backslide. Instead, whenever Nick soiled his diaper, she tattled immediately and made a great show of peeing on the lawn.

Soon after our return, my girlfriends gave us an enormous shower. (So successfully had we kept our adoption secret that the universal response to the invitations was "This is a joke, right?") Clara looked crestfallen when we didn't take her to the party, and her absence was pointedly noted. "You can't ignore your old friend Clara," said a shower guest, and my guilt, already at an all-time high, reached a feverish pitch.

Thanks to the overwhelming generosity of friends and family, our once tasteful living room was soon cluttered with garish sherbet-colored plastic baby gear, and it looked like we had been invaded by Candyland. While Duke, Clara, and I struggled to adjust, Sophie was downright jubilant. Perhaps because she was reveling in her sister's misery, perhaps because she had already suffered through the arrival of Clara and what could be worse than that? Or perhaps she sensed a window of opportunity; she could be the baby's dog. Sophie agreeably lapped up his spit-up formula, fetched his rattles when he threw them, and parked under his high chair hoping for a discarded teething biscuit to come her way. What was her reward for her diligence? Baby first pulled himself to a standing position by grabbing her fur.

Sophie and Clara enjoyed a rare moment of unity when Nicholas discovered their water dish and began splashing merrily like it was a wading pool. The pugs looked up at me accusingly: "How could you allow this?"

I apologized profusely and moved the dish to a safer place.

By the end of the first month, Nicholas crept around full speed on his belly, and anytime I made a move in the house, I was pursued by my three needy floor creatures. Clara progressed to Stage Three of grief: Bargaining. "I'll do anything," she said. "Look how much smarter I am." I had to concede, at this point, Clara was infinitely more ingenious. Laurie came to visit her new nephew. I was trying to take a picture of the two of them together. Clara had never experienced a photo session in which she did not play a starring role, and she did not intend to be upstaged. As soon as she saw my Polaroid, she went into her Kate Moss routine. I got one blurry picture of my son before the wily Clara realized that what she needed was a prop. She casually picked up the baby's pacifier and began sucking. Laurie and I doubled over and ran through my only roll of film getting that shot. Clara perked up. Maybe she hadn't lost her touch.

She was so encouraged by her triumph that she struck a deal without my knowing it. I woke up one morning and discovered Clara asleep in our bed, head on the pillow like a human. I'd never tolerated this sleeping arrangement, but Clara informed me this was the price I had to pay for my treachery. I couldn't refuse and neither could Duke. "Daffodil, you're such a martyr," he said with a sigh as she snuggled in between us. "You're so sensitive."

This is not to suggest that my younger pug skipped the fourth stage of grief—Depression. No, Clara brooded pitifully whenever I took Nick in the car and left her at home. But reality was on her side. It was far simpler for me to take the responsive little dog shopping than it was to wedge the baby into his car seat, load the trunk with an umbrella stroller, diaper bag, bottles, Sassy Seat, and enough toys to divert him during the expedition. So gradually Clara's joie de vivre returned.

Alas, when Sophie sensed that Clara wasn't suffering quite as much as she would have liked, she fell into a dark funk. To cheer her up, Duke gave her the remains of a can of tuna fish. Nicholas came crawling in and decided that it might be fun to play with the shiny can. He reached. Sophie growled and snapped. Nick wailed. I screamed, "No!" and grabbed the child. Around this time, Betty the social worker came to visit for a postadoption checkup. To my horror, Nicholas tried to confiscate Sophie's Milk-Bone and she snapped at him. I imagined that the report would read, "Baby mauled by killer pug," but Betty, a dog lover, took it in stride. "You're going to have to learn to get along with your new brother," Betty warned Sophie.

I called Blanche in a panic. "Once he can walk, Sophie will realize he's not another dog," she assured me. "But for now you may have to crate her if she gets out of line."

I didn't have the heart. Instead, I decided to take Sophie and Clara with me to my office every day for a few hours. Clara was pleased to learn that the vitamins with her picture on the bottle were selling briskly in California grocery stores. Sophie was relieved to get away from Nicholas's insanely irritating electronic toys that barked, quacked, mooed, oinked, and me-owed. (Why is the toy industry obsessed with barnyard sounds? We do not live in an agrarian society. My son is not going to encounter a cow or a duck on Venice Beach.) Sophie still believed that Nicholas was a big white pug, but once he began cruising on two legs, hanging on to her fur or the furniture for support, she had doubts. One morning he dropped his teething biscuit and Sophie snatched it. He tried to take it away from her, and she growled. Undaunted, Nicholas picked up his red plastic baby baseball bat and bopped Sophie on the head. An uneasy truce was reached.

Eventually, Clara reached the fifth stage of grief: Acceptance. Her best skill has always been her adaptability, and once she realized that she still attracted ten times more attention from passersby on the boardwalk than Nick did, she trotted agreeably beside the stroller and permitted him to hold her leash. She even allowed him to share her car. Clara did look back at him smugly from the front seat as if to say, "Ha, Ha, you're in a car seat, and I'm not," and if the entire family went on an outing, she insisted on riding shotgun on my lap instead of joining her brother and sister in the back. But she was basically cooperative. It helped that Nicholas adored her. Clara stood with her front paws on the edge of his high chair, and he carefully placed Pepperidge Farm goldfish, the gourmet delight of the baby universe, into her mouth. Among his first words: "Clara." (He still refuses to say "Sophie.")

My husband believes that during the adjustment period Clara had a revelation. "She looked at the little blond boy knocking down towers of blocks, and suddenly it came to her: 'So that's what I am. I'm a human child,' " Duke said. "She never identified with Sophie and is pleased to have confirmation of her true identity." I concluded he was right after Clara hopped onto our bed, stretched out next to Nicholas, and waited expectantly for the bedtime story *Goodnight Moon*.

Life went on and soon Clara had bigger worries. The movie *Men In Black* came out, and to her dismay she discovered that another pug, a somewhat ratty and louche-looking fawn, had landed the key role, as an extraterrestrial. Tommy Lee Jones, playing a secret agent who keeps tabs on aliens on Earth, interrogated the pug who was decked out for his big scene in an unflattering I ❤ NEW YORK T-shirt. I explained to Clara that the part called for a heavy—whereas she is an ingenue—and the pug was vigorously shaken by Mr. Jones. Unmollified, Clara brooded for weeks and threatened to fire her agent, Loretta.

If truth be told, I didn't find mothering a human to be all that different from mothering the pugs—apart from the fact that no one ever nagged me to enroll Clara in a Mommy and Me program or else jeopardize her chances of getting into a good preschool and college. My life, though more hectic, was greatly enriched. Nicholas managed to convince Clara that maybe, just maybe, she had taken me for granted all these years. She mended her sluttish ways, and sometimes she is openly affectionate with me, even when Duke is around. Sophie, tormented by Nick's barking, meowing, and mooing toys, curtailed her incessant yapping, much to our great relief.

I suspect that deep in Clara's heart she realized the situation could be worse. A few months after Nick arrived, we flew back to Baltimore for my grandmother's ninetieth birthday. I left the pugs with Blanche for the weekend and brought the baby along with me when I went to pick them up. Blanche had a two-month-old puppy running around the house, and my son was mesmerized by the tiny creature.

That night over dinner I said to Duke, "Maybe Nicholas needs his own pug."

Clara looked at me with alarm.